LEWIS HENRY MORGAN
AND THE
INVENTION OF KINSHIP

Lewis Henry Morgan, c. 1868. (Morgan Papers, University of Rochester)

LEWIS HENRY MORGAN
AND THE
INVENTION OF KINSHIP

Thomas R. Trautmann

UNIVERSITY OF CALIFORNIA PRESS
Berkeley   Los Angeles   London

University of California Press
Berkeley and Los Angeles, California

University of California Press, Ltd.
London, England

Copyright © 1987 by The Regents of the University of California

Library of Congress Cataloging in Publication Data

Trautmann, Thomas R.
  Lewis Henry Morgan and the invention of kinship.

  Bibliography: p.
  Includes index.
  1. Morgan, Lewis Henry, 1818–1881. Systems of consanguinity and affinity
of the human family. 2. Kinship. 3. Anthropology. I. Title.
GN487.T73   1987   306.8′3   86–24941
ISBN 0–520–05849–6 (alk. paper)

Printed in the United States of America

1 2 3 4 5 6 7 8 9

in memory of
M. S. A. RAO

Contents

Illustrations

Preface

❖❖

This book extends and, I hope, makes good the shortcomings of my analysis of Morgan's kinship project in an earlier book, *Dravidian kinship,* a study of the kinship systems of South India and Sri Lanka. In that book it had been my ambition to analyze the anthropological literature on Dravidian kinship together with such documentary material on it that has survived over the last two millennia, in light of a "genealogical" conception of the object of study. My project led me inevitably to the first study of kinship systems of India, and indeed of kinship systems as such, Lewis Henry Morgan's massive *Systems of consanguinity and affinity of the human family* (1871). The analysis of the Dravidian system was a central problem right from the beginning of kinship as a field of study, for Morgan's book is built around the similarity of semantic patterning of Iroquois and Dravidian kinship.

I was not prepared for what I found. Our ideas about Morgan are shaped by the more readable, much reprinted books he wrote before and after the *Systems.* We think of him as Iroquoianist for his *League of the Iroquois* (1851) and as an exponent of a robust, high Victorian form of social evolutionism in his *Ancient society* (1877). These characterizations are apt but incomplete. In the *Systems* we see more clearly that Morgan's historicism is of two kinds, not one. Besides the stepwise evolutionism expressing belief in a law of progress, there is the treelike historical process of the progressive differentiation of systems through time; the idea, borrowed from comparative philology, that kinship systems—like languages—grow from one or few to many. The coexistence of these two logically distinct historicisms, I have come to find, is quite general in nineteenth-century Euroamerican thought. In any event, what is most striking about the *Systems* is not evolutionism but the philological design of its argument and the invention of what Morgan called "a new instrument for ethnology" analogous to but different from the philologist's comparison of vocabularies: the comparison of the semantic patterning of kinship terminologies, and the study of the relation of these patterns to rules of marriage. These features of Morgan's work have made it of more than antiquarian interest to me. In some respects he is our contemporary, and there are new lessons yet to be learned from his book.

In my examination of the literature on Dravidian kinship I found a common failure to address the problem of identity. It is generally agreed that the many empirical kinship systems of South India and Sri Lanka reported in the literature are so many instances of a single Dravidian system. These instances, however, are only partially similar to one another in lexicon, semantic patterning, and rules of marriage. Are we to understand that the Dravidian is a merely morphological or typological class? In that case it is an analytical construct with no necessary implication of historical interrelationship of the instances. We may decide whether a particular instance is Dravidian by referring it to a list of defining features, such as the equations FB = F, MB ≠ F, and so forth or by comparing it to a type case representing the Platonic idea, as it were, of the Dravidian. In fact it is generally agreed (at least tacitly) that the Dravidian is a genealogical or genetic class, the members of which are related to one another by codescent from an ancestral system. That being so, a quite different method is required: the comparison of all instances of the system in order to abstract the features that we may truly call Dravidian from those that are borrowed or are local innovations.

This way of approaching Dravidian kinship owes a great deal to Morgan. On the one hand, it treats particular Dravidian kinship systems as related to one another in the way that Dravidian languages are, as had Morgan. On the other hand, it implements Morgan's distinction between the (linguist's) comparison of vocabularies and the (anthropologist's) comparison of the semantic patterning of kinships terms. Doing so makes it possible to show, for example, that some systems on the frontiers of the Dravidian region, though non-Dravidian (more exactly, Indo-Aryan) in lexicon, are nevertheless Dravidian in semantics. My study became an attempt to recover and reinvigorate the half-forgotten conceptualization of Morgan's much-admired but seldom-read masterpiece.

I am ashamed to say that I had not read Carl Resek's useful biography of Morgan until after completing *Dravidian kinship* and the section on Morgan that it contains. From Resek's account of how the *Systems* came to be written one learns that Morgan submitted an earlier manuscript version of the book to the Smithsonian Institution, that it was rewritten in response to criticisms of the publisher and his readers, and that it was only in the final, published version that Morgan incorporated the well-known evolutionary series of family forms from the zero of primitive promiscuity to monogamy. Intrigued to know what the first version actually said and how it differs from the published version, and finding some implausibilities in Resek's reconstruction of the events leading to the writing of the final version, I went to the University of Rochester in the spring of 1982 on the first of what was to be a series of visits to examine the Morgan Papers. I was surprised at the extraordinary richness of the collection, not indeed by the measure of my American history colleagues, who are accustomed to brag about the number of linear feet of manuscript collections they have gone through, but in the quality of access it gives, when closely examined, to the development of Morgan's ideas, especially the kinship project as it unfolds over the two central decades of his scholarly life. If this book accomplishes nothing else, I hope it will encourage others to examine this fine collection.

What was originally intended to have been one or two articles on the development of the *Systems* has become this book. It is both more and less than a biography; more in that it aspires to say something about the general condition of the emergent anthropology of the 1860s and the continuing pertinence to kinship studies of Morgan's work; less in that it deals with Morgan's life only as it relates to the kinship project, and only until 1871 when the *Systems* appeared. It is the biography of a book.

I have, of course, made use of the biographies that exist. Resek's *Lewis Henry Morgan, American scholar* (1960) is the standard work, superseding Bernhard Stern's *Lewis Henry Morgan, social evolutionist* (1931). Stern's is in the nature of a preliminary skirmish with the subject. It is little more than a display of Morgan's ideas through a stitching together of quotations, with little archival work and little historical context, although the commentary is sometimes good, especially on the way in which Morgan was inclined to see the Iroquois through a lens provided by the concept of nomadism as the cause of savagery. Stern's grasp of the anthropological issues is the surer, but it is an advantage that has all but disappeared with the passage of time; and it has too many inaccuracies to be of continuing value. Resek's approach is that of an historian rather than an anthropologist. It is based on extensive archival research, and he gives us a more rounded picture of Morgan's life that goes a fair way to restoring it to its historical setting. It is a youthful effort, which races through the material quickly and does not always plumb its depths; but one would not wish to be critical of a book for whose decided contribution one is grateful. By a fortunate chance I was able to see an advance copy of *Science encounters the Indian, 1820–1880* (1986) by the historian of American anthropology, Robert E. Bieder, just as I was completing final revisions of this book. Bieder's work consists of intellectual biographies of Albert Gallatin, Samuel G. Morton, Ephraim George Squier, Henry Rowe Schoolcraft, and Morgan, and it is based on manuscript as well as printed sources. The Morgan biography is, of course, comparatively brief, but its treatment of his intellectual development is good, and the series of pioneer anthropologists with whom he is clubbed in this book establishes the intellectual environment in which he worked better than anything hitherto published. These three biographies nevertheless leave much to be said, and none of them gives an adequate account of the kinship project that was the central scholarly undertaking of Morgan's life. Indeed, it is nothing less than a scandal that more than a century since his death we do not have a major biography of the most significant American contributor of his generation (together with the linguist W. D. Whitney) to what we have come to call the social sciences.

The most important of the earlier writers on Morgan was unquestionably the late Leslie A. White of the University of Michigan. Although I joined the university (in the Department of History) before White's death, I much regret that I never met him. Although one cannot always agree with his rather embattled interpretations— and, indeed, I shall criticize White on Morgan's attitude toward religion in the pages that follow—I should not like to let slip the opportunity to pay homage to the one who has done more to advance our understanding of Morgan than any other, in the face of much indifference and some hostility, and to declare my solidarity with him in his belief in Morgan's fundamental importance. White did a great deal to make Morgan's manuscript material accessible through his annotated editions of the field notes of his Indian researches in the West, the journal of his European trip (which White himself discovered), his correspondence with Adolph Bandelier and other items (see the bibliography). The Leslie A. White Papers at the Bentley Historical Library contain typescript copies that White had made of what appears to be the complete Morgan correspondence numbering,

I estimate, over 2,500 letters, in preparation for a biography that he never, in fact, wrote. White's notes show that he ferreted out many hitherto unknown Morgan letters and arranged for photographic copies to be deposited in the Morgan Papers. His own research correspondence indicates that toward the end of his life he had been preparing an edition of Morgan's correspondence with "distinguished scientists and scholars." One hopes that someone equally as dedicated will take up the publication of the Morgan correspondence, which White so nearly finished.

I cannot say that Morgan scholarship has made great strides since White was among us and subsequent to Resek's biography. The recent literature seems to have gotten stuck on certain issues, such as evolutionism, materialism, racism, and the warfare of science with theology. Important as these are, they have become the whole agenda for Morgan study, making fresh approaches difficult. Rather than engage with this literature point by point, I have found it more fruitful to go directly to Morgan's publications and manuscripts, carrying with me the "philological" reading of the *Systems* that I had formed in the course of my earlier, Dravidian work, and to deal with the canonical themes of the Morgan literature only peripherally (and, doubtless, inadequately). I have wanted to shift the center of Morgan studies to the semanticism and "genealogism" of the *Systems*.

Elisabeth Tooker, fellow laborer in the Morgan Papers vineyard, is an outstanding exception to the above strictures. I remember well my first encounter with her writings on Morgan. On my first visit to the Rochester collection I called up a folder whose catalogue description held out the promise that it contained the solution to the problem, which I felt Resek had not resolved, of the exact nature of Joshua McIlvaine's contribution to Morgan's evolutionary schema at the end of the *Systems*. Opening the folder with trembling hands, I was much chagrined to find within a photocopy of a published note by Professor Tooker, correctly identifying the document it accompanied as the key text. I have subsequently enjoyed many interchanges with her and had the inestimable advantage of her intimate knowledge of the Morgan material and of Iroquois ethnography. "F.M.&B.M.S."—the hope for more and better Morgan scholarship—with which she closed a letter to me, has since become a motto of our endeavors, one result of which is this book.

I am grateful for help from many quarters. Financial support for the research was provided by the National Endowment for the Humanities and the Horace H. Rackham School of Graduate Studies.

University of Michigan. Karl Kabelac, Manuscripts Librarian of the Department of Rare Books in the Rush Rhees Library, University of Rochester, was unfailingly generous with his time and his knowledge of the Morgan Papers and of Rochester's history. I should also like to record my appreciation of the late Alma Creek of that library. William Cox of the Smithsonian Institution Archives, Cynthia McLelland of the Princeton University Archives, Stanley Insler of the American Oriental Society, and my colleague Francis X. Blouin of the Bentley Historical Library were especially helpful in tracking down sources. My friend John V. A. Fine, Jr., gave his enthusiastic encouragement to this project and pressed his mother Elizabeth Bunting Fine into service; I am grateful to her for unearthing material on Joshua Hall McIlvaine.

I cannot express how helpful the voluminous comments of Robert W. McKinley, the kinship theorist, on this and on my previous book have been; I am only grateful to be among the happy few who know the value of his guidance. Other friends read and commented on the manuscript of the book, in whole or in part: Elisabeth Tooker, the Iroquoianist and Morgan scholar; the political scientist Kenneth R. Hoover; the intellectual historians David A. Hollinger, Stephen J. Tonsor, James Turner, and Frederic van Holthoon; and the historian of the ancient Near East, Louis L. Orlin. I was fortunate to have had comments from George S. Stocking, the dean of historians of anthropology, as a reader for California. Robert F. Berkhofer, Jr., Bernard S. Cohen, Geoffrey H. Eley, S. C. Humphreys, J. Mills Thornton, and Aram A. Yengoyan gave me the benefit of their support and their erudition at various junctures, and Walter Lippincott gave sound advice. To Marcella Hauolilani I am grateful for lessons on Hawaiian kinship and for much encouragement. The Institute of Social Anthropology, Oxford University; the Centre for Historical Study, Jawaharlal Nehru University; and the history and anthropology departments of the University of Michigan graciously offered me platforms from which to try out my ideas about Morgan. I am grateful to have had excellent research assistants in Margaret A. Becker and Vichai Chitvimarn. Theodore W. Trautmann drew the original kinship diagram of Morgan's marriage. I thank Jeanette Kay Ranta and Jeanette Diuble for the typing.

This book is dedicated to the memory of M. S. A. Rao, Professor of Sociology, University of Delhi, teacher and friend, whose untimely death has deprived me of the opportunity to take his help, once again, in the writing of a book. His intelligence, his civility, and his humanity will be remembered by many around the world.

Acknowledgments

Manuscript material in the Morgan Papers is quoted at various places, especially in chapters 2, 5, and 6 (including figure 6). The frontispiece and figures 1, 5, 7, and 8 are from photographs supplied by the University of Rochester. Unpublished material by Lewis Henry Morgan, both at the University of Rochester and elsewhere, of which the University of Rochester is copyright holder, is published by permission.

Part of chapter 10 uses material, in revised form, from "Decoding Dravidian kinship: Morgan and McIlvaine," *Man* (n.s.) (1954) *19*: 421–431. Figure 12 first appeared there, p. 428. Reprinted by permission.

Figure 14 is based on *Dravidian kinship* (Cambridge: Cambridge University Press, 1981), p. 84. Reprinted by permission.

1

Kinship and Its Inventors

✦✦

In July 1871, Lewis Henry Morgan, having returned to London from
the Continent in the course of an extended European tour, first saw
his book in print, the *Systems of consanguinity and affinity of the
human family,* recently published by the Smithsonian Institution.
The meeting of author with book stirred deep emotions of pride and
pain, which he recorded in his journal:

> Yesterday I obtained from Mr. Charles Nesley, agent of the Smithsonian
> Institution, 28 Essex St. Strand, a copy of my work on Systems of
> Consanguinity and Affinity of the Human Family. . . . Of course I was
> glad to see it. My last work before leaving home in June a year ago was
> to finish reading the proof sheets. I looked it over with a curious kind
> of interest. It represents about eight years of hard labor, a large expendi-
> ture of money, and is identified in my mind always with the loss of my
> dear children, the irreparable calamity of my life.

The death by scarlet fever of his daughters in the summer of 1862
while he was on a field trip to the American West, collecting systems
of relationship from Indian tribes for the massive tables of kinship
terms around which he built his book, gave it the private iconography
of a memorial to the dead. In the journal entry he goes on at some
length about his struggle to include a dedication to his daughters'
memory and the emotional cost of acceding in the end to the insistence of Joseph Henry, secretary of the Smithsonian and his editor,
that it be omitted.[1]

At some six hundred pages the book was immensely large. Henry's
assistant, Spencer Baird, had told him it cost nearly $8,000 to pub-
lish, that stereotyping of the tables alone cost $16 the page, and that

---

[1] "Extracts from the European travel journal of Lewis H. Morgan," edited by
Leslie A. White, pp. 369–371. The original is in the Morgan Papers.

it was the most expensive work the Smithsonian had ever published. On another occasion he estimated the cost to himself at $25,000 in out-of-pocket expenses and work foregone in his law practice.[2] He was afraid its size would repel perusal, though he believed all of its detail to be material. "It is the hardest kind of reading, and yet it is tolerably well written, and I have no cause to be ashamed of it." It would take a long time before it was much known, he thought, and would likely make its reputation through references in other books on kindred subjects; but the great current interest in the "ages of barbarism" would bring it into notice sooner or later. "It embodies the first collection of facts which tend to show the successive stages of growth in the Family, indicating four of those stages with a good deal of certainty. This I regard as the most remarkable result by far of the investigation."

Every book has a twofold history, private and public, standing as it does in different relation to the sequence of events that constitute the author's life, on the one hand, than it does to the sequence of events that constitutes the public discourse in which it participates, on the other. The moment of publication has magical properties for the author, for it is the moment at which a part of the self becomes objectified and leaves the private for the public domain. The private history of the *Systems* began, according to Morgan himself, in the summer of 1858; the program of research that brought it forth was "formed in an Indian Cabin on the shore of Lake Superior" near Marquette in Michigan's Upper Peninsula.[3] The final version of the manuscript was submitted to the Smithsonian Institution in 1867, but it was not published until 1871, the delays of publication causing the author much frustration and fears of being forestalled by others.

The period in which the private history of Morgan's kinship project unfolded—let us call it the long decade of the 1860s—was a

---

[2] Morgan to Lorimer Fison 6/30/79, Morgan Papers.

[3] MS. of the final version of the *Systems,* Morgan Papers: "At that time, eight years ago, when this programme was formed in an Indian cabin on the shore of Lake Superior, I little imagined the amount of labor its execution would require, or the numberless difficulties that would obstruct its prosecution. Experience is sure to be quick enough with her wholesome admonitions. Beside this, during the first six years of the investigation it was wholly uncertain whether it was a shadow or a substance I was pursuing, but it did not for this reason lose its attractive character. After the schedules in the Tables had been studied and compared, and not until then, did the doubts on the subject disappear." This paragraph does not appear in the printed *Systems.*

decisive one in the formation of modern anthropology. Five remarkable books appear in that decade, books which between them inau-
gurate the public discourse of kinship: Johann Jakob Bachofen's *Das
Mutterrecht* (1861), Henry Sumner Maine's *Ancient law* (1861),
Numa Denis Fustel de Coulanges' *La cité antique* (1864), John
Ferguson McLennan's *Primitive marriage* (1865), and Morgan's *Systems* (1871). I shall examine the interconnections of these works in
some detail in chapter 8. Here, by way of anticipation, it needs to
be said that anthropology's axial age coincided with, and was shaped
by, two simultaneous intellectual revolutions that exercised profound
effects upon conceptions of the human. The decade of kinship was
also the decade of Darwin, bounded by the appearance of *The origin
of species* (1859) and *The descent of man* (1871). I shall, however,
argue that the direct effect of Darwin upon the invention of kinship
was very small (though not insignificant) and quite late in making
itself felt. It was rather the other revolution, cast into the shade for
us by the brilliance of Darwin's achievement and the widespread
consternation it provoked, that irrevocably altered the terms and
direction of that discourse. Thanks to the discovery of fossil man,
the 1860s were the decade of the sudden expansion of the duration
of ethnological time from the cramped confines of the traditional,
Bible-based chronology of history since the Flood. The effects of this
change upon Morgan and his generation ran deep. The most important among them was that it served to set ethnology free of the
tutelage of ancient history and of philology. It will be a major task
of this book to examine the onset and outcomes for kinship of the
revolution in ethnological time.

The work of these pioneers has the character of both discovery
and invention. It may seem odd to speak of the discovery of kinship,
given that the elements of that entity—family, family relationships,
modes of descent, rules of marriage, gender roles—lie immediately
to hand for every human being. On the face of it the pioneers of
anthropology need only have reached out and appropriated kinship
from everyday experience. In fact, the provisions of the kinship
system are nearly everywhere attributed to some immanent order,
whether of Nature or of God or some other, which gives it the
transparency of that which constitutes "the way things are." Like
the air we breathe, it is all around us and we cannot see it. Kinship
had to be discovered, and it was discovered through the discordant,
noncommonsensical kinship of the cultural other. Morgan discovered
kinship through study of the Iroquois; he was astonished to find that

property and office descended among them through females only, interior to the "tribes" or clans into which their society was divided, and that the father's brother was a father and the mother's sister a mother. Facts of this kind served to denaturalize kinship for Morgan and in doing so to make it available to consciousness. For Bachofen this was accomplished by his vision of Mother Law as the deep logic of preclassical myth, in antithesis to the familiar Father Principle animating the societies of the Greeks and Romans in classical times. Maine and Fustel made of the Greeks and Romans themselves a cultural other, ethnologizing them such that they were perceived as strangers rather than as ancestors. For McLennan it was the study of savages, especially contemporary ones, that provided the point of departure for the radical reexamination of marriage. I shall be examining Morgan's discovery of kinship in chapter 3; as will be seen, his encounter with an exotic kinship system had the marks of genuine discovery, of facts that existed independent of his will and whose existence he had not so much as suspected.

Kinship is not only an object of anthropological study, however, something existing outside the scholar's mind which had first to be discovered. It is also something anthropologists do; "kinship" is a verb as well as a noun. The ways in which anthropologists "do kinship" have been invented; they are artifacts of the will. This doing consists of the whole kit bag of methods for the collection, description, and analysis of the facts of kinship. But it consists as well of the prior act of drawing a border around certain aspects of human behavior, isolating them for study and affirming that they do indeed constitute an object, that they cohere. This affirmation is an act of will, because coherence must first be asserted before analysis can be applied to demonstrate it; but analysis rarely exhausts the problems it must resolve before its task of demonstrating coherence is complete. In all these senses kinship was invented, in the long decade of the 1860s. And the most important single source of the practice of kinship, of kinship as it is done, was Morgan. Doing kinship is deeply structured by Morgan's work to this day, much more than it is by any of his contemporaries; and much more (as I hope to show) than its current practitioners realize.

Let us make a beginning by leafing through the book itself.

The *Systems* is a massive book published by the Smithsonian Institution in its *Contributions to knowledge* series as the seventeenth volume. As we have seen, it was the largest and costliest publication the Smithsonian had undertaken, and its size and complexity placed a great burden on its finances. This gave Joseph Henry reason to be cautious in accepting it for publication, and he protected himself by submitting the manuscript to not one review process but two, totaling five readers. In the Advertisement that greets readers when they open the book, they find the following cautiously distant statement over Joseph Henry's signature:[4]

> The present memoir was first referred to a commission consisting of Professor J. H. McIlvaine and Professor William Henry Green, of Princeton, New Jersey, who recommended its publication, but advised certain changes in the method of presenting the subject. After these modifications had been made, it was submitted to the American Oriental Society, and was by it referred to a special committee, consisting of Messrs. Hadley, Trumbull, and Whitney, who, having critically examined the memoir, reported that it contained a series of highly interesting facts which they believed the students of philology and ethnology, though they might not accept all the conclusions of the author, would welcome as valuable contributions to science.

The book consists of 600 pages. Over 200 of them are taken up by three synoptic tables of "schedules" of "systems of consanguinity and affinity" or "systems of relationship"—or, as we would say nowadays, kinship terminologies. These systems of relationship (I shall adopt the shorter of Morgan's phrases) had been collected by Morgan personally through fieldwork among American Indians and by correspondence with missionaries and others in distant parts of the world. The results of these labors are very unevenly distributed. The 139 schedules, each containing entries for some 200 different relationships, are grouped in the following way:

Table I: Systems of consanguinity and affinity of the Semitic, Aryan, and Uralian families (39 schedules)

Table II: Systems of consanguinity and affinity of the Ganowánian [i.e., American Indian] family (80 schedules)

Table III: Systems of consanguinity and affinity of the Turanian and Malayan families (18 schedules plus two late-arriving schedules in a supplement)

---

[4] *Systems,* p. iii.

The text is in effect a commentary upon the tables, so that the whole of the book is subdivided into three parts, each part consisting of several chapters of text and a table. One may, as an approximation, describe the geography of the *Systems* by saying that Part I is devoted to peoples of Europe and western Asia, Part II to American Indians (confined, really, to those of the United States and Canada), and Part III to Asia from India eastward, and parts of Oceania.

The units of Morgan's larger groupings of systems of relationships are not geographical, however, but linguistic, and the families of which he speaks are historic groupings of peoples as known, in the first instance, through philology.

Turning to the argument of the book, succinctly summarized in the preface, we find that *philology* is the first word with which Morgan addresses his readers. The design of the book is a philological one; indeed, Morgan's ethnology is the continuation of philology by other means.[5]

> Philology has proved itself an admirable instrument for the classification of nations into families upon the basis of linguistic affinities. A comparison of the vocables and of the grammatical forms of certain languages has shown them to be dialects of a common speech; and these dialects, under a common name, have thus been restored to their original unity as a family of languages. In this manner, and by this instrumentality, the nations of the earth have been reduced, with more or less of certainty, to a small number of independent families. . . .
>
> The remarkable results of comparative philology, and the efficiency of the method upon which as a science it proceeds, yield encouraging assurance that it will ultimately reduce all the nations of mankind to families as clearly circumscribed as the Aryan and Semitic. But it is probable that the number of these families, as finally ascertained, will considerably exceed the number now recognized. When this work of philology has been fully accomplished, the question will remain whether the connection of any two or more of these families can be determined from the materials of language. Such a result is not improbable, and yet, up to the present time, no analysis of language, however searching and profound, has been able to cross the barrier which separates the Aryan from the Semitic languages—and these are the two most thoroughly explored—and discover the processes by which, if originally derived from a common speech, they have become radically changed in their ultimate forms. It was with special reference to the bearing which the systems of consanguinity and affinity of the several families of mankind might have upon

---

[5] The same, pp. v–vi.

this vital question, that the research, the results of which are contained in this volume, was undertaken.

To this inability of philology to complete its project of uniting the various families of mankind into one, Morgan brings to bear what he elsewhere calls a "new instrumentality for ethnology," the comparative study of systems of relationship. Where the comparison of vocabularies establishes families of historically related languages but is powerless to show the historical relations between language families, comparison of systems of relationship reveals historical relationships within and also between language families. The language families are many, but there are only two systems of relationship: the *descriptive* and the *classificatory*. The peoples of Table I (Semitic, Aryan, and Uralian) possess the descriptive system; those of Tables II and III (Ganowánian or Amerindian, Turanian, and Malayan), the classificatory.

This well-known and much-discussed pair of terms generalizes and rationalizes the aforementioned peculiarity Morgan encountered among the Iroquois—namely, that the father's brother is a father, the mother's sister is a mother, and so forth. Morgan sees this as a matter of "reducing consanguinei to great classes by a series of apparently arbitrary generalizations" and applying "the same terms to all the members of the same class,"[6] whence the system is called classificatory. More specifically, the decisive thing for Morgan is that collateral relatives are "classified" (merged) with lineal ones—the father's brother with the father, and so forth. In the descriptive system, on the contrary, primary terms such as *father* and *mother* are restricted to their primary sense and not expanded to include collaterals. All other terms are secondary. The system derives its name from the tendency in systems of the Semitic, Aryan, and Uralian group to *describe* "collateral consanguinei, for the most part, by an augmentation or combination of the primary terms of relationship." English is a rather poor example of the type; Erse and Welsh in which the equivalents of *father's brother* and *mother's brother* (rather than *uncle*) are the models Morgan has in mind. Even in the case of English *uncle*, however, what we see is a limited generalization, one that does not cross the all-important distinction between lineals and collaterals. We shall see in chapter 3 just why that barrier was so important to Morgan.

---

[6] The same, p. 12.

Morgan believed that these systems originated in a remote antiquity and hoped to demonstrate "the stability of these forms, and their power of self-perpetuation in the streams of the blood through indefinite periods of time."[7] Thus the many particular cases of the descriptive system are related to one another by codescent from a common ancestral system of relationship, and so also for the cases of the classificatory system. Morgan's new instrument for ethnology advances philology's project of demonstrating the genetic connection of all peoples to one another beyond the limit philology seemed to have reached, to the extent of reducing the multiplicity of language families to two groups, though it fell short of the final goal of showing the unity of the human family as a whole.

Morgan believed in the unity of the human family (which his title attests) as a truth of religion and of science and in opposition to polygenism or the separate creation of the races, which was being hotly debated in his day. It served a particular purpose of his, however, that the comparison of systems should have resolved them into two instead of one. The new instrument for ethnology was designed for that purpose—namely, to show (where philology could not) the unity of the American Indians and their Asian origin. In Part II comparison of American Indian schedules leads to the conclusion that there is essentially one system of relationship among them; in Part III the systems of southern and eastern Asia and Oceania are shown to be essentially the same as the American Indian system. These are so many instances of the unitary classificatory system, whereas the European and western Asian schedules of Part I are shown to be cases of a unitary descriptive system. The nonidentity of the two systems is necessary to dispose of the unnamed alternative to the hypothesis Morgan seeks to prove: that the Indians came to America via the Atlantic, from some part of Europe or from the Hebrews of the Old Testament.

In the final analysis, however, the difference between the two systems is resolved by means of a "conjectural history" of the family as I shall call it, using the phrase that Dugald Stewart invented to praise Adam Smith and that Radcliffe-Brown appropriated to castigate Morgan. The conjectural history of the family is an evolutionary theory of a "sequence of customs and institutions which mark the pathway through the ages of barbarism; and by means of which he raised himself from a state of promiscuous intercourse to final civili-

---

[7] The same, p. vi.

zation."[8] This theory as to the causes of the classificatory and descriptive systems of relationship is a late addition to the argument of the *Systems,* and Morgan advances it somewhat tentatively and as a finding that he believes his readers will find disagreeable. In this scheme the facts that my father's brother is (is referred to by the same term as) my father and my mother's sister is my mother find their explanation in the hypothesis of a former custom of several brothers sharing a wife, or several sisters a husband. I shall examine the origin and character of this theory in chapter 7. Here I need only remark that although Morgan devised this theory and added it to the argument of the *Systems* at the last minute, it nevertheless fulfills a concern of his that was of very long duration: to show that savagery or barbarism stood to civilization as an earlier stage in the story of progress. "The experience of the two conditions are successive links of a common chain of which one cannot be interpreted without the other."[9]

Thus "the Work." Let us now step back in order to broaden our perspective, and examine its place among the works in their entirety. The canon of Morgan's writing includes a number of articles and five books. Of the books, the best-known are his first book, the *League of the Iroquois* (1851), and the second to last, *Ancient society* (1877). The *Systems* falls in between, and so does *The American beaver and his works* (1868); *Houses and house-life of the American aborigines* (1881) came out in the last year of his life.

The pattern is one of striking modernism when one compares Morgan with Bachofen, Maine, Fustel de Coulanges, and McLennan. Whereas the latter are anthropologists of the library, Morgan's work rests in significant degree upon original fieldwork, first among the Iroquois (for the *League*), then among the Indian tribes of Michigan and the American West (for the *Systems*), again in the ruined pueblos of New Mexico (for *Houses and house-life*), and even among the beaver populations of the wilderness of Michigan's Upper Peninsula (for *The American beaver*). To be sure, held against the heroic standard of Cushing's fieldwork among the Zuni or Malinowski's in the Trobriand Islands, or the more practicable standard of a year of participant observation that has since become the norm, no one of Morgan's field experiences will measure up. From a twentieth-century vantage point, however, it is possible seriously to underesti-

---

[8] The same, p. vi.
[9] The same, p. vii.

mate the role of fieldwork in Morgan. As I shall show in chapter 3, Morgan's first encounter with the Iroquois showed him that the existing histories of the Iroquois were hopelessly unreliable. The experience was a formative one; again and again he sought to get the data of his work by direct interrogation and observation rather than by ransacking libraries. The interjection into the ethnological discourse of facts of an utterly new kind was the first of Morgan's achievements to be appreciated by his contemporaries. They were not mistaken. Although on each of the occasions mentioned the fieldwork is measurable in weeks or months rather than years, it is nevertheless at the center of what Morgan has to say and constitutive of all that is best in his work.

His disposition toward the field, further, gives a very modern cast to the way in which Morgan's work develops. He begins with a tribal monograph, the *League,* research for which, however, leaves unresolved puzzles—exogamous "tribes" or clans, descent through females only, father's brother a father and mother's sister a mother—which generate broader, comparative studies. The *Systems, Ancient society,* and *Houses and house-life* are the outcomes. The works record the successive attempts to rationalize by generalizing the original intense, meaningful, and baffling encounter with the cultural other.

Having perused the works, let us take a brief look at the life.

Lewis Henry Morgan (1818–1881) grew up in the village of Aurora in western New York state, the son of a prosperous landowner. He was educated at Cayuga Lake Academy in Aurora and at Union College, Schenectady. After graduation in 1840 he read law and was admitted to the bar. In 1844 he moved to Rochester, where he resided for the rest of his life. As a lawyer for Rochester businessmen who invested in railroads and iron works in Michigan, he made a modest fortune that enabled him to retire from his profession and devote himself fully to scholarship. He bequeathed his fortune and his papers to the University of Rochester.

The first period of his ethnological work runs from his admission to the bar to his marriage (1842–1851), which was the period of his early research on the Iroquois. Morgan's membership in an association of young men that called itself the New Order of the Iroquois led him to a search for the constitution of the Iroquois confederacy on which to model the constitution of his club. He sought it at first in the existing histories and then in the testimony of the Seneca

Iroquois of nearby Tonawanda Reservation. His initial understanding of Iroquois kinship appears in the series of "Letters on the Iroquois" published in 1847 in *The American review,* reprinted with slight changes in the *League of the Iroquois* (1851), the book in which he draws together the ethnological work of the preceding decade.

There follows an interval in which his Indian interests lay dormant while he applied himself to his law practice and to the raising of a family. He continued his commitment to scholarship, however. In 1854 he founded a literary association called The Club with his close companion and Presbyterian pastor, the Rev. Joshua Hall McIlvaine, and others. Two years later he joined the American Association for the Advancement of Science and was encouraged to resume his ethnological research. The following summer, in preparation for the annual meeting of the AAAS, he returned to his Iroquois material on kinship, reinterpreting it and attempting to generalize the Iroquois pattern to other Amerindian tribes. This paper, "Laws of descent of the Iroquois" (1857), was his first attempt to conceptualize what has become the argument of the *Systems,* but, as we shall see, it was a false start.

Morgan himself dates the beginnings of the *Systems* to the summer of 1858. Business generally obliged him to spend part of his summers in Marquette, Michigan, on the shores of Lake Superior. At the time in question he sought out information on Ojibwa kinship and found strong similarities to the Iroquois system of relationship. The following summer a returned missionary from South India supplied him with information on Tamil terms of relationship, and again he found strong similarities with the Iroquois. Morgan accorded great significance to these events, for they proved, in principle, that the Iroquois pattern was common to the American Indians generally and was found in Asia as well. Successive formulations of the new conception of the common pattern of Amerindian kinship are found in a privately printed circular letter of January 1859, accompanying a schedule or questionnaire of "degrees of relationship" by which he hoped to gather kinship systems for comparative study by correspondence; an unpublished paper, "System of consanguinity of the Red Race, in its relations to ethnology," read at the August meeting of the American Association for the Advancement of Science; and, following Morgan's first acquisition of substantial information on the Tamil and Telugu systems of relationship, a thirteen-page article, dated October 1st, 1859, in a new version of the circular letter and schedule, which now had the backing of the Smithsonian Institution. This last is in effect an embryonic *Systems*; the essential conception is as we find it in the published book, lacking only the conjectual history of the family.

The research and writing up of the first version of the *Systems* occupied the period from 1859 to 1865. The collection of schedules of systems of relationship proceeded apace, and the lion's share of the American schedules were collected by Morgan himself during the summers of 1859–1862, or as circumstances brought Native American representatives to the East. The returned schedules and drafts of the synoptic tables of the schedules are preserved in the Morgan Papers. Also to be found there are two manuscript versions of the *Systems*, the first submitted in 1865 and the revised, final version submitted in 1867, as well as a scattering of early drafts and draft revisions intermediate between the two versions.

From 1865 to 1871, then, was the period in which Morgan rewrote the *Systems* to meet the criticisms of the Smithsonian and its readers, adding to its basic argument the conjectural history of the family. It was also the period in which he awaited publication with mounting impatience for four years after delivering final copy. To avoid being forestalled he published his evolutionary theory in an article, "A conjectural solution of the origin of the classificatory system of relationship" (1868). The same year he brought out his book on the beaver, based on observations made during his summer trips to Marquette.

In his final decade Morgan composed *Ancient society*, which subsumes his kinship work within a broad treatment of social evolution along four dimensions: inventions and discoveries, government, family, and property. It is, as J. W. Powell observed, his "final conclusion and philosophic treatment" of the subject adumbrated in the *Systems*, and it brought his work considerable international attention.[10] He

---

[10] J. W. Powell, "Sketch of Lewis H. Morgan, President of the American Association for the Advancement of Science," p. 117. This article, published in the last year of Morgan's life by one who knew him well, appears to reflect Morgan's own interpretations and valuations of his work. Speaking of the *Systems* he says, "This first volume was essentially a volume of facts, and only a brief and rather unsatisfactory discussion of the facts was undertaken. Mr. Morgan's final conclusion and philosophic treatment of the subject was reserved for a subsequent volume"—that is, *Ancient society*. The position taken in this book is that the *Systems* is far more than a collection of facts, but the epistemology from which it was so viewed will be matter for discussion at the end of this chapter and in chapter 2.

also wrote *Houses and house-life of the American aborigines,* which deals with themes he had had to exclude from the *Systems* concerning the relation between family structure and the forms of domestic architecture. His contemporaries recognized the importance of his accomplishments and of the field of study he had discovered. The American Association for the Advancement of Science formed an anthropology section and made him chairman of it; he subsequently became president of the AAAS and a member of the National Academy of Sciences.

Morgan's intellectual development is unusually accessible to study thanks to the paper trail he left us, more so than for any of the other pioneer anthropologists save perhaps Bachofen. The conception of kinship contained in the *Systems* is traceable over a long period of maturation, measuring a quarter of a century from his first knowledge of Iroquois kinship gained in 1846 to the publication of the *Systems* in 1871. The writings, published and unpublished, record the stages of that maturation with exceptional clarity. Some of these have already been mentioned. There are others.

Morgan was a well-organized person with tidy habits of work. He kept his field notebooks and bound them in six volumes. These include his early Iroquois field notes, which are being edited and annotated for publication by Elisabeth Tooker, and the notebooks of his western field trips of 1859–1862, of which Leslie A. White has published selections. Undoubtedly the single most important item in these volumes bearing upon the development of Morgan's kinship theories is the "Notes of a trip to Marquette, Lake Superior, July 1858," which elucidates a major turning point in his thinking in the course of researches on the Ojibwa.

There are also two manuscript volumes which Morgan had bound in 1859, titled *Record of Indian letters.* It is in the nature of an address book and log of correspondence for his kinship research. In the opening pages there is a carefully worked-out history of his kinship research dated 19 October 1859.[11] This rare fragment of

---

[11] The two volumes of manuscript journals have the title *Record of Indian letters* on the spine; on the title page we read, "Record of the Inquiry Concerning the Indian (American and Oriental) System of Relationship And the Correspondence in Relation thereto L. H. Morgan 1859." It alludes, with ponderous humor, to Morgan's belief that the American Indian system of relationship was identical with that of the Dravidians of India; thus the people whom Columbus encountered in the New World *were* Indians after all. The valuable autobiographical passage in the beginning of the first volume has been published by Leslie White: "How Morgan

autobiography is extended somewhat by the introduction in the *Systems,* in which he recounts the "causes which induced this Investigation."[12] In addition, there are a number of items having an indirect bearing on the development of Morgan's kinship work, including unpublished papers and an inventory of his and his wife's books in the Morgan Papers. And there is a large correspondence connected with this research, including returned schedules of kinship terms in the Morgan Papers, and correspondence preserved in the Smithsonian Institution concerning the publication of the *Systems.*

Two biographical sources are of particular value because they come from principal players in the drama. First, there are Morgan's self-representations, including the autobiographical fragments referred to earlier. Second, there is the funeral address by Morgan's close friend, the Rev. Joshua Hall McIlvaine. Both repay close study. They are very different from each other.

McIlvaine casts the accomplishments of Morgan's scholarly life in the heroic mold of Newtonian science. He emphasizes the originality and other active qualities of Morgan's mind in the formation and adoption of hypotheses, which are then tested against the facts; "for the power of generalization was one of the most distinguished traits of his mind."[13] Speaking of a hypothesis that would explain the classificatory system, McIlvaine said,

> With this instrument in his hand, he now proceeded precisely as Newton did with his hypothesis of gravitation, which gave him his grand principle of ratiocination. He reasoned: If this hypothesis be correct, then such and such facts will be found in the physical and stellar worlds. Then he would raise his telescope and look, and there invariably the facts predicted by the hypothesis would be found. Thus he marched through the physical universe, making discoveries in every direction, like a mighty conqueror subduing and overrunning and taking possession of a hostile country. Precisely in the same way our friend now reasoned from his

---

came to write *Systems of consanguinity and affinity*." Although Morgan himself did not publish this passage, it is a carefully written, formal statement intended to be a proof of Morgan's priority should he be forestalled in print by another scholar.

[12] *Systems,* p. 3.

[13] McIlvaine, *The life and works of Lewis H. Morgan, LL.D., an address at his funeral"* (21 December 1881), p. 50, 52–53. McIlvaine had developed the Newtonian image long before, in language that the funeral address clearly borrows, in *A discourse upon the power of voluntary attention, delivered before the Rochester Atheneum & Mechanics' Association* in 1849 (see pp. 19–20).

grand generalization and hypothesis. He said: If it be correct, then such a fact or facts I shall find; and he also would raise his mental telescope and look for them in the past experience of mankind, where they were sure to be found. Thus he discovered literally thousands of new facts, and was enabled to render intelligible thousands previously known, but which hitherto had been inexplicable.

The aggressive role which McIlvaine ascribes to Morgan's mind contrasts sharply with Morgan's self-representations. Morgan habitually describes the critical junctures of his research as having come about through a series of happy accidents, as if to say that he was the lucky beneficiary of mere chance. Thus in the unpublished autobiographical piece in the *Record of Indian letters* he says of the way in which his Iroquois research developed from the Indian fraternity to which he belonged, "The interest awakened in me in this matter was the result, as in all similar cases, of special circumstances having more the appearance of accident than deliberate intention."[14] He represents himself as having been "surprised" to find that the Ojibwa system was substantially the same as the Iroquois, although his field notes make it clear that he sought out Ojibwa informants in the expectation that they would be found to follow the Iroquois pattern. He says, "My astonishment was greater than I can well express to learn that the Tamil system and the American Indian system were substantially identical."[15] As we shall see later, however, when we have occasion to examine the circumstances more closely, McIlvaine is surely right when he recalls, to the contrary, that Morgan predicted that he would find examples of the American Indian system of relationship "among the Tamil people and Dravidian tribes of Southern India."[16] Again, on another occasion Morgan represents his taking up the subject of the American beaver as a happenstance, an alternative amusement to fishing during the summers in the Michigan wilderness, but in the next chapter we shall see reason to think that the decision to do so was far less casual than Morgan allows himself to say. Morgan is scrupulous about recording intellectual debts and is factually honest to a fault; but because of what he omits to say in the overall presentation of his life, he often conveys the very misleading impression that his accomplishments were the result of fortuitous

[14] White, "How Morgan came to write *Systems*," p. 260.
[15] The same, p. 266.
[16] McIlvaine, *Life and works*, p. 50.

conjunctions of forces, and that his mind was the more or less passive recorder of impressions from without.[17]

To be sure, the difference between McIlvaine on Morgan and Morgan on Morgan is largely accounted for by the very different relation in which each stands to the subject: it is McIlvaine's place to praise and Morgan's to be modest. (Indeed, McIlvaine is modest to the point of complete silence about the critical role *he* played in Morgan's work, for the hypothesis of which he speaks in the funeral address was suggested to him by McIlvaine himself, as we shall see.) But in Morgan's case I believe there is far more than conventional authorial modesty involved. For the theory of mind that informs Morgan's writing about kinship systems and how they come into existence informs as well his conception of scientific knowledge and, as I have come to believe, his representations of his own work. That theory is the complete opposite of the picture of mind in McIlvaine's funeral address, vigorously fashioning hypotheses and deploying them as a power with which to subdue Nature and force her to yield up new facts. Morgan's is a theory that emphasizes the tutelage of nature, to whose promptings the mind must be attentive for true knowledge to form, and it is distrustful of the mind's active powers as such. Generalizations that follow natural suggestion are true; those that are mere products of thought are likely to be arbitrary, artificial, and false. Here, however, we are trenching upon matters that are the proper business of chapter 2. Let us leave it at this for the moment, that with no intent to deceive us Morgan is a reliable guide to the facts of his life but a poor guide to their interpretation.

The plan of this book is, first, to expound two basic elements of Morgan's thinking that underlie his kinship work: his theory of mind and his conception of ethnological time. The next five chapters will trace the private history of the kinship project to the completion of the final version of the manuscript of the *Systems*: the early work on the Iroquois (chapter 3), the period of dormancy (chapter 4), the discovery of Ojibwa and Tamil (chapter 5), and the writing of the first and second versions of the *Systems* (chapters 6 and 7). I shall then look at the state of the public discourse on kinship in the 1860s established by Bachofen, Maine, Fustel de Coulanges, and McLennan (chapter 8), and the consequences of the revolution in ethnological

---

[17] Many of the features of Morgan's self-representation carry over into Powell's "Sketch of Lewis H. Morgan" (see note 10) and thence into later interpretations.

time for ethnology and related disciplines (chapter 9). Finally (chapter 10), I shall return to the *Systems* to describe its publication and essay an evaluation of its achievement.

2

Scale of Mind, Scale of History

✦✦

Before coming to the kinship work itself it will be useful to examine those larger dimensions of Morgan's thought, alluded to in the previous chapter, that environ his interest in "systems of relationship." There are two issues to address here. The first is the concept of mind that conditions both his work and his self-representations. The second issue is the revolutionary expansion, in the middle of Morgan's career, of the scale of human history, the expansion of what I shall call *ethnological time*.

At the center of Morgan's work is the notion of the "scale of mind"; it is the organizing principle of his anthropology, and because it unites mankind with the animals in a continuous series, it makes his anthropology consistent with, and in truth a subset of, his zoology. Examination of Morgan's zoological ideas will shed light on his anthropological conceptions and hence on his kinship work.

These zoological ideas are expressed in a handful of works, the most prominent being *The American beaver and his works* (1868), the research and writing of which was more or less simultaneous with that of the *Systems*. There are in addition three minor pieces. As early as 1843, as he was turning twenty-five, one of his earliest articles appeared in the *Knickerbocker,* entitled "Mind or instinct." An unpublished paper, "Animal psychology" (1859), was delivered before The Club of Rochester nearly a decade before the beaver book, and after it, in 1872, he returned to the mind versus instinct theme in a critical review of a book by P. A. Chadbourne on instinct in *The nation,* nearly thirty years after the *Knickerbocker* article. What is striking about this smallish, chronologically dispersed body of writing is the constancy of its leading ideas, especially given that the Darwinian revolution takes place within the period of time it covers. Morgan's zoology, governed by the scale-of-mind idea, shows very little development over time, and we will not go seriously

wrong if, as a simplifying assumption to facilitate exposition, we take
it that all his zoological writings express a unitary, unchanging concept of mind.

The 1843 *Knickerbocker* article particularly repays scrutiny. Its
full title states the leading concern of all Morgan's zoological writing:
"Mind or instinct, an inquiry concerning the manifestation of mind
by the lower orders of animals." It opens thus:[1]

> The cultivation of the intellectual endowments of man has raised him to
> such a degree above the other orders of animated existence, that he
> claims the exclusive possession of the Thinking Principle; forgetting,
> while he surveys the monuments of human intelligence, that they are but
> the evidence of his advancement from the savage state; and that while
> he remained in that primitive condition he might be considered, in fact,
> as many degrees below his present position in point of mental capacity,
> as above that of the most sagacious animals; forgetting also that had he
> continued in a state of nature, like some of the tribes of Africa or
> America, leaving others to judge of his intelligence from the rude vestiges
> of his civilization exclusively, they could scarcely attribute to him more
> intellect than they would to the beaver, or even to the ant.

Here in a few words Morgan throws up the scaffolding of his life's
work. The tribes of America and the beaver are to become major
preoccupations of his. The European or Euroamerican, the unmarked
universal *man* of the passage, is the standard of civilization; and the
savage state is to civilization as the most sagacious animals are to
the savage state, in point of *mental capacity*. Mind, then, becomes
the central issue for Morgan, both unifying and differentiating the
animal world as a whole, and man as a part of that world.

There are, to be sure, differences between humans and the other
animals. "Animals, unlike men, do not improve materially in different generations, because they generally require no artificial means to
promote their happiness; neither have they the gregarious principle
to the same extent as man; but some of those which have, exhibit
the extraordinary intelligence which will presently be cited."[2] It is
all, at bottom, a matter of degree. Morgan proceeds to show that
"the principle called INSTINCT manifests the same intellectual qualities as MIND," to wit memory, the process of abstraction, imagina-

---

[1] "Mind or instinct, an inquiry concerning the manifestation of mind by the lower
order of animals" (November 1843), p. 414.

[2] The same.

tion, reason or judgment; wherefore instinct is nothing other than mind itself.[3]

> The general deduction follows, that the same thinking intellectual principle pervades all animated existences; created by the DEITY, and bestowed in such measures upon the different species as appeared in His wisdom requisite for the destiny and happiness of each; thus establishing a scale from man to the lowest orders of animalculae; and the successive steps downward from the man of the highest intellectual range to the man of the lowest, are no farther than from the latter to the most intelligent animal; and from him successively to the lowest in the scale of intelligence.

We recognize at once the traditional figure, old as Aristotle, since made scientific and Christian, of the *scala naturae*. In fact Morgan's scale of mind is but one more special case of the traditional scale of nature. The figure of the scale—a ladder or staircase—is marvelously expressive. The succession of rungs or steps bespeaks both continuity between the forms that occupy them and their differences from one another; and the difference of levels expresses hierarchy. Together with continuity, difference, and hierarchy goes what Lovejoy calls "the principle of Plenitude": that there is no empty step, no missing link in the Great Chain of Being, since God's creation is perfect and as such contains all possible forms. Morgan's zoology exhibits all the features of the traditional, pre-Darwinian conception of the order of nature. Though the figure is a traditional one, Morgan's *is* a special case of it, and we must specify the character of this particular variant.

A further characteristic of this family of scalar figures that has become apparent through the modern critique of evolutionism is its unilineal character. It has proved impossible to show that all life forms can be arranged in a single sequence in respect of all dimensions of variation, and in particular to combine physical and mental scalar values consistently in a single scheme. In the whole body of his work, zoological and ethnological, Morgan shows very little interest in physiological features, and almost never are matters of physical form productive of scalar values. Everywhere the chosen dimension is that of mind. Morgan speaks variously of the "scale of intelligence," the "intellectual scale," the "scale of mental power," and the "scale of mind" rather than, for example, the "scale of

---

[3] The same (December 1843), p. 514.

creation" or the "scale of nature"; and again of the "thinking principle" or, simply, "mind" as that which links man with the other
animals. The most widely read of his books, *Ancient society,* makes
the centrality of mind especially clear. The titles of its four parts
speak of the "growth of intelligence through inventions and discoveries," the "growth of the idea of government," the "growth of
the idea of the family," and the "growth of the idea of property."
In the opening pages he lays down his essentially mentalist theme:
"Mankind commenced their course at the bottom of the scale and
worked their way up from savagery to civilization through the slow
accumulations of *experimental knowledge,*" wherefore his book
will show "the rudeness of the early condition of mankind and
the gradual evolution of their mental and moral powers through
experience."[4]

Morgan held a number of very specific ideas about the nature of
the mental powers that together constitute a philosophy of mind.
Briefly, he held that the mind is a unit, without parts, "not a conglom-
erate of constituent parts, but an essence, not resolvable into parts."
Thus, for example, it is the whole mind that remembers, "and not a
particular fraction of it."[5] As we cannot resolve the intellectual powers into parts, we must assume a unitary mind that is immaterial and
distinct from the body; "a principle or essence not divisible into
parts, or faculties, or organs."[6] It is a form, then, and is reducible
neither to its physical container nor to its content. "The mind is a
vortex, into which images and ideas are continually entering, and
from which they are constantly vanishing. The perpetual flow of the
mind suggests the idea of a revolution of some kind; and rather
around a shifting centre, than upon a primal axis."[7] Of its ultimate
nature, however, we know nothing. It is a "mental or spiritual essence
which is distinct from the body, but associated with it in a mysterious
manner."[8] It is immortal and irreducible to any other principle. It is
the element that takes cognizance of sense impressions. Through
"natural suggestion," "the promptings of nature," or "the teachings
of nature" the mind acquires knowledge and grows in intelligence.

[4] *Ancient society,* pp. 3, 4.
[5] "Animal psychology" (unpublished), Morgan Papers, pp. 10–11; compare
American beaver, p. 250.
[6] "Animal psychology," p. 9.
[7] The same, p. 8.
[8] *American beaver,* p. 250.

Morgan attributes to mind an active role in the process of acquiring knowledge, which occurs in the act of pursuing subsistence—in making more than in thinking per se. Mind is subject, however, to the tutelage of Nature, which in one manuscript passage Morgan calls "the great teacher." Thus knowledge—insofar as it is true—has a naturalistic quality, and mind progresses in knowledge insofar as it is attentive to these suggestions of nature, but it errs when it strays from nature's suggestions and follows its own will or fancy. This belief encompasses Morgan's view of scientific work including his own, and it appears as early as the 1843 article with which this chapter opened: "There is nothing unnatural in this theory [of a scale of intelligence uniting man with the other animals]; so far from it, it appears to be suggested by nature itself."[9] By implication, a theory that is unnatural would be false. This doctrine of natural suggestion will become a critical issue in Morgan's interpretation of kinship terminologies.

Morgan's psychology was formed under the guidance of the Scottish philosophical tradition, which was dominant in the America of his day, including the Common Sense school. It cannot be said that Morgan was of a philosophical turn of mind, or even that he was well read in philosophy. His library, as we know from the inventory he made of it, was strongly oriented toward concrete matters having a bearing upon the "struggle for subsistence"—agricultural journals, Patent Office reports, the reports of the various exploring expeditions, and so forth. It contained few works of philosophy. John Locke appears to have been a favorite, judging from the fact that the inventory lists two copies of the *Essay on human understanding*. Still, putting together such scattered bits of evidence as we have, we may say that a large number of the philosophers whose work he owned or whom he cited belong to the Scottish tradition: Adam Smith, Lord Kames, Thomas Reid, Dugald Stewart, Sir James Mackintosh, John Abercrombie, and Sir William Hamilton.

In particular, the concept of "natural suggestion" that is of fundamental importance in Morgan's work recalls the use of "suggestion" by the founder of the philosophy of Common Sense, Thomas Reid. Language for Reid consists of signs of two kinds, "such as have no meaning but what is affixed to them by compact or agreement among those who use them" or artificial signs, and "such as, previous to all compact or agreement, have a meaning which every man understands

---

[9] "Mind or instinct" (December 1843), p. 515.

by the principles of his nature," or natural signs.[10] "Suggestion" is the link between perception of the natural sign and the thing it signifies. "We all know," says Reid, "that a certain kind of sound suggests immediately to the mind, a coach passing in the street; and not only produces the imagination, but the belief, that a coach is passing."[11] This "suggestion," then, has nothing of the indistinctness and uncertainty it has in ordinary language; the connection between a certain kind of sound that is the natural sign of a coach and the coach that it signifies is clear and certain, and the mass of knowledge acquired through experience of such suggestions is equally clear and certain. The connection between the natural sign and the thing signified is "established by nature, but discovered only by experience."[12]

> The whole of genuine philosophy consists in discovering such connections, and reducing them to general rules. . . . What is all we know of mechanics, astronomy, and optics, but connections established by nature, and discovered by experience or observation, and consequences deduced from them? All the knowledge we have in agriculture, gardening, chemistry, and medicine, is built upon the same foundation. . . . What we commonly call natural *causes* might, with more propriety, be called natural *signs,* and what we call *effects,* the things signified. The causes have no proper efficiency or causality, as far as we know; and all we can certainly affirm is, that nature hath established a constant conjunction between them and the things called their effects; and hath given to mankind a disposition to observe those connections, to confide in their continuance, and to make use of them for the improvement of our knowledge, and increase of our power.

Morgan's zoology and ethnology, concentrating on the growth of knowledge not so much through contemplation and reflection as through interaction with external nature in the production of subsistence, are in deep harmony with that philosophy.

This focus upon productive interactions with nature as the source

---

[10] Reid's analysis of natural signs and of suggestion is much more complex than I can indicate here. Reid, *An inquiry into the human mind,* in *The works of Thomas Reid,* p. 117.

[11] Reid, p. 111. See the discussion in S. A. Grave, *The Scottish philosophy of common sense,* p. 178.

[12] The same, pp. 121–122. I do not mean to say that Morgan read of these matters in Reid's work, for which there is no evidence; but the dominance of the Scottish tradition in his age would have made these ideas available to him in many ways.

of "the growth of ideas," together with the disposition to minimize the difference between humans and other animals upon the chosen dimension of intelligence, leads Morgan's interest to fix upon the higher end of the scale of mind, upon these "most sagacious animals" that show human qualities of gregariousness and the use of art to promote their happiness: animals such as the ant, the bee, the nesting birds, and the beaver. Hence when business interests took him in 1855 on the first of several trips to Marquette, Michigan, he spent his free time studying the vast engineering works of beavers under wilderness conditions, his researches leading eventually to the *American beaver* book in 1868. As we have seen, in his autobiographical statements Morgan has a way of giving the impression that he was led to his work by a series of happy accidents rather than by his own design. Thus in his account of how he came to write *The American beaver* he says, "I took up the subject as I did fishing, for summer recreation."[13] But we see from the 1843 article that his choice of the beaver (over the fish, let us say) as an object of study was strongly predetermined and was more thoughtful than Morgan allows himself to say. The beaver is an engineer; his works are artificial constructions made in the pursuit of subsistence, which demonstrate the existence of a mental principle. Not only are beaver capable of artifice, for Morgan, but in different environments they show different behaviors that argue for a reasoned response to differences in nature. Thus the beavers of Michigan make canals, but those of the Red River of the North, where the river channels run through very steep banks, make mudslides but not canals. We might almost say that for Morgan the beaver is a cultural animal and shows cultural variation between different populations, following the suggestions of nature.

Morgan was fond of saying that the animals are "mutes, not brutes." Thus it is lack of language, not reason ("the thinking principle") that distinguishes the lower animals from man. Beyond this there is no commonly accepted frontier between man and the other animals that Morgan does not throw into doubt, where he does not directly deny it. In the 1843 article he suggests that animals may even have a moral as well as an intellectual nature, and in thus emphasizing the kinship of man and the other animals he is drawn toward vegetarianism:

---

[13] *American beaver,* p. ix.

Let us not boast too much of our moral qualities, although the Deity did design that we should subsist in part upon flesh; although we have the marks of this design upon us, the same as the bear and the wolf, and have the sanction of the Scriptures; for although the final cause of this is wise, it is no excuse for cruelty; and probably an enlightened moral sense would teach us to abstain entirely from animal food, if we can live without it.[14]

In his 1859 paper he repeats this idea and, among friends, broaches the further idea that the "Mutae" have immortal souls like humans and speaks approvingly, if regretfully, of the doctrine of the transmigration of souls:[15]

I have often thought that the ancient philosopher, whoever he was, who first promulgated the doctrine of the transmigration of souls, was worthy of immortal renown. Such a shield for the protection of the inferior animals against the rapacity of man was never before devised by human genius, and perhaps will never be again. Great is the pity then, that like the shield of Achilles it now exists only in poetry.

Vegetarianism, imperishable souls in animals, transmigration: a latent Hindu lurks inside the Presbyterian! Even possession of language does not radically part man from the other animals, who have means of communication of some kind; nor is the idea "that man alone is a progressive animal" allowed to pass unchallenged. Man, indeed, progresses in knowledge from age to age, but the limits of human understanding—the mental capacity of individuals—"have not advanced one hair's breadth within man's historical period." Conversely, we cannot assert that the bee and the ant "do not teach their offspring, and thus hand down traditional knowledge, acquired within their sphere of life, from generation to generation."[16] The boundary between Art and Nature is pushed down the scale of mind to include, tentatively, the most sagacious animals, nature's engineers.

A final characteristic of this zoology that we must note is Morgan's tendency to relativize the scale of mind, such that its inescapably hierarchical character is softened and qualified. He denies that the

---

[14] "Mind or instinct" (December 1843), p. 515.
[15] "Animal psychology," pp. 25–26.
[16] The same, p. 24.

other animals were created for man's use, asserting rather that God created each species for its own happiness and endowed it with mental powers sufficient to achieve it; he has adjusted a balance between these races and bestowed rights upon every species which no other may violate and escape the consequences.[17] Morgan's conception of the scale of mind does not treat the minds of animals as merely diminished likenesses of the human mind; rather, it entertains the possibility that they may have powers proper to them which mankind lacks.[18]

> Man, who stands at the head of the animal series, is about as far removed from the zero of matter, the ultimate atom, as he is from the totality of matter, or the Universe; and the subjects of knowledge as well as the means of enjoyment below the ken of his rougher intellect and coarser senses, which may be open to the more delicate perceptions, and exquisite senses of the tiny insect, may for aught we know, or have reason to disbelieve, be as great and wonderful, as the subjects of knowledge, and means of enjoyment which fall within mans sphere. As time is purely a relative term it has doubtless an expansion as we descend the scale, which furnishes in itself an increased means of knowledge. A range for the development and exercise of the thinking principle is thus laid open; which the different species were created to occupy. Thus the field of knowledge of the thinking principle is vastly expanded by a diversity of organic forms, through which it is constituted to manifest itself; and the sum of the powers of all the species is far greater, than those of any single one. It would seem, then that a full comprehension of the powers and capacities of the thinking principle necessarily involves a consideration of its manifestations throughout the animal kingdom; for the sum of the capabilities of this principle are not possessed by any species, but dwell in the animal races as a totality, recognising the lost, as well as existing species, and rendering possible intelligences higher than man endowed with the same principle. This view of the subject tends rather to exalt than debase our estimate of that intellectual and immortal gift of God which furnishes, in itself, a higher evidence of his power and wisdom, than the Universe of matter, and the laws impressed upon it at the moment of creation.

The scale of mind, then, admits "a diversity of powers" such that "the archetypal animal mind cannot be deduced from the human

---

[17] The same, p. 25.
[18] The same, pp. 11½–11¾.

alone"; whence an adequate science of mind must "comprehend the whole range of its manifestations throughout the animal kingdom."[19]

Morgan's anthropology is logically entailed by his zoology. If the task of an adequate science of mind is to address the problem of intelligence in lower animals and its relation to that in humans, a science of man has as its essential problem the relation of the savage state, conceived as a level of intelligence, to civilization. That is to say, the problem of the cultural other and its relation to the self is constructed by Morgan in a certain way—namely, as the problem of the relation of savagism, understood as an intellectual stage below civilization, to civilization itself.

As we have seen, the idea that the savage state is as many degrees below that of civilization as it is above that of the most sagacious animals was part of Morgan's thinking as early as his 1843 article. But the idea that the savage is to the European or Euroamerican as the animal is to the savage—that the Bushman is to Daniel Webster as the elephant is to the Bushman, as Morgan put it to the members of the Club[20]—was an idea by no means new and shocking. Indeed, there was wide agreement among white Americans of his day over the idea. The scale of nature concept and its applicability to the problem of the savage state was the common sense of the age. It was not in dispute; it was the very starting point of ethnological discourse. Arguments broke out over a different question—that of the unity of the human race.

One tradition, rendered scientific by the craniological measurements of the Philadelphia physician Samuel George Morton, propounded a physiological source—brain size—for the supposed intellectual differences between the races posited by the scale of nature

---

[19] The same, p. 3.

[20] The same, p. 22. In this paper the relation between man and the other animals has become somewhat problematic: "The hiatus between man and the species next below him is far greater than can be found in any other part of the scale; and it is sufficiently great to suggest, at least, that some intermediate species, and perhaps several of them, have dropped out in the course of the early ages, or that some existing species have been degraded beyond redemption. But with such conjectures we have nothing to do. I shall content myself, however, with suggesting, that the difference in intellectual power in degree between the highest specimens of man, and the lowest, between Daniel Webster, and a Bushman, is very probably as great, as between the Bushman and his neighbor the elephant; and so on down to the end of the scale."

(or scale of civilization) idea. In a country where and at a time when ethnological issues were immediate and pressing policy questions as well, there were many for whom such ideas had a fatal fascination. As the slavery question heated up in the decade leading to the Civil War, Morton's craniology was appropriated by Josiah Nott and George Gliddon, together with the polygenist writings of the cele- brated Harvard biologist Louis Agassiz, to form a fully blown scien- tific racism.[21] The belief that God had created the races separately and that they remained more or less fixed ever since was the cor- nerstone of this position.

Morgan and, indeed, others in his circle regarded slavery as un- natural and abhorrent and strongly adhered to the more orthodox view of the unity of the human race—which is to say, its unity of creation. From this flowed the doctrine of the unity of the human mind, which meant that the relation between the savage and the civilized had a quality altogether different from that of the relation between the savage and other animals. In the unpublished paper on animal psychology read to the Club in 1859 Morgan says,[22]

Man, indeed, progresses in knowledge from generation to generation, but yet the limits of the human understanding have not been advanced one hairs breadth within man's historical period. All the capacities of the entire race of man existed potentially in the first human pair. Man progresses in knowledge not only as an individual, but from age to age. He alone is able to perpetuate his intellectual achievements by means of a written language, thus making every discovery a foundation on which to mount up to a new discovery. This gives to him an advantage almost inconceivably great, and is sufficient of itself to account for the wide distance between him, and the next highest species. Notwithstanding portions of the human race have thus risen to the heights of civilization,

---

[21] Of the publications of Samuel George Morton, Morgan certainly had read *Crania americana; or, a comparative view of the skulls of various aboriginal nations of North and South America* (1839) and *Crania ægytiaca; or, observations on Egyptian ethnography, derived from anatomy, history and the monuments* (1844); notes on both appear in the *Record of Indian letters* in the Morgan Papers, and the first is cited in *Systems* (pp. 259, 268–269). He also knew Josiah Nott and George Gliddon, *Types of mankind* (1854) and *Indigenous races of the earth* (1857), and Louis Agassiz' "The diversity of origin of the human races," which first appeared in the *Christian examiner* (July 1850) and was reprinted by Nott and Gliddon. Stephen Jay Gould, *The mismeasure of man*, chap. 2, reviews this literature and shows that Morton's measurements were subject to unconscious bias.

[22] "Animal psychology," p. 24.

other portions, as the Bushman & the Hotentot, still sit in the darkness of ignorance and intellectual imbecility. The Bushman, however, is of the human genus; and logically, the point of comparison between man and the species next below him, commences with the Bushman just as legitimately as with the European.

A similar sentiment, but one in which the relation of the savage to the civilized man has been temporalized, being put into evolutionary series to one another, appears years later in *Ancient society*:

> Since mankind were one in origin, their career has been essentially one, running in different but uniform channels upon all continents, and very similarly in all the tribes and nations of mankind down to the same status of advancement. It follows that the history and experience of the American Indian tribes represent, more or less nearly, the history and experience of our own remote ancestors when in corresponding conditions.[23]

Morgan did hold the belief that certain ideas, whether as arbitrary creations of the intellect or as products of natural suggestion, could somehow be somatically stored and transmitted from generation to generation. In the *Systems* he holds that the classificatory system of relationship, once formed, is transmitted "in the streams of the blood" and gives us an outlandish list of customs that, because of their universality among Amerindians, are "customs of the blood"—to wit, that of saluting by kin, that of wearing the breechcloth, and that of sleeping at night in a state of nudity.[24] We have here a doctrine of racial knowledge. Again, in *Ancient society* he says that the primary institutions develop over time from a few primary germs of thought. "Modern institutions place their roots in the period of barbarism, into which their germs were transmitted from the previous period of savagery. They have had a lineal descent through the ages, with the streams of the blood, as well as a logical development."[25] Although Morgan entertains the belief that institutions, arts, and customs are imprinted upon their physiological substrate, this is not a doctrine of permanent, somatically encoded and transmitted intellectual differences among the races. On the contrary, Morgan expressly believes that the intellectual differences among peoples are remediable, and that the savage can be raised to civiliza-

---

[23] *Ancient society,* p. xxxi.
[24] *Systems,* p. 274.
[25] *Ancient society,* p. 4.

tion. On the issue of mental capacity—the *limits* of intelligence—his 1859 paper makes it clear that this is a constant that is the same for all races throughout history: "All the capacities of the entire race of man existed potentially in the first human pair."

In *Ancient society* we find a single sentence expressive of a slightly different view, a concession to the craniological tradition: "With the production of inventions and discoveries, and with the growth of institutions, the human mind necessarily grew and expanded; and we are led to recognize a gradual enlargement of the brain itself, particularly of the cerebral portion."[26] The view that the human brain has increased in size over the long reaches of time available to the evolutionary process is a modern one, and it is separated from the craniological publications of Morton and his intellectual progeny both by the time revolution and by Darwin. A leading argument of the scientific racists had been that the races were the same at the beginning of human history as they are today—as proved by the modernity of the racial types depicted in ancient Egyptian art. Thus their position required both the short chronology and the fixity of species and races. Once the time revolution had invalidated the one and the Darwinian revolution the other, the position collapsed. It then became possible to come to terms with the supposed craniological evidence of racial differences without also embracing polygenism.[27] Morgan does appear in the passage cited to be accepting Morton's dubious findings of graded craniological differences among races that reproduce, more or less, the scale of mind; but for him, unlike the scientific racists, growth of the mind *causes* enlargement of the brain, rather than the size of the brain being the cause of supposed intellectual differences among races. Although some of Morgan's ideas have racist associations, and although he seems to have accepted the conventional white American estimate of the intellect of blacks uncritically (and with nothing of the generosity of spirit we meet in his writings about American Indians), his position cannot properly be called racist for want of two essential ingredients of that view: the permanence of intellectual differences among races and their physiological cause.

---

[26] The same, p. 37. For a somewhat different interpretation, see George W. Stocking, Jr., "The dark-skinned savage: the image of primitive man in evolutionary anthropology," in *Race, culture, and evolution* (see pp. 116–117).

[27] Stocking, "The persistence of polygenist thought in post-Darwinian anthropology," in *Race, culture, and evolution,* argues that a complex of ideas that he calls "polygenist thought" survives the demise of polygenism.

In his later work, *Ancient society*, Morgan abandons the notion of a unitary savage state and adopts the categories of savagery and barbarism, each of these further subdivided into a lower, middle, and upper status. This proliferation of "ethnical periods," however, does not alter the fact that at the heart of all Morgan has done lies the dichotomy of savagism and civilization. Morgan takes from a well-established Euroamerican discourse on savagism[28] the ideas that the foundation of savagism is the hunter state, as contrasted with the agriculture of the plow. The hunter state entails nomadism, which chains the Indian in slavery to a savage way of life and prevents the growth of knowledge that would enable him to rise above it. The hold of this idea on Morgan was very strong; so strong that in his early writings on the Iroquois he treats the latter as hunters even though he describes their agriculture and refers to the stockaded villages in which they lived. In later writings he admits distinctions between Roving Indians (hunters), Village Indians (agriculturalists), and the partially Roving and partially Village tribes. The Iroquois are of the intermediate type; the most advanced stage is that of the Village Indians of New Mexico, the Aztecs, the Mayas, and the Incas. Even so, Indian agriculture, though admitted to the precivilizational stages, is minimized. It is really a cultivation of gardens, a horticulture with hoes, not the plow agriculture of civilized man.

Thus although Morgan's ideas on this matter show change and development, central to the matter is the concept of the stultifying effect of the hunting state and the civilizing effect of plow agriculture of Euroamerican type. These ideas have direct implications for public policy.

Throughout his adult life Morgan showed an interest in philanthropic and political activity in favor of the Indian, which was of a piece with his scientific ideas about Indians; indeed, his whole scientific endeavor, in his own conception, had a policy bearing. Morgan's philanthropic impulse was strong and attached itself to the struggle of the Senecas with the Ogden Land Company in the 1840s, and a subscription effort to send two Indian girls to school. He befriended the Seneca youth Ely Parker and helped him in his career. In 1841

---

[28] On this subject there is a sizable literature. Especially noteworthy are Roy Harvey Pearce, *Savagism and civilization;* Robert F. Berkhofer, Jr., *The White Man's Indian;* Ronald L. Meek, *Social science and the ignoble savage;* and P. J. Marshall and Glyndwr Williams, *The great map of mankind: perceptions of new worlds in the Age of Enlightenment.* The savagery/barbarism/civilization schema is drawn by Morgan from this discourse.

he applied for the subagency of the New York Indians, but he did
not get the post. Later he unsuccessfully sought appointment as
commissioner of Indian Affairs under Lincoln, and it is very likely
that his stint as New York assemblyman was intended to be a preparation for the Indian Affairs post. From time to time he wrote on
Indian policy, most notably and eloquently to defend the Indians
during the outcry over the annihilation of Custer's force at Little Big
Horn.[29] The leitmotif of these activities is education, cattle herding,
plow agriculture, and industry as the hope of an otherwise doomed
race. The government must not simply feed the Indians as an alternative to fighting them; it must civilize them.

The anthropology and zoology I have described are embedded
within geological and cosmological ideas that are not so fully worked
out and that, therefore, are not easy to identify. The most encompass-
ing of Morgan's ideas is that the evolutionary process is a progressive, unilineal one. The evolving subject, of course, is mind. He tells
us in one tantalizing passage that the progress of knowledge is predetermined and without end. As to its beginning, he never speaks
otherwise than in the orthodox terms of a creation by God. His view
of the order of nature was, as we have seen, entirely traditional and
not fundamentally changed by the Darwinian revolution. He knew
and admired Darwin; but if he was persuaded of the mutability of
species he does not say so, and regards Darwin's theory as a special
case of evolutionism that, so far from being a novelty, is traceable
to Horace and above all Lucretius, who is for Morgan evolution's
first theorist.[30]

Morgan's scale of mind concept undergoes little change in the
course of his life; to use his own language, it develops from primary
germs of thought already apparent in the 1843 article, and its successive expressions stand in unfolding relations to earlier ones. Quite
different is the case of Morgan's view of the scale of human history,
which in the middle of his career underwent a change that was
sudden, decisive, and of far-reaching consequences for his anthropology. In Morgan's own estimation, *the* intellectual revolution of his
generation was the explosion of the traditional biblically based
chronology.

---

[29] "The hue-and-cry against the Indians" (1876).

[30] The first version of *Ancient society* (MSS. dated in 1872 and 1873 in the
Morgan Papers) include a chapter called "Roman genesis of human development,"
which expounds Lucretius' system.

If we turn to the first pages of Genesis in the massive family Bible deposited in the Morgan Papers, we find printed in the central column of notes the words "Before CHRIST 4004." Other dates appear against other passages, offering a comprehensive chronology of the Bible. This chronology is that of James Ussher, archbishop of Armagh; it was first published in 1650 (*Annales Veteris et Novi Testamenti*) and had been printed in the margins of Protestant English Bibles from the beginning of the eighteenth century. Ussher's was but one of a family of biblical chronologies that, in spite of many differences of detail, belonged to the same order of magnitude.

In this particular version of the short chronology, the one with which Morgan had grown to manhood, the creation of the world and of the human race had occurred scarcely six thousand years previous. Indeed, ethnological time began a good bit after the Creation, for it is only subsequent to the Flood, or again to the Confusion of Tongues with which the Tower of Babel incident concluded, that ethnic and linguistic diversity, the stuff of ethnology, begins. The dispersal of the different nations of man across the earth proceeded from the descent of the sons of Noah: Shem, Ham, and Japhet. The Flood, in this chronology, began in 2349 B.C., allowing little more than four thousand years in which the earth might be peopled from the Asiatic cradle of the race.

Morgan abandoned this traditional chronology in the 1860s along with many others of his generation in the wake of archaeological discoveries of prehistoric man that rendered a short chronology untenable, replacing it with an ethnological time frame that was indefinitely long. Later I shall examine the timing, circumstances, and effects of this revolution on Morgan and his contemporaries. For the moment it will suffice to frame the problem by indicating Morgan's position early and late in his scholarly life.

In an early paper, the "Essay on geology" (1841), Morgan puts the relation of scientific theories of the earth's origin—the Neptunian theory of Werner and the Plutonian theory of Hutton—to the biblical account of Creation thus:[31]

> The Mosaic account of the creation declares, that "in the beginning God created the heaven, and the earth." From this it would at first appear, that as the creation itself was a miracle, it precluded all enquiry as to the manner of the formation of the Earth.—And elsewhere "the earth was spoke into existence."—But on the other hand, in the next verse it reads,

---

[31] "Essay on geology" (unpublished, Morgan Papers), p. 10.

"the earth *was* without form, and void; and darkness rested upon the face of the deep." How long the earth continued without form, and in this chaos, we have no means of knowing; This then, is the great inlet of the theories and speculations of which we have been speaking, so ready is the mind of man to pass through the smallest aperture in search of truth, or to urge the explorations of science with the daring of genius, almost to the beginning of time.

In a note to this passage he adds, "Mr. Comstock in alluding to this field for conjecture remarks, 'We may believe without the least violation of the sacred text that the materials of which the earth is composed, were created a thousand, or a million of years, before they were brought into a form fit for the habitation of man.' Com. Geo. P 315."[32]

Thus Morgan embraces the reconciliation of Genesis and Geology which allowed an indeterminately lengthy age to the earth prior to the first day of Creation, or the beginnings of life as we know it. Creation itself, however—and therefore ethnological time—remained confined within the cramped, six-thousand-year span of the prevailing Protestant chronology. Indeed, for many of Morgan's generation the breakup of the biblical chronology occurred in two distinct phases: the establishment of a long chronology for earth history in the 1830s, and a long chronology for human history in the 1860s. To get a fix on this process we may view the publications of the geologist Charles Lyell as landmarks, for Lyell had a great influence on nongeologists, defining geological doctrine and propagating it beyond the bounds of the community of practitioners. His *Principles of geology*, 1830–1833, speaks eloquently for the antiquity of the earth and of the fossil record, but the modernity of human beings. The assimilation of humanity to the fossil record is accomplished thirty years later, with the publication of *The antiquity of man* (1863). Thus for Morgan and others of his generation who were born around 1820, the opening out of the age of the earth was completed in their youth, before they had begun to publish. The opening out of ethnological time fell upon them in mid-career, however, after they had committed themselves to positions that assumed a short chronology, and consequently it required a profound change of course.

In the last decade of his life we find Morgan a confirmed believer in the new, long chronology for ethnological time. The opening

---

[32] The reference is to Comstock's *Geology*.

paragraphs of the preface to *Ancient society* indicate the premier importance to his life's work of the time revolution:[33]

> The great antiquity of mankind upon the earth has been conclusively established. It seems singular that the proofs should have been discovered as recently as within the last thirty years, and that the present generation should be the first called upon to recognize so important a fact.
>
> Mankind are now known to have existed in Europe in the glacial period, and even back of its commencement, with every probability of their origination in a prior geological age. They have survived many races of animals with whom they were contemporaneous, and passed through a process of development, in the several branches of the human family, as remarkable in its courses as in its progress.
>
> Since the probable length of their career is connected with geological periods, a limited measure of time is excluded. One hundred or two hundred thousand years would be an unextravagant estimate of the period from the disappearance of the glaciers in the northern hemisphere to the present time. Whatever doubts may attend any estimate of a period, the actual duration of which is unknown, the existence of mankind extends backward immeasurably, and loses itself in a vast and profound antiquity.

The effect of the explosion of ethnological time upon the anthropological problem, the problem of savagism, was dramatic:[34]

> This knowledge changes materially the views which have prevailed respecting the relations of savages to barbarians, and of barbarians to civilized men. It can now be asserted upon convincing evidence that savagery preceded barbarism in all the tribes of mankind, as barbarism is known to have preceded civilization. The history of the human race is one in source, one in experience, one in progress.

Our problem in the pages that follow will be to determine exactly where the revolution in ethnological time overtakes Morgan, and to what effect. It will be clear from what has been said so far that it overtakes him in the midst of his kinship project; thus in examining the history of that project it will be important to keep it in mind that Morgan's original formulation assumes a short chronology. Our problem, then, is to specify how the short chronology shapes the kinship project, and what changes in it were wrought by the time revolution.

---

[33] *Ancient society*, p. xxix.
[34] The same, pp. xxix–xxx.

3

A Lawyer among the Iroquois

+++

In retrospect it would seem to Morgan that the kinship project had its beginning in 1858 "in an Indian cabin on Lake Superior," when he discovered (as he believed) the identity of the Ojibwa system of relationship with that of the Iroquois. But he recognized that the remote origins of the project belonged to the period of his first discovery of the Iroquois pattern. "When I first came upon this peculiar [American Indian] system of consanguinity, which was as early as the year 1846 among the Seneca Iroquois," he writes in the *Record of Indian letters*, "I did not so much as surmise that it extended beyond this Indian family, and much less that it might have important ethnological use. In other words I supposed that it was a system of their own invention."[1] In its very nature the kinship project was a program of generalizing the Iroquois system to other groups, and the earlier discovery of the Iroquois system belongs to the prehistory of that project so conceived. It is this prehistory we must now examine.

The harvest of Morgan's early Iroquois research is contained in his first book, *League of the Ho-dé-no-sau-nee, or Iroquois,* published in 1851. For a hundred years and more it has remained the best single overall treatment of Iroquois social structure and culture, and has frequently been reprinted not for its historic interest as a classic of anthropological writing but for its present usefulness as an introduction to Iroquois life. The *League of the Iroquois* has proved a very popular book, and deservedly so, second only perhaps to *Ancient society* among Morgan's writings.

As a tribal monograph that served to launch an ethnological

---

[1] *Record of Indian letters,* vol. 1, Morgan Papers; published in White, "How Morgan came to write *Systems of consanguinity and affinity*," p. 260. The account is dated 19 October 1859.

career, the *League* has a precocious modernism that places it in series
with such books as Rivers' *The Todas* (1906), Radcliffe-Brown's *The
Andaman Islanders* (1922), and Evans-Pritchard's *The Nuer* (1940),
to mention only the better-known instances of a prolific type. Our
readings of the *League* are inevitably shaped by these posterior texts,
by whose light we find the style perhaps a bit rotund, the substance
sound though occasionally intruded upon by Victorian values, but
the form, though imperfect, entirely natural and to be taken for
granted.

It takes an effort of the imagination to see that for Morgan himself,
lacking examples upon which to model his work, the choice of a
form in which to cast his Iroquois material cannot have been obvious
at all. Of the senior ethnologists whom he admired, Gallatin's publications were strictly and severely philological and Schoolcraft's
usual genre was the miscellany—which is to say, formlessness. Two
illustrious close contemporaries with ethnological interests suggest
the range of possibilities available to Morgan. Herman Melville's
adventures among the Marquesan Islanders takes the form of a travel
book in *Typee*; Francis Parkman's obsession with the American
wilderness and its inhabitants takes the form of narrative history, his
many volumes composing an epic history of the titanic struggle of
the three races, French, English, and Indian. Morgan chose neither
the first-person travel-adventure form nor the historical narrative but
instead devised a largely synchronic, structuralist account of which
the conceptual core was the sociopolitical structure (Book I, "Structure of the League"), with satellite chapters devoted to other topics
(Books II and III, "Spirit of the League" and "Incident to the
League"), notably religion and material culture.

Morgan's rejection of narrative history as a form and his spotty
control of the documentary sources of Iroquois life go hand in hand.
In the *League* the use of the older French sources is confined largely
to an introductory chapter on Iroquois history, which, in its per-
functory manner, conveys the feeling that the author wants to put it
behind him so he can get at the meat of the thing. The limited
character of Morgan's use of historical narrative and of older histories of the Iroquois has to do with his discovery that the understanding of the political system of the Iroquois he had obtained from
history books was badly flawed, as I shall shortly show. He judged,
one senses, that the study of histories would merely perpetuate old
errors.

The process of researching and writing the *League* deserves a full-length study of its own. Here, as for the *Systems,* the surviving sources are unusually rich. There are, above all, Morgan's field notebooks in the Morgan Papers at the University of Rochester, and related materials such as the correspondence. We also have the papers of Ely S. Parker, the Seneca informant, translator, and collaborator of Morgan, including schoolboy essays and other materials that document his early efforts to cast his experience of Iroquois life into the medium of the dominant culture.[2] I venture to think that for few anthropological texts do we have surviving papers of the informant as well as the anthropologist. Such a study will have the advantage of Elisabeth Tooker's excellent elucidation of Morgan's research on the structure of the Iroquois league (which I shall draw on later in this chapter) and her forthcoming edition of Morgan's Iroquois notebooks.[3] This is a task for an Iroquoianist. In order to show how the later emergence of Morgan's kinship project is foreshadowed in the *League,* however, I must give a brief account of its composition, however inadequate it is doomed to be.

The publication of *League of the Iroquois* in 1851 closed a chapter in Morgan's life. The book synthesized information he had been gathering on the Iroquois for the better part of a decade, since his admission to the bar in 1842. It draws upon matter that had previously been published as articles: "Letters on the Iroquois," serialized in the *American Whig review* from February through December 1847, and his illustrated reports accompanying Iroquois artifacts he donated to the State Cabinet of Natural History in 1848, 1849, and 1851, published in the annual reports of the New York State Museum, especially the text of his report of 1849 (which was also reprinted under the title, "The Fabrics of the Iroquois" in *Stryker's American register and magazine* in 1850). These now were brought together in a book. Reflecting on this period much later, Morgan says, "My principal object in writing this work, which exhibits abundant evidence of hasty execution, was to free myself of the subject."[4] The same year he drew up a will, married, and compiled an inventory of his and his wife's books; from it we learn that he gave his bride,

---

[2] Ely Parker's papers are in the American Philosophical Society Library and the H. E. Huntington Library.

[3] Elisabeth Tooker, "The structure of the Iroquois league: Lewis H. Morgan's research and observations."

[4] White, "How Morgan came to write *Systems,*" p. 262. Morgan's will, inventory of books, and Bible are in the Morgan Papers.

Mary Elizabeth Steele Morgan, a copy of the deluxe edition of the *League*. He also purchased a family Bible and entered into it his and his wife's family history. With the publication of the *League,* he says, "I laid aside the Indian subject to devote my time to my profession."[5] Thus the *League* was to have been the swan song of Morgan's ethnological career. It was not the end, of course, but the beginning. At the time, it had been his intent to put ethnology aside in order to raise a family and to practice law in earnest.

Three principal ingredients went into the making of *League of the Iroquois*. First, there was Morgan's training as a lawyer, which provided him with a certain way of looking at things and a specified learned tradition to resort to in giving intellectual order to his field experiences of Iroquois life. Second, there was the literary and social organization to which he belonged in his bachelor days, the Grand Order of the Iroquois, which provided him the pretext for his research. Finally, there was his collaboration with Ely Parker, which gave him access to the Iroquois.

Following his education at Cayuga Academy in the western New York village of Aurora where he had grown up, and at Union College in Schenectady from which he graduated in 1840, he read law under the direction of a lawyer and was admitted to the bar. Whatever the content of that training (some of it can be known through citations in his writings)—which cannot have been extensive—the fact of his having been so trained is decisive for his ethnology.

It is no accident that of the inventors of kinship Morgan was a practicing lawyer, Maine a professor of legal history and Legal Member of the Governor-General's Council in British India, Bachofen a scholar of Roman law and magistrate in his native Basle, and McLennan also a practicing lawyer. Only Fustel de Coulanges was not a lawyer in any formal sense, but in his case we nevertheless also see a great interest in questions of legal history. Indeed, we may say that kinship as object of study was created not *ex nihilo*, nor again from common sense, but from law. Law supplied the matter of kinship and its first analytic categories and techniques. The starting point, then, was not a naive view of the substance of kinship but a learned one obtained from books.

A consequence for anthropology, and one that is especially salient in Morgan's thought, is the fact that the kinship structure of ancient Roman society has played a large role in the formation of analytical

---

[5] The same.

constructs for the science. Roman law lies at the beginning of modern European law or, as Europeans liked to say, the law of "civilized nations," and could be conceived as the first formulation of scientific law rather than the expression of an exotic society. For these reasons kinship constructs peculiar to Roman society have entered the law and have carried over into anthropology: such concepts as those of *agnates, cognates, consanguines,* and *affines,* and the practice of tracing kinship relations from a central *ego*; even some of the ways of diagramming kin relations that anthropologists use derive from law books, as we shall see, and come ultimately from Roman law. At the same time, the early theorists of kinship in the 1860s were examining Roman (and Greek) kinship as an ethnological case, and in chapter 8 we shall see that the formative conflict, so to say, of the new field was about Roman kinship, under the rubric of the Patriarchal Theory. In Morgan's case, in the *League* Roman law is part of the unexamined ground of perception from which he perceives the Iroquois case; only later does Roman kinship itself become a case for study.

Morgan's legal career did not immediately flourish; indeed, it began in the midst of a long depression set off by the Panic of 1837. He whiled away his enforced leisure in Aurora by helping in the management of the family farms, speaking on temperance in nearby villages, and writing three articles (none of them ethnological), which were published in *The Knickerbocker* in 1843.[6] He also joined a secret society of young men who had attended Cayuga Academy, called the Gordian Knot but soon to be transformed into the Grand Order of the Iroquois, or New Confederacy of the Iroquois, as it was variously called.

Years later, when he had come to believe that the Iroquois system was representative of a general American Indian system of relationship, he looked back on the events that led to its discovery as a series of happy accidents. The passage is so characteristic that I cannot forebear to quote it at length:[7]

> The interest awakened in me in this matter was the result, as in all similar cases, of special circumstances having more the appearance of accident

---

[6] "Aristomenes the Messenian" (January 1843); "Thoughts at Niagara" (September 1843); "Mind or instinct" (November-December 1843). The first piece of an ethnological character appeared in September 1844: "Vision of Kar-is-ta-gi-a, a sachem of Cayuga."

[7] White, "How Morgan came to write *Systems,*" pp. 260–262.

than deliberate intention; and they took their rise so far back that I am constrained, in this connection, to recapitulate the principal facts. The year 1842 found me at home at Aurora, Cayuga County, admitted as an attorney, but not yet ready, from the depression of all business, to commence practice. Having leisure I became a member of a literary club, organized in Cayuga Academy, called the "Gordian Knot," and made up of a few thorough going young men. We finally concluded to cut this knot, and change our organization into an Indian society under the name of the "Cayugas," as we resided in the ancient territory of this Indian nation and quite near the site of their principal village. As our interest increased, we enlarged the number of our council fires, until we numbered in our membership about four hundred young men: the Oneidas were located at Utica, the Onondagas at Syracuse, the Cayugas in four tribes were located at Aurora, Auburn, Ithaca and Owego; and the Senecas in four at Waterloo, Canandaigua, Rochester and Lima. The fraternity was known as "The Order of the Iroquois." As we hoped at that time to found a permanent order, with a charitable as well as a literary basis, we connected with it the idea of protecting, so far as it lay in our power, the remainder of the Iroquois living in this State; and particularly, the band of Senecas at Tonawanda who then and since the year 1838 had been beset and hunted by the Ogden Land Company, to despoil them of the remaining lands. We visited the Indians at Onondaga and at Tonawanda, and at Buffalo, attending their councils from time to time, and making ourselves familiar with their conditions and wants; but more particularly we engaged, with ardor, in the work of studying out the structure and principles of the ancient League, by which they had been united for so many centuries. We wished to model our organization upon this, and to reproduce it with as much fidelity as the nature and objects of our order would permit. This desire, on our part, led to the first discovery of the real structure and principles of the League of the Iroquois, which up to that time were entirely unknown, except in a most general sense. . . .

I have adverted thus fully to this organization for the reason, that, whatever of interest I have since taken in Indian studies was awakened through my connection with this Indian fraternity.

Although this autobiographical statement is true in every detail, features of its style, especially the use of the "we" and the suppression of the "I" in certain places and omission to mention his own role in these affairs, implement a purpose to depict himself as the beneficiary of events that happened to him and to understate the degree to which Morgan's actions helped bring about those events. Facts he does not mention change the picture. Morgan was an inveterate organizer and leader of literary societies, both before (the Erodephecin Society of his Cayuga Academy days) and after (The Club of Rochester) the period in question. He held the supreme office in the Grand Order of the Iroquois its second and third years, August 1844 to August 1846,[8] directing its not always serious-minded membership into literary and charitable activities that mark the beginnings of his Iroquois fieldwork. Some of his addresses to its meetings are early drafts of material that ends up in the *League,* being in the nature of serious scholarly papers cloaked in a spirit of fun. Indeed, we may suppose that the change of style from the Gordian Knot to the Cayugas was a deliberate one in which Morgan played a major role. J. W. Powell, who seems to have obtained his information from Morgan himself, says as much: "The society was organized for no definite purpose, and failed to interest young Morgan, who at once looked about for some method of expanding the society and extending its influence; and finally, under his management, a new society was organized and styled 'The Grand Order of the Iroquois.'"[9] In sum, Morgan's activity in the organization has all the earmarks of serious play, of a deliberate preparation for a life of scholarship and public affairs under the aspect of light-heartedness, behind which he might at any time retreat as he tried his hand. It was not all that accidental.

If the Grand Order of the Iroquois had this quality of serious play for Morgan, however, it was also, for him and the others, a matter of playful seriousness. Something of the tone of mock solemnity that runs through the surviving records of the Order is evident in these minutes of one of the monthly meetings of the Cayugas of Aurora:[10]

The Warriors met for the initiation of W Hurd. The Council fire in the valley of Shistus. Soon after it was lit up the boundaries of the sacred ground being intruded upon by a pale face, he was sent howling through the forest, causing the rocky banks of fair Cayuga to reecho with his yells. By the presence of mind of one of the Braves the initiation then followed. He was led to the sacred spot by Shenandoah [L. H. Morgan]. After having gone through the regular ceremonies some of the bold and daring warriors sallied forth bringing back with them the produce of the White mans cornfield which was roasted by the glowing coals of the Council fire and served as nutritive aliment to the empty abdomens of

---

[8] Manuscript volume, *Record of T.T. of C.N. of G.C.I.* (Record of Toryoh-ne [Wolf] Tribe of the Cayuga Nation of the Grand Confederacy of the Iroquois), Morgan Papers. "List of Grand To-do-da-hoh's."

[9] Powell, "Sketch of Lewis H. Morgan," p. 114.

[10] *Record of T.T. of C.N. of G.C.I.*

our Warriors. After having chanted the war song and danced the war dance each warrior returned to his wigwam to enjoy the exquisites of somnolency.

Nobler purposes were enshrined in the preamble of the constitution of the Order:[11]

> The institution of an Indian Order having for its object a literary and social confederation of the young men of the State for the purpose of making such order the repository of all that remains of the Indians, their history, manners & customs, their government, mythology and literature; and for the further purpose of creating and encouraging a kinder feeling towards the Red Man, founded upon a truer knowledge of the virtues and blemishes of Indian character; and finally to raise up an institution that shall eventually cast the broad shield of protection, and the mantle of its benevolence over these declining races & lastly our own intellectual & moral improvement is an object both interesting & commendable.

The words "to encourage a kinder feeling toward the Red Man" reappear in the *League*. Although he is too modest to say so, we cannot doubt that Morgan was the leading constitutionalist for the Order.

In the spring of 1844, while visiting Albany, Morgan took the opportunity to examine Cayuga treaties in the office of the secretary of state. A few days later, visiting a bookstore, he happened upon a Seneca young man of sixteen, Hasaneanda, whose English name was Ely S. Parker. He was serving as interpreter to a delegation of three Seneca chiefs from the Tonawanda reserve. Morgan eagerly engaged him in conversation. It was the beginning of a collaboration that was to be celebrated in the dedication of the *League* to Parker, "the materials of which are the fruit of our joint researches." Several translations of speeches in the *League* are specially noted as the work of Ely Parker.

Parker was one of the most remarkable Americans of his generation. Schooled by Baptist missionaries, Parker was a very apt pupil. He went on to Yates Academy in Yates, New York, for further education; it was while he was a student that he and Morgan met. Later Morgan arranged for his admission to Cayuga Academy in Aurora, where Morgan himself had been educated. Parker's mastery of English thrust him into adult situations while still very young.

---

[11] The same.

When Morgan met him, the delegation of Tonawanda Seneca, for whom he was interpreter, met with Governor William C. Bouck; at age eighteen he accompanied a delegation to Washington, where he met President Polk. The depredations of the Ogden Land Company threatened the enforced removal of the Senecas of Tonawanda, and to their struggle against the company Morgan offered the services of the Grand Order of the Iroquois. Ely Parker, in the course of this struggle, was obliged at an early age to master the complexities of lobbying the state and national governments. Like the children of immigrants who, through their ability to pick up English and assimilate Euroamerican ways, in essence, become parents to their parents, Ely Parker became a precocious leader of the people of his reservation. He went on to become a civil engineer, being engaged in canal work in the Rochester area and then taking a position in Galena, Illinois, where he built the post office. In Galena he became friends with Ulysses S. Grant. During the Civil War Parker became Grant's secretary, rising to the brevet of an adjutant general, and may be seen in photographs of Grant's staff. During Grant's presidency he became commissioner of Indian Affairs.[12]

Parker's remarkable family played a role in the making of the *League*. Engravings of full-length figures that appear in the book are captioned "Dä-ah-de-a, A Seneca in the Costume of the Iroquois," and "Gä-hah-ʻno, A Seneca Indian Girl, In the Costume of the Iroquois" (see figure 1). What the captions do not tell us is that the first is Ely's brother Levi Parker; the second, his sister Caroline. Caroline, moreover, made a number of articles of clothing on commission from Morgan for the State Cabinet of Natural History, which appear in the many illustrations in the *League*. She was one of two Seneca girls for whom Morgan's Grand Order of the Iroquois raised a subscription to finance an education at Cayuga Academy, and he was one of the leading contributors. In later years she would teasingly suggest that he got his start in ethnology through falling in love with her.[13] The Parker parents also made objects for the state museum.

---

[12] There is a good biography of Ely Parker by William H. Armstrong, *Warrior in two camps: Ely S. Parker, Union general and Seneca chief,* from which the substance of this paragraph comes. See also the biography by his grand nephew, Arthur C. Parker: *The life of General Ely S. Parker.*

[13] Caroline Parker Mount Pleasant to Morgan, 11/14/76, Morgan Papers: "Mr. H[athaway] told us that when he was very young he fell in *love* with a beautiful

DÄ-AH-DE-A,
A SENECA In the Costume of the Iroquois

GÄ·HAH,·NO
A Seneca Indian Girl
In the Costume of the Iroquois

Fig. 1. Levi and Caroline Parker. (University of Rochester)

The Parker family was, in Morgan's eyes, very progressive. William Parker, the father, had taken up plow agriculture, putting aside the old Iroquois pattern of horticulture under the care of women. The family was associated with the reforming religion of Handsome Lake, which, although it was against assimilation to Euroamerican

---

Indian girl & he thinks that is why he is so interested to write about Indians. I *wonder* if others that writes on Indian subjects ever did the same, well! not one out of ten would be as honest as Mr. H. as to tell of it." The young man in fig. 1 is usually identified as Nicholson Parker, another brother of Ely; however, a list of Parker family names that Morgan made (Manuscript journals, vol. 2, p. 159, Morgan Papers) gives Dä-ah-de-ah as Levi Parker. I am obliged to Elisabeth Tooker for this information.

ways, agreed with Morgan's Presbyterianism in promoting absten-
tion from alcohol, and his treatment of Iroquois religion in the
League is accordingly very positive. The children, as we have seen,
were being educated in English and were becoming Christians. The
Parkers were living proof of the civilizing effects of plow agriculture,
education, and religion. They were also ideally situated to contribute
to the making of ethnographic texts. Being in transition between two
cultures, they constantly had to be ethnographers of each. Much of
the text-making that went into the *League* occurred among the bi-
lingual and bicultural Parker children—above all the eloquent Ely.

The overall form of the *League,* however, was Morgan's, and it
was very much a lawyer's form. The heart of the matter is what may
be called the Iroquois constitution, the structure of the league or
confederacy of the Six Nations that was their polity. The elucidation
of this structure in his book was the serious outcome of Morgan's
participation in the constitution-making of the New Confederacy of
the Iroquois. Let us take a brief look at this process. We cannot do
better than to follow Elisabeth Tooker's exposition.[14]

When the members of the Gordian Knot decided to adopt an
Indian style, they had very little information to go on. They knew
the names of the Six Nations: Mohawk, Oneida, Onondaga, Cayuga,
Seneca, Tuscarora. Thus the original group at Aurora was named
Cayuga, as the town was in former Cayuga territory. When a chapter
was formed at Waterloo, it was appropriate to name it Seneca, in
whose ancient territory it was situated. Gordian Knot members
naturally turned to the available literature, which was histories, especially William L. Stone's *Life of Joseph Brant,* from which they
acquired the erroneous information that Tekarihogea was the title
of the supreme chief of the confederacy, and so named their highest
office. It was in fact merely the first title on the roll call of Iroquois
chiefs. Morgan would later pillory Stone's inaccuracies.[15] The histories gave very little information on the Iroquois constitution, and
the abundance and evident reliability of information he was shortly
to obtain from the Seneca themselves seems to have led to a decisive
turning from the library to the field.

---

[14] Tooker, "The structure of the Iroquois league."

[15] William L. Stone, *Life of Joseph Brant—Thayendanegea* (1838). Morgan's
attack comes much later, in his 1857 paper, "Laws of descent of the Iroquois," p.
140.

Morgan was seeking better information when he met Ely Parker in an Albany bookstore. With Parker as interpreter he interviewed the three Tonawanda Seneca chiefs who made up the delegation. He learned, among other things, that there were forty-eight "sachems" (Morgan's word—an English borrowing from Algonquin, not Iroquois) in all, and that the Seneca had eight sachems and two war chiefs. He further learned that the Seneca were divided into eight "tribes" or "families" (clans, as we would say): Wolf, Turtle, Hawk, Beaver, Deer, Snipe, Bear, and Heron. The offices of the two war chiefs descended in the female line, one belonging to the Snipe tribe and the other to the Wolf.

As Tooker shows, Morgan misconstrued some of this information. He wrongly assumed that because the Seneca had two war chiefs, so did the other of the Six Nations. He seems to have been told that sachemships belonged to the tribes, and he wrongly interpreted this to mean that each of the eight Seneca tribes owned one of the eight sachemships. Further, he interpreted what he had been told to mean that each of the Six Nations had the full complement of eight tribes, whence the forty-eight sachems were drawn from the eight tribes of the six constituent nations of the league. This understanding was fed into the constitution adopted in August 1844. The Cayugas at Aurora now became the Wolf Tribe of the Cayuga Nation, the Senecas at Waterloo became the Wolf Tribe of the Seneca Nation, and other chapters of the growing organization were given names of this kind, on a plan that allowed for a full complement of forty-eight chapters. Chapters of the Wolf and Snipe tribe, and they alone, had the office of Head Warrior. The forty-eight sachems, one from each chapter, were to serve as "Grand Counsellors of the Tekarihogea."

This understanding of the structure of the Iroquois league appears in Morgan's first ethnological publication: "Vision of Kar-is-ta-gi-a, a sachem of Cayuga" (September 1844), signed "Aquarius." It takes the form of a prophetic vision of the Cayuga chief known to whites as Steeltrap, who foresees the establishment of the New Confederacy of the Iroquois in the Cayuga country as consolation, in some measure, for the passing of the old confederacy. Morgan uses the device of a discovered manuscript that "came into the writer's possession in a manner so singular and unexpected as to awaken interest" the nature of which, however, he omits to tell his readers. After the telling of the vision the "original manuscript . . . terminates abruptly" and Morgan continues with a brief lesson on Iroquois sociopolitical structure. The substance of the article consists of the information he got at Albany in the meeting with the Tonawanda chiefs and the Cayuga treaties he saw in the office of the secretary of state.

Morgan himself became Grand Tekarihogea at the general council of August 1844, and he continued in office for two years. Late in the year he moved to Rochester and shortly thereafter organized a new chapter of the Order, the Turtle Tribe of the Seneca Nation. In the fall of the following year a great council of the Six Nations was held at Tonawanda to mourn the sachems who had passed away since the previous council and to "raise up" new sachems in their places. Morgan and a few other members of the Order spent the better part of a week at Tonawanda observing the council's proceedings, interviewing (with Ely Parker interpreting, when necessary) and taking notes; it was the first of a number of field trips Morgan made to the Iroquois of Tonawanda and of other nearby reservations. The result was a much improved understanding of the structure of the league. A few days after the initial visit to Tonawanda, Morgan wrote to ethnologist Henry Rowe Schoolcraft, who had been made an honorary member of the Grand Order of the Iroquois, addressing himself "Unto Alhalla [Schoolcraft's name in the G.O.I.], a wise-man of the Confederacy." The burden of the letter was printed under the title "Iroquois laws of descent" in Schoolcraft's *Notes on the Iroquois*.[16]

In this letter Morgan sketches his revised understanding of the structure of the Iroquois League. There are fifty sachems (not forty-eight), and they are unequally divided among the original five nations of the league, the Tuscarora, who joined the league long after its founding, having no sachem chiefs. There are indeed eight original tribes or families, but each one does not have a sachemship; some have none; others, one or two. The fifty sachems are the only officials in the councils of the confederacy, other ranks of chiefs having no say; "and unanimity as in the Polish diet was always necessary."[17]

---

[16] Morgan to Henry Rowe Schoolcraft, 10/7/45, Schoolcraft Papers, Library of Congress, quoted in Tooker, p. 145. Reprinted in part in Schoolcraft, *Notes on the Iroquois*, pp. 495–497, under the title, "Iroquois laws of descent."

[17] My colleague Mills Thornton draws my attention to John C. Calhoun's *A disquisition on government* (1854), which discusses the Polish constitution, and then turns to that of the Iroquois. "As in the Polish Diet, each member possessed a veto on its decision; so that nothing could be done without the united consent of all" (p. 72). Calhoun's version of the Iroquois league, however, differs from Morgan's. "One chief delegate, chosen by each nation [of the six]—associated with six others

The council is presided over by the Tha-do-da-hoh or Great Sachem of the Confederacy, drawn from the Onondagas, and there is no such officer as Tekarihogea or military chieftain. Accordingly Morgan signs his letter "G[rand] Tha-do-da-hoh of the Iroquois." The Seneca have two head warriors, but the other nations have none.

He also gives full recognition to the matrilineal transmission of office—the beginnings, one may say, of his understanding of the Iroquois kinship system.[18]

> Their laws of descent are quite intricate. They follow the female line, and as the children always follow the tribe of the mother, and the man never is allowed to marry in his own tribe, it follows that father and son are never of the same tribe, and hence the son can never succeed the father, because the sachemship runs in the tribe of the father. It really is quite surprising to find such permanent original institutions among the Iroquois, and still more surprising that these institutions have never seen the light. If I can construct a table of descents with any approach to accuracy, I will send it down to the Historical Society. The idea at the foundation of their law of descent is quite a comment upon human nature. The child must be the son of the mother though he may not be of his mother's husband—quite and absolutely an original code.

Much the same information went into a paper on Iroquois government and institutions delivered in November before the Turtle Tribe of the Seneca Nation in Rochester, and to the New York Historical Society the following April.[19] The new constitution adopted at the August 1846 meeting incorporated a few changes that seem to reflect the improved understanding of the league: the Tuscarora were dropped as a nation, as was the title Tekarihogea, mention of forty-eight sachems, and the two head warriors per nation. The impulse to model the New Confederacy of the Iroquois upon the old no longer ran strong, however, and most changes in this constitution reflected the internal problems of the organization.

By this time, as he was coming to the end of his second term of

---

of his own selection—and making, in all, forty-two members—constituted their federal, or general government."

[18] "Iroquois laws of descent," pp. 496–497.

[19] "Address by Schenandoah on the government and institutions of the Iroquois," Morgan Papers, delivered before the Rochester branch of the G.O.I., 7 November 1845, and the New York Historical Society 6 April 1846. Published under the title, "Government and institutions of the Iroquois," ed. Arthur C. Parker.

office as leader of the New Confederacy, Morgan's interest in the Iroquois polity had acquired a scholarly purpose that went beyond the original needs of his organization, and in the fall of 1846 he wrote the series of articles that appeared in *The American review* beginning in February 1847 under the title, "Letters on the Iroquois, by Skenandoah, addressed to Albert Gallatin, LL.D., President, New York Historical Society." Skenandoah was Morgan's personal style in the Order, and Gallatin was another of the senior ethnologists who, like Schoolcraft, the Order had wooed with honorary memberships. Thus did playfulness serve the interests of earnestness.

In the *League of the Iroquois* (and also in his 1849 report of collections for the State Museum) Morgan stands forth in his own right, shedding the epistolary form, coming out from under the shadow of his elders and discarding his Indian moniker. Let us now examine the book itself, and what it has to tell us of kinship.

At the bottom of the Iroquois constitution Morgan found the "family relationships"; indeed, the league "was established upon the principles, and was designed to be but an elaboration, of the Family relationships." The Iroquois, then, have built up an organizational structure by the elaboration of relationships that are universal and prior to ideas of society and government; relationships in themselves "consistent alike with the hunter, the pastoral and the civilized state." The Six Nations were united into a single family, notionally dwelling together in one longhouse, and the ties of family relationship ran through the civil and social system, from individuals to tribes, tribes to nations, and nations to the league itself, binding them in a common, indissoluble brotherhood.[20]

Thus at the end of a lawyer's enquiry there appears an ethnological object. This object, family relationships, is in Morgan's mind a unitary entity with two parts, in both of which the Iroquois departed from the familiar: (1) the "transmission of all titles, rights and property" and (2) the "mode of computing degrees of consanguinity." The construction of this entity follows Blackstone's *Commentaries on the laws of England,* the lawyer's bible and probably the most important prior text for Morgan's early work on kinship. Blackstone's "Of title by descent" (book 2, chapter 14) joins discussion of "descent, or hereditary succession" with "consanguinity, or kindred" in a unitary treatment. It is illustrated, moreover, by diagrams

---

[20] *League,* p. 60.

that are models and governing images for the emergent anthropology of kinship, above all for Morgan's *Systems* (see figure 2). Let us examine the two dimensions of the Iroquois family relations in turn.

As to the "transmission of all titles, rights and property," what we call matrilineal descent had already made a great impression on Morgan—he thinks it a new discovery in his letter to Schoolcraft—and the problem of accounting for it would prove to be a matter of enduring interest to him. In his first essay of explanation in the *League,* he said that the transmission of titles, rights, and property in the female line to the exclusion of the male was "strangely unlike the canons of descent adopted by civilized nations"; nevertheless, as it seemed to him, it secured important objects. Perhaps the leading one was "the perpetual disinheritance of the son."[21]

> Being of the tribe of his mother formed an impassible barrier against him; and he could neither succeed his father as a sachem, nor inherit from him even his medal, or his tomahawk. The inheritance, for the protection of tribal rights, was thus directed from the lineal descendants of the sachem, to his brothers, or his sisters' children, or, under certain circumstances, to some individual of the tribe at large; each and all of whom were in his tribe, while his children, being in another tribe, as before remarked, were placed out of the line of succession.
>
> By the operation of this principle, also, the certainty of descent in the tribe, of their principal chiefs, was secured by a rule infallible; for the child must be the son of its mother, although not necessarily of its mother's husband. If the purity of blood be of any moment, the lawgivers of the Iroquois established the only certain rule the case admits of, whereby the assurance might be enjoyed that the ruling sachem was of the same family or tribe with the first taker of the title.

In relation to his later work we see here the seeds of two different (and not entirely compatible) theories: that matrilineal succession to office is a protection against tyranny and is thus the expression of nomadic peoples' love of freedom; and that it secures purity of descent against the inherent uncertainty of paternity under a regime of multiple marriage of some kind.

As to the second aspect of the family relationships, the familiar rubric of "computing degrees of consanguinity," the lineaments of Morgan's treatment spring directly from Blackstone. In Blackstone's chapter on title by descent he divides "consanguinity, or kindred"

---

[21] The same, p. 84.

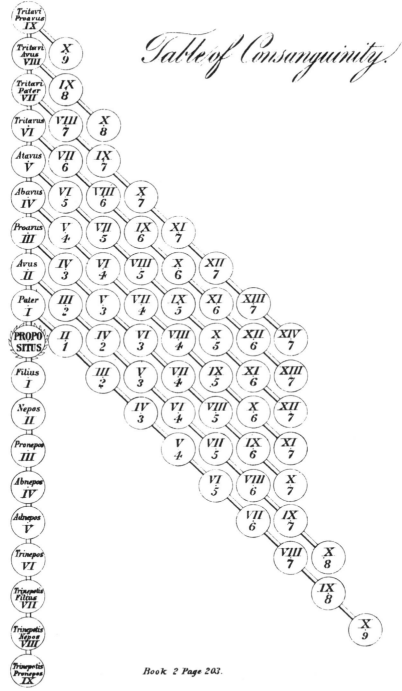

Fig. 2. Blackstone's table of consanguinity.

into two kinds, lineal and collateral. And in the explanation of collateral consanguinity he expounds the two methods of computing degrees of consanguinity—that of the canon law of the Church, which English law follows, and that of the civilians, or the codification of Roman civil law under the emperor Justinian. Blackstone could not, however, explain discordant facts of Iroquois consanguinity for Morgan. In the brief, complicated exposition of it in the *League* Morgan tries to explain it by appeal to the exogamous character of the matrilineal "tribes," thus unifying the description of the Iroquois system of family relationships in both its aspects. This is the passage in full:[22]

> The Iroquois mode of computing degrees of consanguinity was unlike that of the civil or canon law; but was yet a clear and definite system. No distinction was made between the lineal and collateral lines, either in the ascending or descending series. To understand this subject, it must be borne in mind, that of the grandparents one only, the maternal grandmother, necessarily was, and of the parents only the mother, and, in the descending line, only the sisters' children could be of the same tribe with the propositus, or individual from whom the degrees of relationship were reckoned. By careful attention to this rule, the reasons of the following relationships will be readily perceived. The maternal grandmother and her sisters were equally grandmothers; the mother and her sisters were equally mothers; the children of a mother's sisters were brothers and sisters; the children of a sister were nephews and nieces; and the grandchildren of a sister were his grandchildren. These were the chief relatives within the tribe, though not fully extended as to number. Out of the tribe, the paternal grandfather and his brothers were equally grandfathers; the father and his brothers equally fathers; the father's sisters were aunts, while, in the tribe, the mother's brothers were uncles; the father's sister's children were cousins as in the civil law; the children of these cousins were nephews and nieces, and the children of these nephews and nieces were his grandchildren, or the grandchildren of the propositus. Again: the children of a brother were his children, and the grandchildren of a brother were his grandchildren; also, the children of a father's brother were his brothers and sisters, instead of cousins, as under the civil law; and lastly, their children were his grandchildren.
>
> It was the leading object of the Iroquois law of descent, to merge the collateral in the lineal line, as sufficiently appears in the above outline. By the civil law, every departure from the common ancestor in the descending series, removed the collateral from the lineal; while, by the

[22] The same, pp. 85–87.

law under consideration, the two lines were finally brought into one. Under the civil law mode of computation, the degrees of relationship become too remote to be traced among collaterals; while, by the mode of the Iroquois, none of the collaterals were lost by remoteness of degree. The number of those linked together by the nearer family ties was largely multiplied by preventing, in this manner, the subdivision of a family into collateral branches. The relationships, so novel and original, did not exist simply in theory, but were actual, and of constant recognition, and lay at the foundation of their political, as well as social organization.

The vantage point for the description of Iroquois consanguinity is provided by canon law and Roman civil law as the foundation of the laws of the civilized nations. It is not a commonsense view of the family relationships from which Morgan sets out but a learned view that provides a self-consciously scientific ground against which the ethnographic other is perceived, found to be problematical, and explained.

This is the beginning, then, of the contrast in Morgan's later work between Iroquois and Roman systems of relationship, the contrast that in the *Systems* has become emblematic of two vastly extended historic systems of relationship: the classificatory and the descriptive. Here in the *League,* however, the two poles of the comparison are not equal. For the Iroquois "mode of computing degrees of consanguinity" is singular; as Morgan later stated, he thought it at first "an invention peculiar to themselves." The unmarked or barely marked Roman case is in some unspecified sense general and normative. The Roman mode of computing degrees of consanguinity, and its treatment of lineal and collateral lines, are invoked not as elements of another particular culture but as a learned, scientific reckoning of consanguinity, just as "the canons of descent adopted by civilized nations" are the general ground against which the peculiar Iroquois matrilineal transmission of titles, rights, and property is highlighted. The future of the Iroquois-Roman contrast will be to generalize Iroquois such that it becomes an emblematic case on a par with the Roman, but the Roman side will remain the standard and the Iroquois, the problem variant to be explained.

I have attempted to diagram Morgan's explanation of the Iroquois kinship terminology in this first formulation (figure 3). The diagram puts right an error in respect of the descendants of the father's brother: "the children of a father's brother were his brothers and sisters . . . and . . . their children were his grandchildren." The first

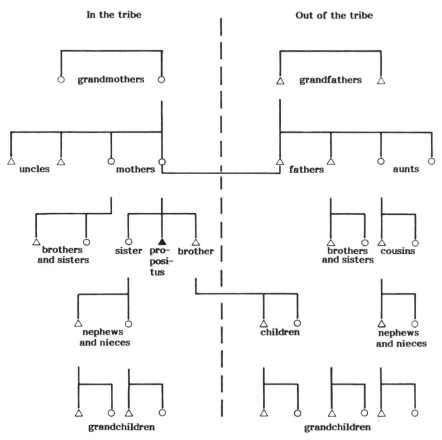

Fig. 3. Iroquois degrees of consanguinity in the *League of the Iroquois*.

clause is correct, but a generation appears to have been inadvertently
dropped between it and the second clause.

Morgan's explanation attempts to link the logic of the matrilineal
tribe (in/out) with the lineal/collateral distinction familiar to him
through the law. This latter isolates the direct line ascending of
parents, grandparents, and so forth and the direct line descending of
children, grandchildren, and so forth of the propositus; and all the
siblings of these lineals are collaterals. The combination is not a
happy one. The explanation is reasonably successful in dealing with
ascending lineals, the mother and mother's mother within the tribe,
and the father and father's father without, whose (same-sex) siblings,
as collaterals, are merged with them by virtue of being in the same

condition as to tribe. The union of these two antithetic ideas breaks down, however, when we deal with descendants; Morgan does not even speak of the (male) propositus' own children, who are lineals, perhaps because of the awkward fact that they were out of his tribe. The most that can be said here is that all second-generation descendants are grandchildren, so that "none of the collaterals were lost by remoteness of degree." The Roman case is like the downward- and outward-sloping branches of a Christmas tree, collateral lines growing ever more distant from the main trunk; in the Iroquois case, however, these collateral lines return to the stem in the grandchildren's generation. Morgan would make these images explicit in the *Systems*. His theory that the tribal organization causes the merger of lineals and collaterals, however, fails before the fact that some grandchildren are within the tribe but others are without.

The argument has a strong naturalistic tendency: the terms of discussion—lineal line, collateral line, fathers, mothers, aunts, uncles, cousins, and so forth—are taken to be categories existing in nature independent of the human will, rather than arbitrary creations of the mind. They are of Nature, not Art. Morgan gives a list of the Seneca vocabulary of kinship after the manner of contemporary philologists such as Gallatin, and he expressly conceives of it as a nomenclature—that is, a set of words that are names for relationships that exist in nature (rather than being the signifiers of concepts). It is significant that he consigns this vocabulary to a footnote:[23]

The following are the names of the several degrees of relationship recognized among the *Ho-de'-no-sau-nee*, in the language of the Senecas:—

Hoc-sote',	Grandfather.
Uc-sote',	Grandmother.
Hä-'nih,	Father.
Noh-yeh,'	Mother.
Ho-ah-'wuk,	Son.
Go-ah-'wuk,	Daughter.
Kä-yä-'dä,	Grandchildren.
Hoc-no-'seh,	Uncle.
Ah-geh-'huc,	Aunt.
Hä-yan-wän-deh,'	Nephew.
Kä-yan-wän-deh,'	Niece.
Dä-ya-gwä-dan-no-dä,	Brothers and sisters.
Ah-gare-'seh,	Cousin.

---

[23] The same, p. 86n.

In spite of this show of philological method, however, the treatment of Iroquois kinship is not a philological one. For the philologist of Morgan's day the object of study would be the Seneca vocabulary itself, as a list of names. Morgan merely indicates in a note that Seneca *Hä'-nih*, for example, is the name for the (naturally occurring) relationship of father, and *Hoc-no'-seh* the name for uncle. But the significant thing that is discussed in the text is not the lexicon of kinship but its semantics—that is, that "the father and his brother [are] equally fathers" and not uncles. This manner of approaching the most striking features of the language of Iroquois kinship is forced upon him by the limitations of the vocabulary list with its underlying linguistic realism, which takes English *father* and *uncle* as names of unalterable natural categories.

The inadequacies of the simple vocabulary list would become glaringly apparent to Morgan years later, when he pressed the Seneca kinship data much harder. He would discover, for example (what he had evidently not understood in the *League*), that the Seneca radically distinguish elder from younger siblings. Rather than the *League*'s vocabulary entry "Dä-ya-gwä-dan-no-dä, Brothers and sisters," he will find that he needs separate entries for *elder brother, younger brother, elder sister,* and *younger sister*; he will find, in short, that he must lengthen the column of English entries in the vocabulary list to render Iroquois distinctions properly. The overall pattern of his treatment in the *League* will remain, however. The vocabulary list will furnish the stuff of kinship, but the analysis will deal not with the names of relationships but with the manner in which relationships are or are not classed together. As we would say, the lexicon of kinship is subordinated to its semantics. This will not be philology but an as yet nameless "new instrument for ethnology." In a word, it will be kinship.

4

Philology in Its Relations to Ethnology

✦✦

The decade leading up to the Civil War was the period in which Morgan created his great work on kinship. When the decade opened he seemed to have brought his Indian researches to an end with the publication of *League of the Iroquois* in January 1851. At its close, in October 1859, his thirteen-page paper on kinship was in its essentials the first version of the *Systems* as we know it. The earlier and greater part of that interval was a period of latency. He tells us, "From the close of 1850 until the summer of 1857 Indian affairs were laid entirely aside."[1] None of the papers he is known to have given during that interval is on Indians, and almost none of the books he bought for his library bears upon Indians; Schoolcraft's multivolume *History, condition and prospects of the Indian tribes,* Squiers' *Aboriginal monuments of the State of New-York,* and Riggs' *Dakota language* are among the very few exceptions. But then, he says,

> in the year 1856, having attended the Albany meeting of the Association for the Advancement of Science, my interest in Ethnology was quickened to such a degree that I resolved to resume the study as soon as the state of my business would permit. In 1857, as a preparation for the Montreal meeting of the Association, I took up anew the laws of descent and consanguinity of the Iroquois, and gave to it a more particular examination than ever before.[2]

The period of quickened ethnological interest from the summer of 1856 to the fall of 1859 during which the basic structure of the

---

[1] Leslie A. White, "How Morgan came to write *Systems of consanguinity and affinity,*" p. 262.

[2] The same, pp. 262–263.

Systems was laid down can be known directly from a number of documents he has left. That period will be examined in the next chapter. In this one I shall examine the period of latency, which leads up to it, in order to establish the general intellectual environment of the 1850s in relation to Morgan's kinship work.

A few years after their marriage Morgan and his wife acquired a house on Fitzhugh Street in the fashionable Third Ward. A son, Lemuel Steele, was born in 1853; a daughter, Mary Elizabeth, at the end of 1855; and in 1860 a second daughter, Helen King. The daughters were to die while he was on one of the four field trips to the West collecting data on Indian systems of relationship; the son, who was mentally deficient, long survived his parents but had no children of his own.

Morgan applied himself to his law practice. His services for the Elys, Rochester's first milling family, had important consequences. On 15 February 1855 the Iron Mountain Railroad was formed to connect the mines of the Lake Superior Iron Company with Marquette on the Lake Superior shore of Michigan's Upper Peninsula. The founder was Heman B. Ely; he and his nephews, Samuel P. and George H. Ely, were major stockholders, and Morgan was among twenty-two other Rochester businessmen who subscribed for smaller amounts. In the following year Congress passed a number of bills allowing several states, including Michigan, to award public lands to companies that completed railway lines between designated points within a certain number of years. Fierce competition for land grants between hastily formed railroad companies ensued, a competition in which the Rochester group had the unforeseen advantage of an early start. As both state and federal governments were involved in rule-making and certification, there was much work for lawyers, and Morgan proved himself indispensable; by the end of this period, in December 1865, Morgan had gotten over a quarter of a million acres of land certified to a successor company, the Bay de Noquet Railroad. Along the way small, cautious investments in various smelting and railroad ventures of the Elys in the Upper Peninsula, including the Morgan Iron Company, of which he was a major shareholder, brought Morgan a small fortune and he was able to retire from business in 1866 to devote himself to scholarship.[3]

Thus on its practical side the trajectory of Morgan's life traces a

---

[3] See Saul Benison, "Railroads land and iron: a phase in the career of Lewis Henry Morgan."

path from the formation of a fortune to the turning of that wealth into the means of knowledge—personal exemplification of the conviction expressed in the closing pages of *Ancient society* that "a mere property career is not the final destiny of mankind."[4] The destiny of Morgan's fortune was to provide freedom from the making of money for a life fully devoted to study; and, after his wife and son had died, to go to the University of Rochester "for the purpose of female education of high grade."[5]

The house on Fitzhugh Street, though in a fashionable district, was a modest one. The only embellishment Morgan allowed himself in the years of his prosperity was, characteristically, the addition of a library. The opening of the library was an item of interest for the local press; and the fact that photographs were taken for viewing in a stereopticon suggests that it was meant for public display as well as private labor. The photographs show a well-furnished room, with tall cases of oak and glass for books and Indian artifacts, on top of which perch busts of Lincoln and other of Morgan's heroes; a chandelier overlooking a circle of chairs drawn around a massive desk; and, in a window, the stuffed beaver whose likeness appears in *The American beaver.*

It was in Morgan's home, on 13 July 1854, that six gentlemen gathered to form another literary club, of which the president of the fledgling University of Rochester, Dr. Martin B. Anderson, was to be the chairman and Morgan the secretary. There is every reason to suppose that Morgan was the instigator; and in any case during his twelve-year reign as secretary there can be no doubt he was the guiding spirit. "His unflagging enthusiasm permeated the membership, and his rule, though rigid, was salutary and even necessary," a member recalled years later.[6] The Club, or the Pundit Club as the wives called it, grew to seventeen members, meeting alternate Tuesdays during the season, fall through spring. It met at the homes of members, often in Morgan's newly built library, and it was in that library that Morgan's funeral services were held, members of the Club in attendance. The address on that occasion was delivered by the one member of the Club then present who had been among the six founding members, the Rev. Dr. Joshua Hall McIlvaine.

---

[4] *Ancient society,* p. 561.

[5] *Matter of Lewis H. Morgan, will,* MS. volume, Morgan Papers.

[6] William Carey Morey, "Reminiscences of 'The Pundit Club,'" p. 106. See also Morgan, "Origin and history of 'The Club'" (unpublished), Morgan Papers.

McIlvaine was Morgan's closest friend and intellectual companion. In the *Systems* Morgan gives us to understand that McIlvaine supplied a crucial suggestion that caused him to develop a theory of the evolution of the family; subsequently Morgan dedicated *Ancient society,* in which that theory is further elaborated, to McIlvaine, "in recognition of his genius and learning, and in appreciation of his friendship." McIlvaine was one of a very few contemporaries who understood Morgan's kinship researches, and it will be necessary to specify so far as possible what exactly was his contribution to the invention of kinship. I shall examine the nature of McIlvaine's contribution to what may be called Morgan's conjectural history of the family in chapter 7. Here we must consider his role in the formation of general ideas that gave shape to Morgan's grand project.

Let us begin with a sketch of McIlvaine's life. He was born in 1815 of Scotch-Irish stock in Lewes, Delaware. He graduated from Princeton College—the College of New Jersey, as it was then called—in 1837 and from the theological seminary in 1840. In 1842 he was ordained by the Presbytery of Albany and served as pastor in several communities in New York state: Little Falls (1842–43), Utica (1843–47), and Rochester (1848–60), to which Morgan had moved from Aurora toward the close of 1844. McIlvaine left Rochester in 1860 to accept a professorship of belles-lettres at Princeton, which he held until 1870. He resigned from Princeton to accept a newly created chair of social science at the University of Pennsylvania, but its benefactor died suddenly and the position fell through. He was obliged to take the pastorate of a church in Newark, New Jersey, where he remained for seventeen years. Returning to Princeton in 1887, now aged 72, he and his daughters Elizabeth and Mary founded Evelyn College for Women, whose course of study was that of Princeton University and which had Princeton professors on its faculty. He died ten years later, in 1897; Evelyn College was not paying its way and was forced to close a year later. McIlvaine was a scholar as well as a pastor, professor, and educational entrepreneur. He wrote four books and a number of articles, seven of them published in the *Princeton review.* There are also several pamphlets consisting of sermons and addresses among his published work.[7]

---

[7] *The national cyclopædia of American biography,* vol. 5, p. 456; *Twentieth century biographical dictionary of notable Americans,* vol. 7; *Princeton Theological Seminary necrological report* (May 1897), pp. 419–420; "The death of Dr. McIl-

He and Morgan had a great deal in common and became fast friends. When he assumed the pastorate at First Presbyterian Church of Rochester, which Morgan attended, he had just published his first book, and Morgan had several articles in print, including the "Letters on the Iroquois," soon to take the form of a book. Both gave addresses before the Atheneum and Mechanics' Association, the leading literary association in Rochester at the time.[8] They were founding members of the Club, and McIlvaine continued to present papers to it after he moved out of Rochester in 1860 on his many visits, during which he generally stayed with the Morgans. In 1856 he became a member of the American Oriental Society. In 1856, Morgan joined the American Association for the Advancement of Science; McIlvaine joined the latter the following year, and we may suppose that the two journeyed to the annual August meeting together.[9] In addition to the inclination toward scholarship and the many similarities fostered by a common religion and domestic culture (both, for example, spoke in the cause of temperance), there was a similarity born of a common adversity, the fact that both had daughters who died in childhood, contributing perhaps to a common commitment to the cause of women's education: McIlvaine and his surviving daughters founding Evelyn College; Morgan leaving his fortune to the University of Rochester to provide for the education of women.

Having spoken of the community of religion between the two men, it becomes necessary to say a word about the much-discussed

---

vaine," *The Democrat and chronicle* (Rochester), 1 February 1897; Frances Patricia Healy, "A history of Evelyn College for women, Princeton, New Jersey, 1887 to 1897," especially chap. 2, "The Founding Family," which includes new material from a relative of McIlvaine; and "Evelyn College was state's first for women," *Princeton recollector,* vol. 1, no. 8 (February 1976). For McIlvaine's publications see the *National union catalogue;* for identification of unsigned articles in the *Biblical repertory and Princeton review,* see *Index volume from 1825 to 1868,* s.v. McIlvaine.

[8] McIlvaine's *A discourse upon the power of voluntary attention* was given on the occasion of the association's reorganization after several years of inactivity and the opening of the library and reading rooms, 28 June 1849. It contains material on Newton that he was to use years later in his funeral address for Morgan, whom he treats as the Newton of ethnology. Morgan's "Diffusion against centralization" was given on 6 January 1852, to mark the association's third anniversary. Both addresses were published.

[9] McIlvaine to Edwd. Eldrige Salisbury Esq., 12/8/55, American Oriental Society archives; *Proceedings of the American Association for the Advancement of Science* (1856), p. xxxvi; (1857), p. liv.

and still vexed question of Morgan's religion and its relation to his ethnology. Clearly we cannot leave the matter where White has left it.[10]

> When we know that Morgan's wife, to whom he was much devoted, was a very narrow, devout, and strict Presbyterian; when we note that Morgan was old enough to vote a full twenty years before *Origin of Species* was published; when we appreciate the fact that virtually all of Morgan's friends and neighbors were good church folk, and that Morgan lived virtually all of his adult life in a community where to be respectable one must attend church; when we take account of all this, the concessions which Morgan made to the clergy and to respectability do not appear very great. And his steadfast refusal "publicly and before men to confess Christ" in the face of such odds is nothing less than heroic.

There is something in the claim that Morgan tempered the public expression of "advanced" beliefs that would be painful to his wife and friends, especially concerning Darwinism; but the argument as a whole overlooks the fact that, after all, he elected to marry a very pious woman and to make a clergyman his best friend.

The question *is* vexed because Morgan was closemouthed on the subject. The testimony of McIlvaine is that Morgan's relation to Christianity was troubled, and this in turn was a source of pain to McIlvaine. In the funeral address, after reviewing Morgan's life work, he turns to the question of his friend's relation to the hereafter, as "certain misunderstandings and misrepresentations have arisen on this subject, chiefly through his extreme reticence."[11] He demonstrates at some length that none of Morgan's scientific views is at odds with Scripture, and goes on to say that Morgan's whole life and character were molded by Christianity, that he admired Christian missionaries, regularly attended the preaching of the Gospel, and was a liberal supporter of the church. Although McIlvaine often questioned Morgan as to his religious beliefs Morgan continued reticent; and when, just months before his death, McIlvaine pressed him as a lifelong friend to tell him his relation to God and the spiritual world, the reply he got was, "I do not claim to have freed my mind from all sceptical doubts, but my heart is with the Christian religion."[12]

---

[10] White, "Morgan's attitude toward religion and science," p. 226.

[11] McIlvaine, *The life and works of Lewis H. Morgan, LL.D., an address at his funeral,* p. 56.

[12] The same, p. 58.

McIlvaine regretted "that he was not able to free his mind from sceptical difficulties so far as to confess Christ before men, as we are all commanded to do, by a public profession of faith," but concluded on the hopeful note that although "it is every man's duty to confess Christ as his Saviour, and to live in full communion with the Christian Church"—as Morgan evidently did not—God may yet have special uses for men who stand in precisely the relations to Christianity that Morgan did. "Certainly we are thus taught to enlarge our charity and our hopes," he concluded, "not to judge men by their conformity to our peculiar shibboleths of dogma, or doctrine; but to judge of them by their lives, and to indulge for such men the most comfortable hopes, especially when they can express themselves as having their hearts in the Lord's kingdom."[13] If Morgan's skeptical doubts were at odds with his heart, McIlvaine's fondness for his friend was troubled before his conception of a Christian's duty.

The problem that vitiates the literature on Morgan's religion is the radical simplicity of the terms of the debate. In Morgan's day, White tells us, "If you were for Theology, you were against Science. Morgan was definitely for Science."[14] It is of little use to recite once again the oft-quoted passages of Morgan's writings that speak of religion. In order to get beyond the sterility of the literature we need to break out of that dead zone in which two simple giants, Religion and Science, fight it out with clubs to the death. We must assume, rather, and contrary to the terms just indicated, that Morgan's religious culture had a formative effect upon his ethnology in some respects which it is our task to discover. And to discover them the monolith of Religion must be abandoned, and we must seek to establish the specific content of the microculture of religion in which Morgan lived and its relation to other religious cultures of the time. I cannot hope to do justice to this question, and in any case it would take us too far from the subject in hand. What follows are a few suggestions of what a proper study of the matter would show without any pretense that we have plumbed its depths.

By the Plan of Union of 1801 the New England Congregationalists and the mainly Scotch-Irish Presbyterians agreed to compromise their differences in church polity in order to join forces in the establishment of new churches in the rapidly growing frontier west of the border between New England and New York. Under this "Presbygational"

---

[13] The same, p. 59.
[14] White, "Morgan's attitude," p. 219.

plan large numbers were added to the Presbyterian Church; but the social ferment of the immigrant population of western New York could not be contained by its staid and learned Calvinism, even under the relaxed conditions allowed by the Plan of Union. Western New York state showed a special appetite for various forms of enthusiastic religion, a distinctiveness that earned it the name of the Burned-over District. The spiritual fires of revivalism swept the region, beginning in the mid-1820s; and the greatest of the evangelists, Charles Grandison Finney, held the greatest of its revivals in 1830 in the pulpits of Rochester, among them that of First Presbyterian, where McIlvaine was later to preach and Morgan to attend. The charisma of the revivalists cast the regular clergy into the shade but brought scores of new members to their churches. Other expressions of a heightened religious enthusiasm ranged from relatively mild forms to the extreme. There was the lively activism of benevolent movements in such interests as temperance, sabbath observance, and Sunday schools. There were also the millennarians, the outstanding example of which were the Millerites, who expected the Second Coming on 22 October 1844; the utopians, such as those of the Oneida Community established by John Humphrey Noyes in the mid-1840s; and the Mormons, followers of Joseph Smith of Palmyra.

Two aspects, perhaps, of the more extreme outcomes of enthusiastic religion in western New York feed into the formation of ethnological conceptions for Morgan. Leading issues for Morgan, especially in his kinship work, are variation in forms of the ownership and transmission of property, and variation in forms of sexuality and marriage. Religious enthusiasts in his midst offered examples of each. Community of property was found in the Millerites and the Oneida Community, and also in the Fourierist socialist phalanxes, five of which were founded around Rochester in the spring of 1844. And religious enthusiasm showed a pronounced tendency to spill over into unhallowed sexual encounters in individual cases and to develop into bizarre regimes of marriage in the new groups, such as the "complex marriages" of the Oneida community and the polygyny of the Mormons.[15]

All these new developments McIlvaine publicly opposed. During

---

[15] I rely here on the classic study of Whitney R. Cross, *The Burned-over District, the social and intellectual history of enthusiastic religion in western New York, 1800–1850.* "Presbygational" is from Robert Ellis Thompson, *A history of the Presbyterian churches in the United States.*

his Rochester pastorate Charles Finney returned to the city to hold revivals in its churches, and early in 1856 the First Church considered whether to invite Finney to speak. Under McIlvaine's guidance the church, after debating the matter at several meetings, decided against an invitation, and McIlvaine read from the pulpit a long statement to the effect that conversions resulting from revivals were not permanent.[16] McIlvaine's opposition to religious enthusiasm in favor of a rational, intellectual religiosity was typically Presbyterian; and it was joined to the doctrinal conservatism of Old School Presbyterianism. The Old School had imposed a split upon the church in 1837–38, during McIlvaine's first year in seminary at Princeton, against the deviations from the Westminster Confession and Catechism they saw in the doctrines of the New School theologians. Three synods in western New York (Utica, Geneva, and Genesee) and one in Ohio (Western Reserve) were declared to be out of communication with the Presbyterian Church—to which, however, individual churches might reunite themselves by applying to the nearest unexcluded presbytery. It is indicative of McIlvaine's Old School affiliation that he was ordained in an unexcluded New York presbytery (Albany) before preaching at churches within the territory of the excluded ones. McIlvaine deplored the schism and lent his best efforts to restoring union; but when Rochester Presbytery forced the issue by deciding for the New School branch in 1854, he led the First Church out in order to join the Old School branch. In the last year of his Rochester pastorate (1860) the Old School General Assembly met in his church.[17]

What a Rochester journalist remembered as McIlvaine's conservatism and "blue Presbyterianism" prompted him not only to deny his pulpit to the most popular revivalist of the age but to attack the spiritualism craze, theatrical performances and dancing parties.[18] In a notable sermon on the Christian family he attacked Mormonism and socialism together—"this latter having, it is said, an establish-

---

[16] Charles Mulford Robinson, *First Church chronicles, 1815–1915,* p. 128.

[17] On the schism see Thompson, *History of the Presbyterian churches,* chs. 10–11; Robinson, *First Church chronicles,* pp. 95–96; George M. Marsden, *The evangelical mind and the New School Presbyterian experience,* pp. 62–63; on McIlvaine see Robinson, *First Church chronicles,* pp. 124–125, 130.

[18] "The death of Dr. McIlvaine," *The Democrat and chronicle* (Rochester), 1 February 1897; Robinson, *First Church chronicles,* pp. 116, 129; McIlvaine, *A discourse upon ancient and modern divination.*

ment in this city"—for reviving polygamy, which the Gospel had abolished.[19] His conservatism also led him into the central quandary of his relationship with Morgan, who, though he regularly attended church services, could not become a church member without confessing Christ.[20]

More important to our purposes than the doctrinal content of the controversy that split the Presbyterian Church is the fact that Princeton Theological Seminary, under the conservative Dr. Charles Hodge, editor of the *Princeton review,* threw in with the Old School. McIlvaine was joined to this movement by many bonds.

This coalition of forces brought a conservative Calvinism into partnership with Presbyterian scholar-educators who held very positive attitudes toward science, and promoted scientific education. Old School intellectuals looked upon nature as a source of knowledge of the Creation and therefore of the Creator second only to revelation, and science as the means by which that truth was known, whence science and scripture spoke of the same truth and could not truly be in conflict with each other. Science, at bottom, is a kind of worship. This conception of, to use Bozeman's happy phrase, doxological science is well expressed by McIlvaine in an 1878 article entitled "The miracle of creation." The ideas are by no means peculiar to him.

For McIlvaine science is the intellectual apprehension of the regularity or lawfulness of the forces of nature, which depend ultimately upon the uniform action of the power or will of God.[21]

Both these grand sources of truth and human well being, religion and science, are from God, though in different ways; and their reciprocal

---

[19] McIlvaine, *The peace of the tabernacle* (1857), p. 17. He regarded a resurgence of polygamy as a real and present danger: "For I doubt not that most of us will live to see an organized attempt in this country, to expunge from our statute books all penalties against bigamy and polygamy."

[20] A pamphlet entitled *A catalogue of the members of the First Presbyterian Church, in Rochester: June 1850* does not list Morgan as a church member, even though in the funeral address McIlvaine says he was Morgan's pastor for twelve years (i.e., from 1848 to 1860). According to First Church records in the Presbyterian Historical Society, Philadelphia, which Elisabeth Tooker kindly examined for me, Morgan's name is not in the membership register for 1832–1903, although Mary's is (admitted 24 March 1852 by letter); nor again is he listed in separate registers for 1864 and 1866.

[21] McIlvaine, "The miracle of creation," pp. 834, 837–838. Theodore Dwight Bozeman's book is *Protestants in an age of science, the Baconian ideal and antebellum American religious thought.*

influence is such that neither can do without the other. On the one hand, the intellectual faculties of man have their deepest roots in his moral and spiritual nature, through which they draw their richest nourishment from the infinite of truth; and thus, in distinction from the mere animal mind, they are rendered capable of growth and development from generation to generation, from age to age. And all science, properly so called, is the intellectual grasp of the raw material of truth, subjecting it to the forms and laws of thought. Science itself, therefore, is truly a blossom and fruit of faith, and cannot attain to its utmost and permanent development except upon the soil of religion. On the other hand, scientific culture is the most powerful and effectual means of developing and purifying the intellect, in order that it may become capable of appreciating the evidences of true religion in distinction from baleful superstitions. This, doubtless, is the reason why Christianity, with its transcendent claims upon the faith of mankind, always prevails wherever science is cultivated, and why there is not even a possibility of any other religion in the bosom of modern civilization.

Where faith, by stimulating the imagination, predisposes the mind to regard what it cannot otherwise explain as miraculous, science comes to exert its benign influence in emancipating the human mind from superstition.

To be sure, the mutually beneficial alliance between Protestant religion and science—between, that is to say, religion that had been purified by science of the superstition of medieval and modern Romanism and the idolatrous lapses of the Jews in ancient times, and science spiritualized by faith—was not, in the aftermath of the Darwinian revolution, an easy one, and science could no longer be relied upon to read the book of nature and find its author. For his finest example of natural theology McIlvaine pressed Louis Agassiz' work on classification into service; but it belonged to an older generation of scholarship. He complained of "the materialists and pantheists of modern science, who would banish the Creator from the world he created,"[22] and insisted on the existence of miracles.

Thus for McIlvaine science and religion were parallel activities directed to the same end, each making up the deficiencies of the other, and neither prospering in the absence of the other, religion without science running to superstition and science without religion, to pantheism and materialism. His "blue Presbyterianism," if such

---

[22] McIlvaine, "Miracle," p. 837.

it was, was joined to a very positive attitude toward science that became defensive only with the advent of *Origin of species*.

The conservative Presbyterian environment that McIlvaine epitomized and in which Morgan grew up, I suggest, molded Morgan in several ways. The emotional austerity and impulse to the mastery of experience through the intellect which both men shared were qualities general to Presbyterianism, qualities that gave it the leadership of the nation's intellectual life even as it was losing ground in membership to the less learned Baptists and Methodists. Other characteristically Old School Presbyterian attitudes in McIlvaine were the sharp hostility to superstitious forms of religion, of which Roman Catholicism was the type, and to Mormonism for its polygyny, which again the two men shared. It is perhaps here that Morgan finds his propensity to view Mormonism and other forms of deviance as atavisms of an earlier age: "Some of the excrescences of modern civilization, such as Mormonism, are seen to be relics of the old savagism not yet eradicated from the human brain," he tells us in *Ancient society*.[23] McIlvaine held the religiously grounded belief in the historic exceptionalism of the Hebrews (as, it must be said, did most Christians), and this probably motivates Morgan's belief that civilization is the achievement of both Semitic and European peoples and that the two are closely related; and, as a corollary, that other peoples are less advanced. As we shall see in chapter 6, these are the underlying ideas that inform Morgan's ethnic classifications and that clarify some of the oddities of his scheme.

In their attitudes toward the less advanced cultures the two distinctly differ, however. McIlvaine is entirely lacking in sympathy for the savage and speaks of him in terms of "permanent degradation and inferiority."[24] Morgan, by some unaccountable personal inclination, is sympathetic and generous. It was Morgan's originality, and not McIlvaine's suggestion, the latter directly tells us, to show that savagism was the original condition of our own ancestors, and to

---

[23] *Ancient society*, p. 61. McIlvaine: "Upon the same ground [individual religious liberty] the Mormon denies our authority to punish him for his loathsome polygamy, and insists upon his constitutional right to sit in on legislative bodies, and to fill our highest judicial and military offices, in the very eye of the nation, with all his harem around him." *A nation's right to worship God*, p. 39, reprinted in *Princeton review*, p. 694. In *A discourse upon ancient and modern divination* he links Mormonism with the spiritualist movement.

[24] McIlvaine, "The organisation of society," MS. in the Morgan Papers, p. 30.

show a larger appreciation of the difficulty and importance of the accomplishments of the ages of savagery and barbarism. This difference between the two men extended to Morgan's sympathetic appreciation of the manifestations of mind among animals, which McIlvaine could not share, holding to the conventional view that the lower animals were created for man's use and that the animal mind, unlike the human, was incapable of growth and development from generation to generation.

These at least would be among the terms of an adequate treatment of the effects of religion upon Morgan's ethnology.

McIlvaine's attitude toward science expressed itself in his participation in the founding of the Club and in the papers he presented there. The first season (1854–55) his paper was on "Limitations of logic," but the next three seasons he gave a series of papers on topics of comparative philology, perhaps limited to Indo-European: "Observations on the Sanscrit language," "The arrowhead inscriptions," and "Comparative philology in its relations to ethnology." It is a great pity that these papers have not survived because they are likely to have been a formative influence on Morgan's kinship work, as one of several forces that gave it a philological design. It is well, therefore, to look at the matter more closely.

Let us begin with a chronology of McIlvaine's philological papers. In the second season of the Club (1855–56), McIlvaine gave the "Observations on the Sanscrit language" on 29 January, a few months after having joined the American Oriental Society.[25] In the third season (1856–57) he spoke on "The arrowhead [i.e., cuneiform] inscriptions" 11 February, reporting Rawlinson's work on the decipherment of the Old Persian and Aramaic portions of the Behistun Inscription of Darius the Great. According to a local newspaper, McIlvaine gave a public lecture on the subject in the Corinthian Hall the following April.[26] In August he attended the Montreal meeting of the American Association for the Advancement of Science with Morgan (the latter having joined the year previous), and is said to have given a paper on the "decipherment of arrowhead inscriptions." Morgan's Indian interests had recently revived, and at the same

---

[25] Titles and dates of these and subsequent Club papers are given in the minute book kept by Morgan, the secretary (MS., The Club Papers, University of Rochester) and in *The Club, si quid veri invereris profer 1854–1937.*

[26] "Dr. McIlvaine's lectures," *Rochester union and advertiser,* 9 April 1857.

meeting he gave a paper on "Laws of descent of the Iroquois"; it was, however, largely a reworking of old material from *League of the Iroquois,* with an attempt to generalize the pattern of Iroquois institutions. It has the *League*'s legalist vision and does not have the philological design his kinship work was soon to take on. Finally, in the fourth season of the Club (1857–58), McIlvaine gave "Comparative philology in its relations to ethnology" 12 January. On 1 March he began a series of public lectures at the Smithsonian Institution which the *Annual report* describes as five lectures on "Comparative Philology in some of its bearings upon Ethnology, and embracing an account of the Sanskrit and Persian Arrowhead Languages"—somewhat inaccurately, to be sure, as cuneiform is a script, not a language, and although Old Persian has been written in cuneiform, Sanskrit has not.[27] That summer Morgan's kinship work took a decisive philological turning, as we shall see in the next chapter.

Thus McIlvaine was exploring the results of comparative philology in a systematic way and had a considered view of its consequences for ethnology. Still, we must not exaggerate the depth or quality of McIlvaine's knowledge of the field he had taken on. He published no philological papers (or, indeed, articles on any subject) in either the *Journal of the American Oriental Society* or the *Proceedings of the American Association for the Advancement of Science*; indeed, the latter has no mention of the philological paper he was said to have given in 1857. His Smithsonian lectures were not published in the *Annual report* as some of the more scientific ones were. I think

---

[27] Smithsonian Institution, *Annual report* (1857), p. 37. (The 1857 issue reported on the lectures given during the 1857–58 winter season.) In the *Rochester union and advertiser* (4 March 1858) it is described as a course of three lectures on "Comparative Philology in some of its bearings upon Ethnology, and embracing some account of the Sanscrit and Persian Arrowhead Language." Some description of its content comes from McIlvaine's letter to the Yale Sanskritist, William Dwight Whitney: "My attention was attracted to the Persian Arrowhead by its relationship to the Skt. I have done little in it but reconstruct Rawlinson's processes of discovery; which Prof. Henry of the Smithsonian Institution, after I had given them in a lecture, assured me were perfectly rigorous, as a specimen of inductive reasoning. I had used the expression that they were 'only less rigorous than those of the physicists.' He said that was an incorrect expression; that from the original hypothesis to the conclusion, the reasoning was perfect; and he seemed to be somewhat surprised, and was greatly delighted to find out that linguists could reason inductively. You are aware that he knows nothing of philology." McIlvaine to Whitney, 3/13/58, American Oriental Society archives.

it likely that Joseph Henry, secretary of the Smithsonian and member of the publication committee of the American Association for the Advancement of Science, who had very austere standards for scientific publication, may have adjudged the paper and the lectures as essentially synthetic and popular expositions rather than original contributions to knowledge. Resek's characterization of McIlvaine as "an accomplished Sanskrit scholar" surely goes too far. In my examination of his published writings and his surviving letters I find no evidence to sustain the idea that McIlvaine's knowledge of Sanskrit was sufficient to enable him to undertake original research. As late as January 1858 he obtained from W. D. Whitney of Yale names of books needed for the study of Sanskrit—that is, as he was preparing the Smithsonian course of lectures but long after the earlier papers on which those lectures were based. It is likely, however, that he knew Sanskrit well enough to follow the literature intelligently.[28] McIlvaine's grasp of comparative philology, it appears, is that of someone who read up on the subject in order to present it in an intelligible way to others; indeed, there is reason to think he took up the subject of philology as his special contribution to the life of the Club. It was in the role of broker to the intelligent public for linguistic science, I suggest, that his contribution to the philological design of Morgan's kinship work lay. The alliance of comparative philology and ethnology, however, was by no means McIlvaine's invention; he can only have brought to Morgan's attention the recent triumphs of a discipline whose bearing upon ethnology contemporaries came to take for granted.

It would be difficult to overestimate the prestige of comparative philology in Morgan's day, because of the striking successes in Indo-European historical linguistics that led the field and its role as a model for emergent social sciences. Indeed, it may be said that by mid-century political economy and comparative philology were the two forms of inquiry into human behavior that, in the general estimation, had risen to the dignity of sciences and had become exemplars for other of the emergent human sciences. They were very different, even competing models. Political economy, especially in its classical, British form, purported to formulate the laws of a uniform human nature, at the core of which was a propensity to exchange and a desire for individual betterment. It resolved society into a congeries

<hr>

[28] Resek, *Morgan, American scholar,* p. 93; McIlvaine to Whitney, 3/13/58, American Oriental Society archives.

of self-seeking individuals. History and culture are banished by means of *ceteris paribus* provisions that treat them as mere sources of friction in the operation of its laws. And it posited a natural equilibrium as the outcome of the interplay of the unfettered individual will. Political economy held out the promise of basing policy on disinterested science rather than partisan passion. The nationalist economics of List and Carey that was favored by Morgan's circle was not typical in these respects.

Quite different was the case of comparative philology. Its famous laws were particularizing, not generalizing; its starting point was the social fact of the particular language, not the individual human agent; its subject was cultural and its method historical. Philology's power was its ability to bring order to the chaos of different languages, its ability to classify languages according to historical relationships. It showed relationships between languages that were unexpected, surprising, independent of the investigator's will or of traditional authority. The ideal end point of philology's program was philosophical rather than political: the comprehensive classification of languages upon historical principles. This would necessarily be a comprehensive account of the historical interrelation of languages, living and dead, and their derivation from the first language. In many ways this project prefigures the shape of a modern, Darwinian conception of the classification of biological species, as Darwin himself recognized.

Philology, then, had an essentially ethnological program, to discern the relationships among nations; and as a model for other emergent disciplines its greatest appeal was for the various elements of what became anthropology. The heart of that appeal was the promise of philology to provide a history for the savage and unlettered peoples who had neither written records nor reliable oral accounts of their own past. Philology would recover a vanished past from vestiges unconsciously preserved in living languages, detectable only to those who could decipher the signs.

In the various stages of Morgan's writing we find not one but three kinds of philology, and in order to clarify the role of philology in Morgan's work and especially in the formation of his kinship project we must distinguish them. The first of these is comparative philology, driven by Indo-Europeanist models, which so interested McIlvaine and nineteenth-century intellectuals at large. Another, which we find in Morgan's earlier work, has its roots in the eighteenth-century philology of conjectural-history speculations upon the origin of language. A third is the tradition of Americanist philology, parallel in structure to Indo-Europeanist philology but emerging earlier and developing independently of it.

These distinctions are necessary because there is an important discontinuity, hitherto unnoticed, between the philology that underlies Morgan's early Iroquois work and the comparative philology of Indo-Europeanist stripe that informs the *Systems,* a discontinuity that needs to be made visible and to be accounted for. In the *League of the Iroquois* there is a chapter on language in which propositions about the nature and origin of language are quoted in *oratio recta* but without attribution. We must assume that their source was so widely known to his contemporaries that Morgan did not feel it necessary to name it. This source was Adam Smith's *Dissertation on the origin of languages,* widely read by Americans of Morgan's generation in the edition of Dugald Stewart.[29] In Stewart's sketch of Smith's life with which the volume opens, he calls attention to the essay as an example of "conjectural history" of which he thought Smith the inventor. Years later as the kinship project was reaching maturity Morgan's language pays homage to Smith's dissertation in his "conjectural solution" of the classificatory system. But Smith's linguistic ideas are found only in Morgan's earlier work; comparative philology would inspire the kinship project.

It was only after the *League* that the Indo-Europeanist-led comparative philology came into Morgan's ken. He was no philologist himself; the book inventory he drew up shortly after the *League* was published shows precious little that a working philologist would require beyond the obligatory Latin and Greek works and a dictionary or two. One book he acquired later, Schele de Vere's *Outlines of comparative philology* (1853), which advertises itself as the "first effort to bring the youthful but promising Science" of comparative philology "before an American Public," provides a benchmark for the popularization of the subject in the United States. This amiable rag-bag of information was cast in the shade by the immensely popular *Lectures on the science of language* (1861) by Max Müller, which Morgan bought promptly and used heavily in the *Systems;*

---

[29] *League of the Iroquois,* book 3, ch. 2. Adam Smith's *A dissertation on the origin of languages* was appended to Stewart's edition of Smith's *Theory of the moral sentiments,* an edition widely read in the United States. The dissertation's proper title is *Considerations concerning the first formation of languages, and the different genius of original and compound languages.*

but the philological design of Morgan's work had been established before it appeared, and also before William Dwight Whitney's lectures on linguistics appeared in the Smithsonian's *Annual reports* (1864), of which Morgan was a regular reader. Other possible sources of philological ideas in his library would be the more technical material found in the *Transactions of the American Ethnological Society,* the *Proceedings of the American Association for the Advancement of Science,* and the annual reports of the Smithsonian. But the premier source was certainly McIlvaine.

There are in addition two broad avenues by which the philological ideas that inform the *Systems* came to Morgan's notice: the polygenism debate that became explosive in the 1850s, drawing comparative philology into the storm center, and the longer tradition of Americanist debate over the origin of the Native Americans in which philology was also deeply implicated. Each of these requires our attention.

As the decade opened, the *Christian examiner* published an article by Louis Agassiz with the provocative title, "The diversity of origin of the human races." This expression of the polygenist thesis profoundly agitated members of the Club, who were unanimous in their hostility toward it. Agassiz embraces two propositions that would hitherto have been thought antagonistic: the Unity of Mankind—that the various races are of one human species—and the Diversity of Origin of the Human Races—that they were separately created. "Who does not recognize *prima facie* that the canoe-birch, white-birch, sweet-birch, and yellow-birch are trees of the same stamp, though they do not pass one into the other, do not mingle, producing, nevertheless, similar fruit?"[30] Thus the most intimate unity may exist without a common origin.[31]

> The comparisons made between monkeys and men by comparative anatomists, when tracing the gradations in nature, have been greatly misunderstood by those who have concluded that, because there were no other types between the highest monkeys and men, these highest monkeys were something intermediate between men and beasts; or that some race particularly disagreeable to those writers was something intermediate between monkeys and human beings. These links between man-

---

[30] Louis Agassiz, "The diversity of origin of the human races," p. 118. For the polygenism-monogenism debate generally see William Stanton, *The leopard's spots; scientific attitudes toward race in America 1815–59.*

[31] The same, pp. 119–120.

kind and the animal creation are only the great steps indicating the gradation established by the Creator among living beings, and they no more indicate a relation between men and monkeys, than between monkeys and beasts of prey, or between these and the ox, or between the ox and the whale.

Thus the races now occupy separate but contiguous steps on the scale of nature, separately created but of one species, "all equal before God, because all of them have been created in his image."[32] Agassiz' argument favoring the diversity of origin of the races is based on a theory of the distinctiveness of the flora and fauna of different geographical regions. Plant and animal varieties are localized and were therefore created in their proper province, but more than that they were created *en masse* (not in single pairs, as the Bible might lead us to think), in numbers proportionate to those of other species and races making up what we would nowadays call an ecosystem. He assimilates the human races to this theory; each was created in a particular natural province and not as a single pair. Agassiz understands "Genesis as chiefly relating to the history of the white race, with special reference to the history of the Jews," and asserts that it does not treat the origin of the human species as a whole, which explains its silence as to the creation of other races.

Agassiz' great prestige as America's leading biologist—Harvard professor, student of the great Cuvier—and his wide popular recognition lent special force to the polygenist position, so distasteful to the pious and so welcome to the slaveholder. And he used science aggressively. He warns off the theologian and the statesman at the outset: "We have a right to consider the questions growing out of men's physical relations as merely scientific questions, and to investigate them without reference to either politics or religion."[33] He then proceeds to tell the theologian how to interpret Genesis, and gives the statesman to understand that policy should look to science:[34]

> What would be the best education to be imparted to the different races in consequence of their primitive difference, if this difference is once granted, no reasonable man can expect to be prepared to say, so long as the principle itself is so generally opposed; but, for our own part, we entertain not the slightest doubt that human affairs with reference to the

---

[32] The same, p. 120.
[33] The same, p. 110.
[34] The same, pp. 144–145.

colored races would be far more judiciously conducted, if, in our intercourse with them, we were guided by a full consciousness of the real difference existing between us and them, and a desire to foster those dispositions that are eminently marked in them, rather than by treating them on terms of equality. We conceive it to be our duty to study these peculiarities, and to do all that is in our power to develop them to the greatest advantage of all parties. And the more we become acquainted with these dispositions, the better, doubtless, will be our course with reference to our own improvement, and with reference to the advance of the colored races. For our own part, we have always considered it as a most injudicious proceeding to attempt to force the peculiarities of our white civilization of the nineteenth century upon all nations of the world.

We find in this argument three assumptions within which the debate over polygeny would rage but which would not long outlive the 1850s. The first of these is the scale of nature idea, in particular its notion of the discreteness of species, here transferred to the level of races. There is not a continuum of individual variation uniting two races; as Agassiz says, the canoe birch does not pass into the white birch. This sense of discreteness will be overthrown by Darwin. The second assumption is that of fixity of species, also to be upset by the Darwinian revolution:

> The monuments of Egypt have fortunately yielded skeletons of animals that lived several thousand years ago; from the same source seeds of plants have been obtained, that have been made to germinate and grow; and from the most minute and careful comparisons of these animals and plants of ancient days with those of the same species now living in the same countries, it has been found that there is no difference between them—that they agree precisely in all particulars as perfectly as the different individuals of the species now living agree together.[35]

The final assumption is that of the short, biblical chronology for human history:

> The monuments of Egypt teach us that five thousand years ago the negroes were as different from the white race as they are now, and that therefore, neither time nor climate nor change of habitation has produced the differences we observe between the races, and that to assume them to be of the same order, and to assert their common origin, is to assume and to assert what has no historical or physiological or physical foundation."[36]

---

[35] The same, p. 116.
[36] The same, p. 124.

Thus the races, as the species, are unchanging; but the proof assumes that the span of human history is little more than five thousand years. This assumption will fall before the time revolution of the 1860s.

Agassiz elaborated his argument in an article on the "Natural provinces of the animal world and their relation to the different types of man" in the notorious *Types of mankind* published by J. C. Nott and George R. Gliddon in 1854. This scientific apology for slavery sold very widely and created a great deal of controversy—so much so that the authors collaborated on another, similar book called *Indigenous races of the earth* produced in a lavish style.

Agassiz, a sterling practitioner of doxological science but a religiously unorthodox one, here identified himself with issues that were religiously and politically repugnant to many northerners of McIlvaine's and Morgan's circle. Philology played a leading role in the controversy that swirled around these publications. Charles Hodge, in a fine critique of Agassiz in the *Princeton review* (which McIlvaine may be expected to have read), invokes all the leading philologists, the Humboldts and the Grimms, Bopp and Bunsen, in the attack.[37]

Several members of the Club spoke out against polygenism, namely, Martin Anderson, Chester Dewey (who gave no less than four papers on the subject), McIlvaine, and Morgan.[38] McIlvaine probably appealed to philology in his paper; Morgan certainly did. Morgan's paper, unpublished but preserved in the University of Rochester, is most interesting. It gives us to understand that Agassiz' theory "has, several times, been brought before the Club, and as often derided with an almost unanimous voice."[39]

Morgan took up the critique of Agassiz not out of interest in the theory itself but because "it lay in my way to desire at least to know

---

[37] Charles Hodge, "The unity of mankind" (1859), p. 147. The authorship of this unsigned article in the *Princeton review* is given in the index for 1825–68.

[38] The papers: Martin Anderson, "On the objections urged against the unity of the human races"; Chester Dewey, "Observations on species," "On the permanence of species in the animal kingdom," "On Agassiz's theory of independent zoological provinces," "On the classification of animals in Agassiz"; McIlvaine, "Species, its technical and philosophical definition"; and Morgan, "Agassiz' theory of the diverse origin of the human race." The latter is preserved in the Morgan Papers. Chester Dewey's "Examination of some reasonings against the unity of mankind" was "rewritten and prepared for the press" by McIlvaine (*The wisdom of Holy Scripture*, p. 60), and published in the *Princeton review* in 1862.

[39] Morgan, "Agassiz' theory," p. 12.

what it claimed to be, as a matter of preparation for the investigation of another question; namely, whether our Indian races are of Asiatic origin."[40] That is, as preparation for the kinship project he wished to investigate the chief alternative to the philological model he had adopted, this being Agassiz' doctrine of separate creation of the races in their proper geographical provinces, which denied the Asian derivation of the American Indians and held that, like the buffalo, they are indigenous. He attempts to give Agassiz' theory its due but finds at its heart a contradiction between the idea of several original pairs and the unity of species. Moreover, while zoology and paleontology are tending toward the theory of the diverse origin of the human race, he says, the new science of ethnology has come into existence "with the avowed object of making herself the champion of the old theory of unity of origin."[41] This ethnology encompasses philology; it "studies languages, institutions, religious systems, architecture, hyeroglyphics [sic], monumental inscriptions, and whatever subject of knowledge may shed any light upon the early footsteps of man upon the Earth."[42] It brings these studies to bear on a project identical with that which comparative philology has at its core:[43]

> Every nation and tribe on the face of the Earth has been visited and questioned of its origin. Every language of living as well as of extinct races has been explored and compelled to deliver up its testimony. Ethnology has thus been enabled to look far back of the historical period into the remote past, and reassociate nations whose unity of origin had fallen out of remembrance. The nations of the Earth have been reduced from a confused multitude, into a limited number of generic stocks; and at the present moment an earnest endeavor is being made to resolve these original stocks into a lower number, and finally into one.

To be sure, the results of ethnology to date have only begun to fulfill its promise:[44]

> Between the primitive or generic stocs [sic], as the black the red and the white races the gulf is at present impassible, with not over much to encourage the belief, that after the lapse of so many centuries it will ever

---

[40] The same, p. 18.
[41] The same, p. 22.
[42] The same, p. 40.
[43] The same, p. 106.
[44] The same, p. 107.

be possible to cross the chasm, and settle the problem on the basis of historical proof, or of scientific induction. The wooly haired negro and the silken haired white man are as far asunder as ever, notwithstanding the efforts of Ethnology, up to the present time, to trace them to the same cradle. Still we are certainly justified in anticipating great results and important discoveries in Ethnology in the future on the basis alone of past achievements. At the present time the Asiatic origin of most of the primitive stocks has been established; and could the proof be made absolute and universal, as it is now partial and probable, it would explode the new doctrine of many Zoological provinces by reducing them to one, if it did not furnish a convincing and unanswerable argument in favor of unity of origin.

Having found zoology wanting as an instrument with which to prove the Asiatic origin of the Indians, Morgan turned to philology. We must look, then, to the state of play in Americanist philology on the questions he took up in the summer of 1856, and to which he addresses the *Systems*: that of the unity, and the Asiatic origin, of the Indians.

A philological approach to the conundrums of Native American anthropology was precociously conceptualized by no less a scholar than Thomas Jefferson, in his *Notes on the state of Virginia* (1782). Asking whence came the aboriginals of America, he offers two practicable routes of migration from the Old World: a European route going from Norway to Iceland to "Groenland" to Labrador, and an Asian route suggested by "the late discoveries of Captain Cook, coasting from Kamschatka to California, [which] have proved that if the two continents of Asia and America be separated at all, it is only by a narrow streight." Language will decide the issue:[45]

> A knowledge of their several languages would be the most certain evidence of their derivation which could be produced. In fact, it is the best proof of the affinity of nations which ever can be referred to. How many ages have elapsed since the English, the Dutch, the Germans, the Swiss, the Norwegians, Danes and Swedes have separated from their common stock? Yet how many more must elapse before the proofs of their common origin, which exists in their several languages, will disappear? It is to be lamented, then, very much to be lamented, that we have suffered so many of the Indian tribes already to extinguish, without our having previously collected and deposited in the records of literature, the general rudiments at least of the languages they spoke. Were vocabularies formed

---

[45] Jefferson, *Notes on the state of Virginia*, pp. 510–511.

of all the languages spoken in North and South America, preserving their appellations of the most common objects in nature, of those which must be present in every nation barbarous or civilized, with the inflections of their nouns and verbs, their principles of regimen and concord, and these deposited in all the public libraries, it would furnish opportunities to those skilled in the languages of the old world to compare them with these, now, or at any future time, and hence to construct the best evidence of the derivation of this part of the human race.

Jefferson's program of collecting and comparing Amerindian vocabularies in the belief that this could prove their common origin and decide their relationship to the nations of the Old World was undertaken by himself and by Stephen Du Ponceau under the auspices of the American Philosophical Society.[46] Thereafter, the classification upon historical principles of the American languages became the fundament of Americanist anthropology, from Stephen Du Ponceau and Albert Gallatin in the first part of the nineteenth century, through Powell's *Linguistic families of North America north of Mexico* (1890) at its end, which "definitively settled most of the classificatory problems for the languages included in his survey."[47] Moreover, nonphilological study of Native Americans, such as Schoolcraft's multivolume compendium (*Historical and statistical information respecting the history, condition and prospects of the Indian tribes of the United States,* 1851–57), was organized by the philological design of Americanist ethnography, by which I mean that the tribes were grouped by language family even though dispersed in space, rather than by geographical units or by the ecological zones (plains, woodland, Northwest Coast, and so forth) that became the dominant frame for Americanists in the twentieth century.

Because of Morgan's early admiration for him, Gallatin is a good

---

[46] See Murphey D. Smith, "Peter Stephen Du Ponceau and his study of languages."

[47] Mary R. Haas, "Grammar or lexicon? The American Indian side of the question from Duponceau to Powell," p. 250, reprinted as "The problem of classifying American Indian languages: from Duponceau to Powell" in *Language, culture, and history; essays by Mary R. Haas.* She points out that the lexicon/grammar distinction in nineteenth-century philology sows the seeds of the distinction between genetic and typological classifications in recent linguistics. It is important to remember, however, that Du Ponceau's polysynthetic class was certainly intended as a demonstration of the genetic connection of all Amerindian languages, and the comparison of grammars was thus a continuation of the program of the comparison of vocabularies.

figure on whom to fasten in order to establish the point to which the
Americanist project had progressed when Morgan's attention turned
toward philology. Gallatin's "Synopsis of the Indian tribes within
the United States east of the Rocky Mountains, and in the British
and Russian possessions in North America" (1836) was an authoritative synthesis of its day, extended to newly elicited vocabularies in
his 1848 article, "Hale's Indians of North-west America, and vocabularies of North America; with an introduction." In the "Synopsis"
he grouped the eighty-one tribes included in the survey into twenty-
eight language families on the basis of shared vocabulary items. This
was very far from the unitary language family the Americanist program had hoped to demonstrate through vocabularies. For Gallatin
this linguistic diversity did not disprove Indian unity; it showed,
rather, that the Indians had dispersed across the New World a very
long time ago, shortly after the Flood. "The diversity which does
actually exist proves only, that the separation of some of the Indian
nations took place in very early times; and the difficulty of accounting
for it is not greater here than on the other continent."[48] And he
embraced Du Ponceau's thesis that where vocabulary failed to show
Indian unity, grammar succeeded. The Indian languages have common features of grammar distinct from those of other parts of the
world which justifies grouping them together as "polysynthetic" languages. Gallatin concludes:[49]

> The uniformity of character in the grammatical forms and structure of
> all the Indian Languages of North America, which have been sufficiently
> investigated, indicates a common origin. The numerous distinct lan-
> guages, if we attend only to the vocabularies between which every trace
> of affinity has disappeared, attest the antiquity of the American popula-
> tion. This may be easily accounted for, consistently with the opinion that
> the first inhabitants came from Asia, and with the Mosaic chronology.

America "received its first inhabitants at a very remote epoch, probably not much posterior to that of the dispersion of mankind."[50]
    Thus philology was already present in every issue to which Morgan

---

[48] Gallatin, "Synopsis," p. 161.
[49] The same, p. 142.
[50] The same, p. 6. Samuel F. Haven, *Archaeology of the United States* (1856) is
indispensable as a guide to the state of the question of Indian origins at the time
Morgan was formulating his kinship project.

addressed himself—or perhaps we may say in every belief that he attempted to sustain by means of science: the unity of the human species, the common origin of the Native Americans and their derivation from Asia. But he would come to think that where the comparison of vocabularies had so far failed to achieve what the Americanist project had hoped of it, a new instrument for ethnology would succeed. Neither vocabulary, then, nor again grammar, but the semantics of kinship would complete the program that Jefferson had begun.

5

Generalizing Iroquois

✦✦✦

In the summer of 1857 Morgan returned to his Iroquois materials in order to prepare a paper for the August meeting, in Montreal, of the American Association for the Advancement of Science, which he had joined the previous year. His paper, "Laws of descent of the Iroquois," shows no evidence of new fieldwork since the *League of the Iroquois*. Morgan is returning to old material, but he does so with the intention of rethinking it. What is new in this paper is the attempt to draw out the implications of his Iroquois work for the understanding of American Indians at large. He had at first thought that the peculiar system of consanguinity he found among the Seneca in 1846 was their own invention. Now for the first time he perceives the Iroquois system as a case of a general American Indian pattern. He sets about generalizing Iroquois, and the Iroquois become the lens through which his ethnographic vision focuses upon other peoples.

The 1857 paper is Morgan's first attempt to formulate a general view of kinship, and accordingly it deserves our close scrutiny. It was, however, to prove a false start. Morgan would abandon it and begin again when his informants for Ojibwa resisted his best efforts to obtain from them confirmation of the theory he brought to the field in the summer of 1858. The kinship project would be completely and definitively reformulated in a year of intense creativity bounded by the confrontation of his Iroquois material first by the Ojibwa and then by the Tamil the following summer. Morgan has left us a record of extraordinary clarity by which to track the developments of his *annus mirabilis*. Before doing so, however, we must see in this 1857 paper what exactly was the content of the general theory of Indian kinship he carried with him to the wilds of Upper Michigan the summer after he had written it. We shall then examine the documentation for his development of a new sense of the problem of kin nomenclature as a "domestic institution" of great durability, worthy of thorough scientific investigation.

The presentation of the Iroquois case with which the 1857 paper opens shows no major change in conceptualization from the treatment found in *League of the Iroquois*. The object that is to become kinship continues to be defined in lawyer's terms, as a "law" or "code" of "descent," which in the Iroquois case differs from both the civil and canon law chiefly in two respects: descent "followed the female line" rather than the male, and the collateral lines "were finally brought into or merged in the lineal" rather than being kept separate and becoming ever more distant with every remove from the common ancestor.[1] Here as in the *League* the tribal (that is, clan) organization, descent through the female, and the degrees of relationship (that is, merger of collaterals with lineals) are thought of as aspects of a unitary code of descent inhering in Iroquois family relationships—that is, as necessarily coexisting.

Morgan's elaboration of these aspects of the Iroquois code of descent again follows the *League*. He sketches the division into tribes and their union in the nations and these in turn in the league. He emphasizes the "bond of kindred blood" that obtains among members of the same tribe though they be of different nations, giving "an element of union among the five nations, of remarkable vitality and power."[2] Conversely, an Iroquois man could not marry a woman of his own tribe, even in another nation: "All of the members of a tribe were within the prohibited degrees of consanguinity."[3] Here he might have made an argument that the rule of marriage outside the tribe subserves intertribal solidarity (he suggests it later on), similar to his previous point about descent; however, he sees a different social purpose at work. The "central idea of their laws of descent" is "to place the father and mother in different tribes, and to assign the children to the tribe of the mother."[4] Here as in the *League* the principal object is "the perpetual disinheritance of the male line," especially as relates to the title of chief or sachem. The treatment of what we would call the kinship terminology is again as we found it in the *League*. The collateral line was merged partly with the lineal in three removes from the common ancestor and completely in four.

[1] Morgan, "Laws of descent of the Iroquois," pp. 132–133.
[2] The same, p. 133.
[3] The same, p. 134.
[4] The same.

Having expounded the Iroquois system, Morgan comes to the point of his paper, which is to use this code of descent, "or any other original, well-defined, Indian institution," as a test of "the truthfulness of history" and as an instrument "to solve the great problem of the origin of the Indian races."[5] Thus does Morgan embark upon the quest for proof of the unity and Asiatic origin of the American Indians that shapes and directs his kinship work culminating in the *Systems*. The remainder of his paper should be thought of as the sketch of a research program, in which theorizing runs far ahead of results in hand.

The general direction of that program is clear: it will concern itself with "the primary institutions" of Amerindian life, which bear the impress of "the nomadic or hunter state":[6]

> Let us observe that the primary institutions of a people are necessarily permanent from age to age, and only change when the whole constitution of society is changed. While in the nomadic or hunter state, institutions of this character are as permanent as the state in which they are developed. It is only by the entire and absolute transmutation of a race from the hunter to the civilized condition, that such institutions can be eradicated; and even then they rarely disappear entirely, as witness the tribes of the Athenians. Not even language itself will be found to be more stable than the domestic institutions within certain limits. Now it is very possible that a primary institution of an aboriginal people, may, if diligently explored among the races of the earth now living in the nomadic or hunter state, lead to important deductions in relation to the ultimate affinity, as well as origin, of generic races. And these results would repose with solidity upon the necessity permanence of such institutions, as this fact of permanence excludes the idea of accidental coincidence.

Morgan puts his Iroquois ethnology to good use in his critique of William L. Stone's *Life of Joseph Brant*. This book was one of Morgan's first introductions to Iroquois life, when the New Confederacy of the Iroquois was in search of information about the structure of the old upon which to model itself; and as we have already seen, Morgan began to learn its limitations when he met Ely Parker and acquired direct access to the Seneca. The book purported to prove that Brant was a sachem among the Iroquois. Stone "attempts to show that his father was a Mohawk sachem of the Wolf tribe, and

---

[5] The same, pp. 139–140.
[6] The same, p. 140.

thus devolves the title on him by descent"; but considering that sachemships belong to the (matrilineal) tribes, "had he succeeded in showing that his father was a sachem, that fact would have insured Brant's disinheritance."

This palpable hit emboldened Morgan to try for another, this time the prevailing view of the Aztecs, among whom, "according to most writers, the crown descended either to a *brother* or to a *nephew* of the deceased emperor, and not to his *son*." He singled out Prescott for criticism:

> Had the researches of this elegant writer brought him in contact with the real institutions of the Aztecs which controlled this question of descent, he would have discovered, there is every reason to believe, that the people were divided into tribes, with laws of descent precisely similar to those of the Iroquois: that no Aztec could marry into his own tribe; that the children were of the tribe of the mother; and that all titles were hereditary in the tribe, and descended in the female line.[7]

Morgan's Aztec theory is found, in embryo, as early as the *League,* in which he repeatedly gives us to understand that the Iroquois, by virtue of the civilizing benefits of their league, had advanced to a state second only among the American Indians to that of the Aztecs. He also adumbrated there his theory of the matrilineal transmission of the crown of Mexico. He continued to develop this theory more or less to the end of his life; but in these elaborations the purpose is not to show to what heights the Iroquois had risen by comparing them to the Aztecs, but to show that Aztec institutions were continuous with those of other Indians, and not with those of civilization.[8] It was a campaign to read the evidence of Aztec life through the lens of the Iroquois ethnography or, later, that of the "village Indians"

---

[7] The same, p. 141.

[8] Morgan's principal piece on the Aztecs is a memorable polemic, "Montezuma's dinner" (1876), which is an attack on Hubert Howe Bancroft's *Native races of the Pacific states.* His interpretation of Aztec life is part of a larger conception expressed in his many articles on the domestic architecture of the Indians ("The 'seven cities of Cibola,'" "Architecture of the American aborigines," "Houses of the mound-builders," "A study of the houses of the American aborigines," and "On the ruins of a stone pueblo on the Animas River in New Mexico"), culminating in the book that appeared in the last year of his life, *Houses and house-life of the American aborigines* (1881). The great historian of the Aztecs, Charles Gibson, subjected Morgan's work to a critique of uncharacteristic asperity in his youthful article, "Lewis Henry Morgan and the Aztec 'Monarchy.'"

of New Mexico, rather than through the European lens of the Spanish annalists. The Aztecs are to be known not in European terms of monarchs, empire, vassals, and palaces, but in Indian terms of sachems, confederacies, (matrilineal) tribes, and longhouses or the "joint-tenement" dwellings of the Pueblo Indians. It was a miss, but not without value in directing archaeological research away from European patterns and toward American ones.[9]

When he turns to the Indians of the United States, we see exactly where Morgan's research program stands:[10]

> This division of generic races into tribes, with descent in the female line, has prevailed very generally throughout the Indian family. Besides the Iroquois, and with every probability the Aztecs, we may mention that the Creeks, were divided into ten tribes; the Chickasaws into six; the Ojibeways into thirteen; and the Delawares into three. As the last two were the principal branches of the Algonquin family, it is reasonable to infer that similar laws of descent prevailed throughout all of its subdivisions.

Moreover, he finds this code of descent in Micronesian islands and, perhaps, in Australia and New Grenada, South America. He then turns to Asia:[11]

> Whether this code of descent came out of Asia, or originated upon this continent, is one of the questions incapable of proof; and it must rest, for its solution, upon the weight of evidence, or upon probable induction. Its existence among American races, whose languages are radically different, and without any traditional knowledge among them of its origin, indicates a very ancient introduction; and would seem to point to Asia as the birth-place of the system. The writer has no means of ascertaining whether similar laws of descent existed among the Tartar races. It is to the Tartar branch of the Mongolian family that attention would first be excited, from the pertinacity with which some of them have adhered to the nomadic state, and from the similarity of domestic habits to be found in the hunter life. Among the classic races we should hardly expect to find any similar institutions, and yet in the account given of the Lycians, of Asia-Minor, by Herodotus (Herod. Lib. I, c. 173), we have a glimpse at a system of descent, which, as far as it is explained, is analogous to that of the Iroquois.

---

[9] On this subject Leslie White's long introduction to his edition of the Bandelier-Morgan correspondence is indispensable.

[10] "Laws of descent," p. 141.

[11] The same, pp. 144–145.

The geographical distribution Morgan anticipates for matrilineal tribes here is what he will later find for classificatory systems of relationship in the *Systems,* and to the same effect: the Indians are shown to be unitary and derived from Asia. They are neither autochthonous, as Agassiz would have it, nor descended from the Ten Lost Tribes of Israel, the most prominent alternative view.

This distribution is in turn provided with an explanation, based on the nomadic or hunter state. "The hunter state is essentially one of individual freedom; and this freedom, as well as the mode of life to which it was incident, became a passion to which the Indian mind was attuned from its lowest depths."[12] The tribal organization, with descent of the office of sachem in the female line and limited to the tribe, was eminently adapted to the hunter state. The original tribe might divide and subdivide, creating more sachemships and spreading over a larger territory, yet still be bound by the ties of consanguinity, and the several tribes intermingled through and through by intermarriage; and they could form confederacies by retracing "the steps by which they had been weakened through subdivision."[13] There were many examples of these Indian confederacies, including the league of the Iroquois, the Powhattan confederacy, the Sioux league of the Seven Council Fires, and the alliance among the Aztecs, Texcucans, and Tlacopans at Mexico. "We have never known of an Indian monarchy" on any part of the continent, "unless we accept the pretended Aztec monarchy." Conversely, however, "break down this barrier of descent in the female line, and allow the sachem to perpetuate his power in his own family, and it is easy to see that a consolidation of tribes under one sachem would be the result; and this process of consolidation would progress by conquest, until despotism would succeed to freedom, and the hunter state would be overthrown."[14] The argument rests, then, on a theory of the evolutionary sequence of political forms, from oligarchy—which is the Indian form of government of sachems—through despotism to freedom (democracy). At one end of this sequence lay the hunter state; at the other, civilization.

Whereas for the most part Morgan's theorizing consists in training an Iroquois lens upon other Native Americans, his theory about the hunter state as first cause of the tribal organization derives in the

---

[12] The same, p. 145.
[13] The same, p. 146.
[14] The same, pp. 146–147.

final instance not from his direct experience of the peculiarities of
Seneca society but from a prior Euroamerican discourse about civilization and savagism, which itself provided a lens through which the
Iroquois case was viewed. In this discourse the essence of the hunter
state is not hunting, as a mode of acquiring a subsistence, but
nomadism, as a condition of constant movement. It is this which
allows Morgan to link the Tartars, who are nomads but not hunters,
with the American Indians. Nomadism has for him the admirable
quality of being an expression of a fierce love of freedom; but as far
as the development of the mind is concerned, it is a kind of forgetfulness akin to that which attends a lack of the knowledge of writing.
Nomadism is the geographical equivalent of illiteracy, and both are
barriers to the growth of the mind. Agriculture and education, by
implication, are the cure of savagism and the causes of civilization.

The weakness of this conception, as others beginning with Stern
have observed, is that it fits particularly poorly just those peoples
upon whom Morgan concentrates, as the Iroquois raised substantial
amounts of corn, beans, and squash and lived in stockaded villages.
It fits the Aztecs more poorly yet. Morgan was obliged to recognize,
on other occasions, that the Iroquois were not completely "roving
Indians" but were partly roving and partly "village" Indians, and
the Aztecs wholly village Indians. As he does so, he redraws the
conceptual boundary between savagism and civilization somewhat
differently; he distinguishes Indian agriculture as horticulture and
distinguishes it from the agriculture of the plow. In his later work,
Ancient society, savagery itself subdivides into Savagery and Barbarism, and each of these into a Lower, Middle, and Upper status.
The nomadism theme becomes muted and modified.

Morgan referred to the thirteen tribes of the Ojibwa in support of
his assertion that a division into "tribes, with descent in the female
line, has prevailed very generally throughout the Indian family." The
assertion ran far ahead of the facts he had at his disposal and shows
that he was strongly predisposed to accept evidence of exogamous
clans as evidence of matrilineal ones. He was soon to have an opportunity to test it at first hand. He would find that it was wrong in
respect of descent in the female line, and his research would turn to
the other aspect of the code of descent: the reckoning of degrees of
consanguinity—that is, the merger of collaterals with lineals.

Business interests took Morgan to Marquette, Michigan, on Lake
Superior in the summer of 1855, and thereafter for several summers.

Morgan had given his "Laws of descent of the Iroquois" paper in August 1857 and repeated it the following February before the Club, a few weeks after McIlvaine had spoken on "Comparative philology in its relations to ethnology." The following July Morgan again went on business to Marquette, this time with a hypothesis to test. It is our good fortune that Morgan was a tidy, methodical scholar who not only kept his notebooks but also bound them in six volumes and bequeathed them to the University of Rochester. Through these we can follow the next stage of his work in which he takes his theory to the field, and the dramatic change of direction that ensues, in great detail.

Morgan left Rochester on 2 July. On the train from Suspension Bridge he met a delegation of twenty-eight Sioux on their return journey from Washington, and he seized the opportunity to question them about "their laws of descent, and degrees of relationship." It was not a successful encounter. As to the theory of tribes with descent in the female line,[15]

> They denied that they were divided into Tribes after the manner of the Iroquois, which I explained to them. . . . Among them at the present time, the son succeeds the father as chief, and if there should be no son, a brother or a nephew. . . .
>
> I asked the oldest man among them through an interpreter if among them the son had always succeeded the father as chief. He said he had so far as he knew; that a brother or a nephew succeeded only in default of a son.

Morgan's theory was faring badly, and he was trying to save it by positing matrilineal tribes in the Sioux *past,* with a subsequent alteration of their ancient institutions to the patrilineal pattern. This tendency toward historical displacement of the matrilineal tribes theory was to have important consequences for Morgan much later.

As to the degrees of relationship, Morgan obtained information that sounded tantalizingly similar to the Iroquois case: "The sisters who have children, are mothers to each others children, and the children are brothers to each other. The same with two brothers." But he got contradictory answers as he pursued the matter and decided that none of these statements could be relied upon. "It is evident that they reckon their degrees in some manner as the Iro-

---

[15] "Notes of a trip to Marquette, Lake Superior, July 1858," MS. journals vol. 2, Morgan Papers. Entry dated Detroit, 4 July 1858.

quois did, and I think it will be found to be [the] same thing though modified in consequence of the absence of Tribes or totems."[16]

Morgan proceeded to Marquette, and there commence on 13 July a series of dated entries in his notebook on his Ojibwa inquiries, which allow us to follow his thought processes as his theory meets with frustration in some respects and encouragement in others. He comes out of the encounter with a much revised theory, in which the matter of matrilineal descent is pushed to the background and the mode of reckoning degrees of consanguinity comes to the fore. Something else of moment happens at the same time: he begins to find, in the course of conversations with his informants, that the questionnaire he has been using is inadequate, and he finds himself obliged to develop a new one.

Let us begin on the matter of the questionnaire, for that is where Morgan's Ojibwa notes begin. The first installment consists of six pages of Ojibwa vocabulary. It opens, "The following vocabulary was taken July 13, 1858 at Marquette through William Cameron Jr. from his mother a Chippeway woman and an old Chippeway. Cameron was absent fishing. He is a Scotsman & disowned by his family."[17] There is a table of vowel sounds and then the vocabulary proper, English words in the left column, Ojibwa in the right. The English column begins, reading down, "God, Devil, Man, Woman, Boy, Girl, Infant, Father, Mother, Husband, Wife, Son, Daughter, Brother, Sister, An Indian," and continues with parts of the body, implements, divisions of time, meteorological and geological phenomena, food items, trees, animals, and so forth.

This innocent-looking entry has in fact a rather long and illustrious pedigree. A printed questionnaire for the collection of vocabularies of Indian languages had been devised to implement the Jeffersonian program for Americanist philology under the auspices of the American Philosophical Society, of which Jefferson had been president.[18] Stephen Du Ponceau, himself a president of the society, compiled a manuscript book of Amerindian vocabularies from the returns and used it as the basis of a prize essay on the subject that represents the

---

[16] The same.

[17] The same, entry for Marquette, 13 July.

[18] See John F. Freeman, *A guide to manuscripts relating to the American Indian in the library of the American Philosophical Society*, index, entries for Jefferson vocabulary list.

beginning of this branch of scientific work.[19] He and several others—
especially Albert Gallatin and Horatio Hale—contributed to the elaboration and refinement of such questionnaires, which tended toward
standardization as the government sought advice from philologists
in preparations for sponsored explorations of the West and in the
Pacific. In size and content Morgan's manuscript vocabulary for
Ojibwa resembles those published in Gallatin's "Synopsis" (1836)
and also those in his 1848 article, "Hale's Indians of north-west
America, and vocabularies of North America" in the *Transactions
of the American Ethnological Society,* a journal Morgan had in
his own library. In any event, the presence of a standardized questionnaire—or "schedule," as he would call it—is a sign that Morgan had
prepared himself for his Ojibwa inquiries in a manner he had not
done in his Iroquois work of over a decade previous. Specifically he
had sought out the best instruments of Americanist philology for his
own work.

The form of this schedule springs from views about the nature of
language that to twentieth-century sensibilities will seem quaint and
even crude. The English words of the left column are taken to be the
names of things for which other languages have corresponding but
different names. Words, then, are the labels for categories that are
given in nature and are the same for all peoples. Words have the
character of sound strings or "vocables" joined to the things they
designate by convention. The proper business of the philologist is to
compare vocables in different languages, similarities between languages in words for the same things being evidence of close historical
relationship between those languages. Consequently in Gallatin's
articles, to take an example, the data are marshalled in parallel
columns of words with the English words to which they correspond
in the leftmost column. Holding meaning (natural kinds or categories) constant, then, the Americanist reads words in rows, across
different languages, in the search for similarity of vocables. Modern
views of language are shaped by the Saussurian doctrine of the sign
as the union of signifier (sound string) and signified (category under-

---

[19] See Freeman, *A guide,* no. 60; also Murphy D. Smith, "Peter Stephen Du
Ponceau and his study of languages." The prize essay was *Mémoire sur le système
grammatical des langues de quelques nations indiennes de l'Amerique du nord,*
Paris, 1838, which was given the Volney Prize by the Institut de France. His
contributions to Americanist philology were legion, however, as one learns in the
Smith article.

stood as idea rather than as thing), both of which are conventional, objects of art in a relation to nature that is problematic. In light of the nominalism of twentieth-century linguistics, the realism of nineteenth-century philology appears simplistic. Nevertheless, the very crudeness of the research instrument had the effect of simplifying the data in a way (holding meaning constant) that was very helpful to the development of the science in its infancy. The great accomplishments of historical linguistics were built upon just such vocabulary lists as these.

Morgan's kinship work as it developed would depart from the model he had sought from Americanist philology in two significant ways. He would first have to overcome the extreme poverty of the schedule in respect to family relationships. The list of eight English terms of the standardized vocabulary was in its brevity no better than the homemade list he published in the *League*—and constituted, in fact, an obstacle to knowledge. As long as the relationships on which he quizzed his informants were limited to a handful of English words such as *brother* and *sister,* for example, Morgan would not readily discover that in many Indian languages including Seneca and Ojibwa a radical distinction is drawn between the elder and the younger siblings.[20] One dimension of Morgan's departure from the philologist's standardized schedule, then, consists of the multiplication of distinctions expressed in the leftmost column of English names for the family relationships.

---

[20] Gallatin, in his 1848 article ("Hale's Indians of North-west America, and vocabularies of North America; with an introduction") made several observations on Indian kinship terms which Morgan may have noticed. He states, "All those who have investigated the subject appear to have agreed in the opinion that, however differing in their vocabularies, there is an evident similarity in the structure of all known American languages, bespeaking a common origin" (cxix). He then notes, among other things, the precision "exhibited in the different names, by which all the American nations distinguish the various degrees and modifications of relationship; such as, the elder brother, the elder sister, and the younger ones; the paternal or maternal uncle, &c." (cxxxi); and again, "as a feature common to all the American nations, that women use different words from men for those purposes; and that the difference of language between men and women, seems in the Indian languages to be almost altogether confined to that species of words, or others of an analogous nature, and to the use of interjections" (cxxxii); and finally, "that, in several of the languages, nouns expressive of relationship are always connected with possessive pronouns, and cannot be used alone and independently." These propositions taken together partially prefigure the shape of Morgan's kinship project in its American Indian component.

The second departure from the philological model consists in the designation of the object of study. For Morgan the cognate vocables—the similar words in horizontal rows of synoptic tables of vocabularies—were the business of the philologist. What he discovers, through his lengthened schedule of family relationships, is that the same word (vocable) recurs in the same vertical column (language) against different relationships. His project, then, becomes the study of the way in which relationships existing in nature are, as he would say, "classified" (merged under the same name or vocable) or "described" (not merged). The object of study is the semantic patterning or ordering of natural categories between languages, not the similarity of their vocabularies. His project has the same objective as philology—that is, the tracing of historical relationships—but it employs semantic rather than lexical means.

In addition to the lengthy Ojibwa word-list in the notebook entry there is also a narrative account of the interview of 13 July. It opens with a list of seventeen or eighteen Ojibwa tribes, the names in both English and Ojibwa; Mrs. Cameron is found to be of the Crane Tribe. All members of the same tribe are relatives or consanguinei, and no man may marry a woman of his own tribe, though now the rule is sometimes broken. "The children always follow the Tribe of the mother"—the matrilineal theory apparently upheld. Morgan pursues the hypothesis of matrilineal succession of chiefs. The chief, he is told, is succeeded by his brother, if he has one; if without a brother, by a nephew in preference to a son, who succeeds in default of the others. Morgan is unsure of his information, however, which falsifies the hypothesis of matrilineal succession: "This I doubt on further questioning. I am satisfied the office of chief belongs to the Tribe, & cannot pass out of it, so that the son cannot inherit." There follows a table of "Degrees of Relationship": there are now eighteen numbered English terms of relationship in the left column, substantially those of the Seneca list; but it is supplemented by interlinear and marginal entries that show recognition of kinds of relationships he had not previously reckoned with, including a radical distinction of elder and younger siblings. Pursuing his inquiries further, Morgan found that his informants could not fully understand, and he reserved further questioning against the return of William Cameron, Sr.

Five days later, on 18 July, Cameron had not yet returned, and Morgan had to be content to interview another son, Dugald, and "a Chippeway woman." He recorded a long list of Ojibwa geographical names, words for birds and fish, and so forth, but nothing on kinship.

After a further five days' wait, on 23 July, Morgan at last was able to interview the senior William Cameron. In answer to Morgan's questions he confirms the matrilineal theory:

> These chiefs must always be of the same tribe. Two sisters marry & have children. These children are of the tribe of the mothers, they are brothers and sisters to each other, & call the two sisters mothers. The sisters mother & her sisters would be equally grandmothers to her children. The father of the sisters and his brothers are grandfathers to her children. The proof of both & all of these cases Cameron cited in his own family. The other degrees reserved for the present.

A few pages later there is a list of "Degrees of Relationship" much longer than the previous one, with English entries numbered from one to forty-seven, and many marginal notes. The schedule is now becoming more adequate to its task. For example, instead of *uncle* and *aunt* we now have father's brother, father's sister, mother's brother, and mother's sister.

On what seems to be another occasion (date not specified), Morgan satisfied himself on the identity of Iroquois and Ojibwa, in respect of the "degrees of relationship."

> Having fixed the names of the several relationships it was an easy matter to put it to the test. E.g. Having ascertained that 2° cousins were esteemed relatives, the questions would be whether they were nephews and nieces to the cousins interchangeably, if so of the children of a brother and of a sister. The first question was, if Mrs. Camerons sister had children [corrected from: a child]—what relationship would subsist between them and her children. She said through her husband as interpreter—brothers and sisters. So also would the children of two brothers be brothers and sisters to each other. Of this we had proof in the test. Jack La Porte, a half breed was her fathers brothers son, & she called him her brother, & he Cameron his step brother. He made his home with them as a relation. The next was, would would [*sic*] be the relationship between herself, and her mothers brothers children. She said they would be cousins, & not brothers and sisters as in the other cases—and that if these cousins had children they would be nephews & nieces, and that the children of these nephews and nieces would be her grandchildren. This is the precise code of the Iroquois.

Although the generality of the Iroquois pattern of degrees of relationship appeared to have been sustained by the Ojibwa pattern, the theory of "descent through the female" received a setback:

Mrs. Cameron insists however in contradiction of what she said before, that the children followed the tribe of the father & not of their mother, & said said [sic] that her father and grandfather were both of the Crane Tribe. This needs further inquiry, but I think it cannot be so, and that her grandfather must have broken the law, & married a Crane. Her children are of the Crane Tribe like herself, but Cameron is a Scotchman & of no Tribe.

On the manner of succession to chiefships, "Mr. Cameron thinks that all of the six chiefships are hereditary in the Tribe, and descend to a brother or a nephew, but said he had never made [it] so much a subject of inquiry as to be sure."

The following page, which appears to be the work of a later occasion, speaks of further conversations with Cameron and his wife, and through them with other "Chippeways." The consensus is that the *son* succeeds the father, not the brother or the nephew. Morgan struggles to retain the matrilineal theory by displacing it to the Ojibwa past, as he had done with the Sioux. Jesuit missionaries and the government have interfered with the civil affairs of the Indians, he reasons, introducing European ideas as far as they could, so that at present the ethnic or tribal life of the race is pretty much destroyed; few pure Chippeways are at hand. "It is not safe to take their present usage & customs as conclusive upon the question of ancient usage." He continues:

I am inclined to think from the fact that they have the tribal organization in all its fullness and force, together with the degrees of consanguinity the same as the Iroquois, that original descent was limited to the female line. For example, the children of two sisters are brothers and sisters to each other, but the children of a brother, and those of a sister are cousins: now with descent in the female line, the children of the sisters would be of the same tribe, and the children of a brother out of the tribe, and for that reason, not so nearly related, the tribal relation being one [corrected from: nearly as strong as that] of kindred blood in itself. [Inserted above the line: Still this would be the same with descent in the male line.] There are other reasons tending in the same direction, and until I can ascertain from other sources how the matter was originally, I shall feel persuaded, that descent among the Chippeways must have followed the female line.

It was a desperate move to save a theory from falsification by the evidence. The theory on this point still needed evidence, and its sole warrant was the supposed necessary connection of the different elements of the Iroquois code: tribal organization, descent through females, degrees of relationship. But there are signs that Morgan was beginning to see these as independent variables. One such in the passage just cited is the interlineal comment: "Still this would be the same with descent in the male line." Morgan silently buried the matrilineal theory in the Upper Peninsula and pursued the matter of kinship terminology. He would revive it later, however, in its historicized form.

Thus in the summer of 1858 Morgan had established, as he believed, the identity of Iroquois and Ojibwa in respect of "degrees of relationship" if not in respect of "descent through the female." The significance of Ojibwa for his project was that it was of a different linguistic stock from Iroquois—that is, that philology could not show genealogical connection between them through the comparison of vocabularies. In this one step Morgan had in principle generalized the Iroquois system to other American Indians, extending philology's project by means of what he would call a "new instrumentality." It remained only to collect similar data from languages of other linguistic stocks to complete the proof of Indian unity. This he set out to do. He also set out in search of proof for the second part of his thesis, the Asiatic origin of the Indians, and he found it in the Tamil system of South India, which he came to know in late August of the following year. That event, in principle, generalized the Iroquois pattern to Asia, and it remained only to fill out the proof with information from other Asian stocks. In its major features Morgan's great project was complete by the fall of 1859, and he formulated it in a circular letter dated 1 October 1859, which accompanied the schedule of degrees of relationship that he sent out in search of the supporting data.

This, then, was the critical year in Morgan's kinship research, from the discovery of the Ojibwa degrees of relationship in the summer of 1858 to the discovery of Tamil in the summer of 1859. Morgan committed his remarkable vitality and capacity for hard work to the project wholeheartedly, developing its methodology and theory and collecting large amounts of data.

Methodological development consisted in the perfection of a schedule of degrees of relationship, which Morgan would use in his own fieldwork and would send to others for information on distant peoples. He made a trip to the Tonawanda Reservation in November for the express purpose of testing out a revised schedule and in doing so to collect new data on Seneca degrees of relationship for the first time since 1846. The perfected schedule exists in three forms, the first privately printed by Morgan and dated January 1859, a second privately printed form dated 1860, and a version issued by the Smithsonian Institution in 1860 and later published in the *Smithsonian miscellaneous collections*.

The perfected schedule of degrees of relationship was an instrument for the compilation of the extensive tables of systems of consanguinity and affinity that are so prominent a part of the published *Systems*; indeed, the tables become for Morgan the thing itself, and the text is but a commentary on them. The tables bear a distant resemblance to Gallatin's and Hale's vocabularies, from which they take their inspiration, in that the vocabularies of several languages are ranged synoptically against uniform categories expressed in English. They nevertheless differ from the pattern as well.

I shall illustrate Morgan's innovations by commenting on the Smithsonian version of the schedule, the first page of which is reproduced in figure 4. What is immediately apparent is that, unlike the entire family of questionnaires Americanist philology had given birth to, Morgan's "schedule of degrees of relationship" has three columns instead of two. The structure of each deserves our close scrutiny.

The leftmost column shows a great expansion of the number of English degrees of relationship.

Morgan had been content to collect a handful of equivalents for English kinship terms in his early Iroquois research, and again in his 1857 paper on the Iroquois code of descent, but the encounter with Ojibwa changed all that. In the Marquette notebook we see Morgan coming to the realization that the number of degrees of relationship to be taken into consideration must be greatly expanded for adequate analysis and comparison. The third of his Ojibwa vocabularies has 47 numbered entries plus additions, and the notebook closes with a Latin vocabulary containing 84 numbered and 20 unnumbered entries. The notebook of the November trip to Tonawanda contains 190 Seneca entries in twelve pages. The final Smithsonian version of the printed schedule has 218 numbered entries under the heading "Description of Relationship," followed by 16 entries on "Relationship of the Descendants of Brothers and Sisters to each other." Thus the grid which Morgan constructed became very extensive. He also made its mesh very fine. We find in it many possible distinctions and relationships between ego and alter that are not known to Euroamerican common sense, such as that between "My Elder Brother, (said by a Male)" and the same said by a female. Although no questionnaire can anticipate all possible distinctions and kinds of relationship,

Degrees of Relationship in the Language of the Nation.

MADE BY (Name.) (Residence.) (Date.) 1860.

VOWEL SOUNDS.—ä, as in art; ă, as in at; ĕ, as in met; ĭ, as in it; ŏ, as in got; ŭ, as oo in food.

☞ *Please mark the accented syllables.*

INSERT NATIVE PRONOUNS—MY..........OUR..........HIS..........

Description of Relationship.	Name, or Native Word, in English Letters.	Translation of the same into English.
1. My Father........		
2. " " Mother........		
3. " " Son........		
4. " " Daughter........		
5. " " Grand-Son........		
6. " " Grand-Daughter........		
7. " " Great-Grand-Son........		
8. " " Daughter........		

Fig. 4. Schedule of degrees of relationship.

9. My Great-Great-Grand-Son.....................

10. " " Daughter...........................

11. " " Elder Brother, (said by a Male)...........

12. " " (" " Female)..........

13. " " Elder Sister, (" " Male)............

14. " " (" " Female)..........

15. " " Younger Brother, (said by a Male)...........

16. " " (" " Female)...........

17. " " Sister, (" " Male)............

18. " " (" " Female)...

19. " " Brothers....................

20. " " Sisters......................

21. " " Father's Brother.................

22. " " Elder Brother.................

23. " " Younger Brother...............

24. " " Brother's Wife................

25. " " Sister....................

Fig. 4. *continued*

Morgan's was a very good instrument with which to launch the systematic, comparative study of kinship terminologies.

The left column of the schedule is, then, an expansion of the simplex English terms of kinship that had appeared in the philologists' schedules, terms such as *father, mother, brother, sister, son, daughter, husband,* and *wife.* In the *Systems* Morgan will call these the eight primary terms and regard them as among the earliest human inventions. The simplex terms, however, are swamped in the schedule by such complex terms or phrases as "My Father's Brother" or "My Elder Brother (said by a Male)," also conceived to be relationships existing in nature, which these locutions *describe* rather than name. Hence the column is titled "Description of Relationship." The metalanguage he devises here will become the model for Morgan's conception of a system of relationship that is at once *natural* and *descriptive,* both scientific and based on the promptings of nature (see chapter 6).

The second column, which is blank, has the rubric "Name, or Native Word, in English Letters." Morgan expects that particular native words or names will be repeated in this column such that they classify (merge) degrees of relationship that in nature are distinct. For example, the Seneca word *hä⸰-nih* will appear against both "My Father" and "My Father's Brother," thus collapsing natural distinctions of which the decisive one is that between lineals and collaterals.

The third column, also blank, is headed "Translation of the same into English." In the example given, Seneca *hä⸰-nih* will be translated as *my father* at every occurrence in the middle column. The translation gives the real meaning of the word and allows us to track the mergers of different degrees of relationship.

The structure of the schedule thus encodes the kind of discourse we have already encountered in the *League,* when Morgan says that the father and his brother are equally fathers. This is or will shortly become in Morgan's mind a doctrine in some respects the same as what is now called "the extensionist hypothesis"—that is, the doctrine that the name for father has been extended to the father's brother, as we shall see in the next chapter. The entries of the "translation" column are generally, though not entirely, simplex English terms that allow us to track the mergers. The entire conception that underlies the schedule is extraphilological in that what is being laid bare is the distinction or merger of the naturally occurring degrees of relationship. Thus the analysis that proceeds from it will concern itself with the translations of native words—that is, their meanings—rather than the words themselves conceived as sound strings making up a vocabulary, the philologist's proper object of study.

Collection of data on the most ambitious scale began immediately the perfected schedule was printed. Morgan obtained lists of missionaries to the various Indian tribes, and, beginning in January and continuing through the early months of 1859, he posted schedules, accompanied by a printed circular letter explaining the purpose of the inquiry,[21] to missionaries of the American, Presbyterian, Baptist Union, Methodist Episcopal, and Southern Baptist mission boards, and to Indian agents. He also sent the circular letter and schedule to missionaries of the American Board in Hawaii and some of the Micronesian islands; to India; to the American minister in Japan; to the U.S. commercial agent in the Amur River area (which he thought to be the point from which the ancestors of the American Indians had set out for the New World); and even to E. G. Latham in London "to forward to Dr. Livingstone in Africa." He seized opportunities to gather information personally whenever they presented themselves. On 9 April in Washington on a business trip, for example, he interviewed a delegation of Winnebagos. Then, on 16 May, he set out for Kansas and Nebraska on a six-week field trip for the exclusive purpose of collecting schedules of kinship terms from the western tribes. He obtained schedules of terms from twelve tribes (Kaw, Pottawattomi, Ottawa, Peoria, Shawnee, Delaware, Mohekunnuk or Stockbridge, Wyandotte, Pawnee, Dakota, Iowa, Otoe). By comparison, the results of the mail campaign were meager, although the Rev. Stephen R. Riggs, author of the *Grammar and dictionary of the Dakota language* in Morgan's library, was the first to comply with

---

[21] This circular is dated January 1859. (It is one of two: the second, dated 1 October 1859, follows the discovery of Tamil, and consequently the formulation of the kinship project in it is quite different.) This circular contains a paper entitled "Laws of consanguinity, and descent of the Iroquois" that makes the state of play at that time perfectly clear. Morgan says, "Descent in the female line does not appear to have been universal among our Indian races" (p. 11); but conversely , "Of the universality of the Iroquois system of relationship upon this continent, we have more evidence" (p. 12). Gilchrist's bibliography wrongly gives the date of this circular as 1852 ("Bibliography of Lewis H. Morgan," p. 85); Stern (*Lewis Henry Morgan, social evolutionist,* p. 205) repeats the error and turns Morgan's circular into a book. A definitive bibliography of Morgan is much to be desired.

a schedule "worked out in the most complete and scholarly manner,"[22] and the Rev. C. C. Copeland and the Rev. C. Byington sent schedules of Choctaw terms, which met him on his return from the West. From these schedules he constructed a table, ancestral to the synoptic tables in the *Systems.* They "reveal at a glance the identity of the system in all these nations, and at the same time show conclusively the genetic connection of the people themselves."

Then came the momentous encounter with Tamil, whose semantic pattern is indeed very similar to the Iroquois. He describes the incident at some length in *Record of Indian letters* entry of 19 October 1859:[23]

> I come now to the most interesting and extraordinary event in the history of this inquiry; a discovery which attests the value of this new instrument in ethnological research, and which also affords some promise of its great future usefulness. Having ascertained that Dr. Henry W. Scudder of the Arcot Mission in Southern India was in this country, I enclosed a schedule and letter to him, and requested him to furnish me the Tamil system of relationship. After some correspondence I received a final answer containing the principal features of the Tamilian system of consanguinity in the month of August last and shortly after my return from Springfield. My astonishment was greater than I can well express to learn that the Tamil system and the American Indian system were substantially identical; and that too, in the most special and intricate features which characterise the two systems. On the 15th day of August last I replied to Dr. Scudder at length laying the two systems side by side, and expressing the belief that we had now been able to put our hands upon decisive evidence of the Asiatic origin of the American Indian race. Shortly after this I visited Dr. Scudder at Milton, Ulster Co. N.Y. and obtained both a Tamil and Telugu schedule as far forth as he was able to furnish this without consulting a native. He informed me that he had had occasion to verify with a qualified native scholar the several relationships which he gave me, and that I might rely upon their entire accuracy. The systems of the Tamil and Telugu races, who number about twenty four millions of people, are substantially identical.

Morgan represents himself as being surprised by the identity of Tamil with the American Indian system. His friend McIlvaine, however, recalled the event differently in his funeral address. He stresses

---

[22] Leslie A. White, "How Morgan came to write *Systems of consanguinity and affinity,*" pp. 264–265.
[23] The same, pp. 266–267.

the Newtonian character of Morgan's scientific activity, recalling that Morgan had predicted that Tamil would furnish the needed proof.[24]

> During this period he lived and worked often in a state of great mental excitement, and the answers he received, as they came in, sometimes nearly overpowered him. I well remember one occasion when he came into my study, saying, "I shall find it, I shall find it among the Tamil People and Dravidian tribes of Southern India." At this time I had no expectation of any such result; and I said to him, "My friend, you have enough to do in working out your discovery in connection with the tribes of the American continent—let the peoples of the old world go." He replied, "I can not do it—I can not do it—I must go on, for I am sure I shall find it all there." Some months afterward, he came in again, his face all aglow with excitement, the Tamil schedule in his hands, the answers to his questions just what he had predicted, and, throwing it on my table, he exclaimed, "There! what did I tell you?" I was indeed amazed and confounded; and still more as his predicted results poured in upon him from a great multitude of independent sources. And thus his second generalization was triumphantly verified. The system was found to prevail in all its essential features throughout the Turanian and Polynesian families of mankind.

Although there are some inaccuracies in McIlvaine's account of Morgan's project as a whole, I see no reason to deny him the validity of his own experience. Indeed, there is other evidence to indicate that Morgan specifically targeted Tamil as a likely prospect well in advance of the events of August. One would not guess from his own narrative, for example, that he had sent a circular and schedule to Scudder "for Tamil," as a notebook entry says, as early as 1 March— that is, in the opening weeks of the mail campaign and some six months prior to the event in question. The next entries in the notebook also target South India: Walter Elliott of Madras and the Rev. R. Caldwell of Tinnevelly are listed as having been asked to supply schedules of "Tamil, Telugu, Canarese, Mahratta, Parsee, Hindoostanee, Malayalim" also on 1 March 1859. Robert Caldwell is the author of *A comparative grammar of the Dravidian or South-Indian family of languages* (1856), a work Morgan knew at this period.

The most intriguing evidence that Morgan had targeted Tamil

---

[24] Joshua Hall McIlvaine, *The life and works of Lewis H. Morgan*, pp. 50–51.

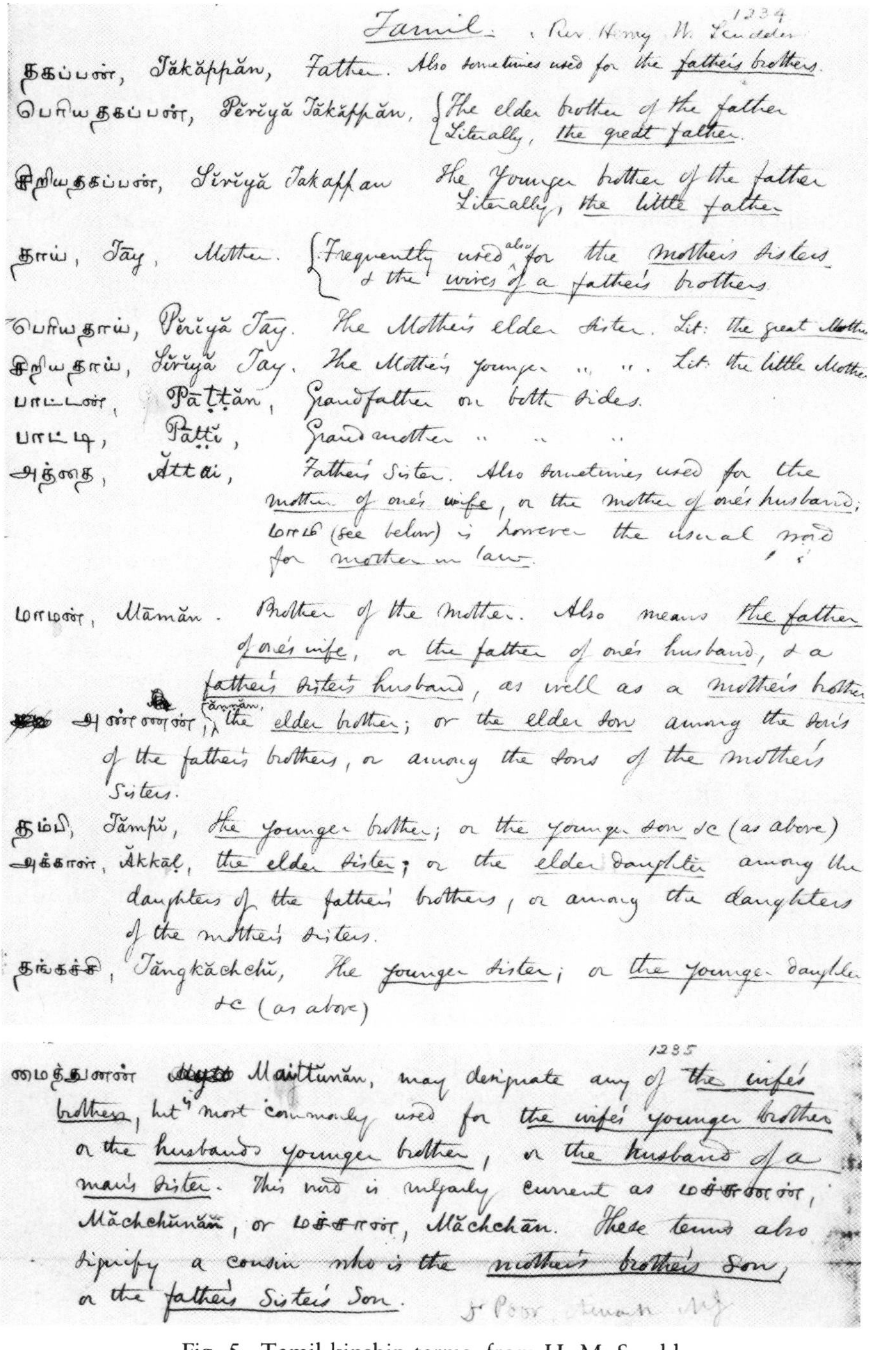

Tamil: Rev. Henry M. Scudder

தகப்பன், Tăkăppăn, Father. Also sometimes used for the father's brothers.

பெரியதகப்பன், Pĕrĭyă Tăkăppăn. {The elder brother of the father. Literally, the great father.

சிறியதகப்பன், Sĭrĭyă Tăkappan. The younger brother of the father. Literally, the little father.

தாய், Tay, Mother. {Frequently used also for the mother's sisters & the wives of a father's brothers.

பெரியதாய், Pĕrĭyă Tay. The Mother's elder sister. Lit: the great Mother.

சிறியதாய், Sĭrĭyă Tay. The Mother's younger ". ". Lit: the little Mother.

பாட்டன், Pā̆ṭṭăn, Grandfather on both sides.

பாட்டி, Paṭṭĭ, Grandmother ". ". ".

அத்தை, Ăttai, Father's Sister. Also sometimes used for the mother of one's wife, or the mother of one's husband; மாமி (see below) is however the usual word for mother in law.

மாமன், Māmăn. Brother of the mother. Also means the father of one's wife, or the father of one's husband, & a father's sister's husband, as well as a mother's brother.

அண்ணன், Ăṇṇăn, the elder brother; or the elder son among the sons of the father's brothers, or among the sons of the mother's sisters.

தம்பி, Tămpĭ, the younger brother; or the younger son &c (as above)

அக்காள், Ăkkāḷ, the elder sister; or the elder daughter among the daughters of the father's brothers, or among the daughters of the mother's sisters.

தங்கச்சி, Tăngkăchchĭ, the younger sister; or the younger daughter &c (as above)

மைத்துனன் Maittŭnăn, may designate any of the wife's brothers, but most commonly used for the wife's younger brother or the husband's younger brother, or the husband of a man's sister. This word is vulgarly current as மச்சுனன், Măchchŭnăn, or மச்சான், Măchchăn. These terms also signify a cousin who is the mother's brother's son, or the father's sister's son.

Fig. 5. Tamil kinship terms, from H. M. Scudder.
(Morgan Papers, University of Rochester)

மைத்துனி Maittŭnŭ (Vulgarly மச்சினிச்சி, Măchchŭnĭchchŭ, or மச்சானி, Măchchŭni) may designate any one of the wife's sisters, but is most commonly used for the wife's younger sister. Also means a man's younger brother's wife; also a Cousin, who is the mother's brother's daughter, or the father's sister's daughter.

கோழுந்தி, Kŏzŭntŭ, The wife's elder sister
கோழுந்தன், Kŏzŭntăn, The husband's younger brother (also commonly called மச்சினான் See above)
நத்தனார், Nattănăr, The husband's sister, whether elder or younger
மாமன், Mămăn, A Mother's brother; Also a Father in Law; Also a father's sister's husband.
மாமி, Mămŭ, A Mother's brother's wife; Also a Mother in Law.
மருமகன், Mărŭmăkăn, A Son in Law; Also, The Son of a man's sister; or the Son of a woman's brother.
மருமகள், Mărŭmăkăl, A Daughter in Law; Also the daughter of a man's sister; or the daughter of a woman's brother.
பேரன், Pĕrăn, A Grandson.
பேர்த்தி, Pĕrttŭ, A Granddaughter

Fig. 5. *continued*

occurs in a marginal note in the field notebook of his fateful trip to Marquette in the summer of 1858. In the midst of the longest list of Ojibwa degrees of relationship, against entries for elder and younger brother and sister, there occurs this note in the right margin:

Tamil language
Older Brother, Ar-non
Younger   "   Tum-be

This is, of course, Tamil *annan* (eB, elder male parallel cousin) and *tampi* (yB, younger male parallel cousin), in an ad hoc transcription that shows that it cannot have come from Caldwell or H. M. Scudder; it could perhaps be Morgan's own rendering of a returned missionary's vocalizations of the words. I do not know the source of this

information or of Morgan's early surmise that Tamil would prove
to be similar to Iroquois; but the fact itself seems certain.[25]

As to the interpretation of the new data, Morgan's theory of
systems of relationship underwent a considerable evolution during
this period, which we can pinpoint by examining papers he wrote
just before and just after he received H. M. Scudder's information
on Tamil and Telugu. The first of these is his paper of early August,
delivered at the Springfield, Massachusetts, meeting of the American
Association for the Advancement of Science but not published; the
second is the circular letter statement dated 1 October, a month and
a half later.

---

[25] As this book was being prepared for press, new evidence tending to confirm
the idea that Morgan had a prior connection with India has come to light through
William C. Sturtevant, Elisabeth Tooker, and Sally McLendon, who are working
on a catalogue of the Iroquois material objects Morgan collected for the state,
illustrated and described in the *League*. A hitherto completely unknown dimension
of Morgan's activity comes to light in a passage of the *Transactions of the New
York State Agricultural Society* for 1859, discovered by Ray Gonyea of the New
York State Museum: "A large assortment of agricultural and horticultural tools
from India, all of which have been in actual use, have been recently presented to
the Society by L. H. Morgan, of Rochester. Thus the farm tools of the time of Jacob
and Laban, are placed alongside those in common use among our New York farmers
to-day, and while in the main we are thus led to see the march of improvement
which through the long centuries has been made, we cannot fail to be surprised at
finding in this lot of rude tools some contrivances for which patents have been
granted at Washington within a few years" (p. 760; list of items at pp. 756–758).
A box of objects from this collection survives, discovered by Charles E. Gillette of
the museum. The tools bear tags in Telugu and come from Cuddapah District in
the present Andhra Pradesh. Sturtevant suggests that Isaac N. Hurd may have been
Morgan's contact in South India. Hurd, a fellow member of the New Confederacy
of the Iroquois, accompanied Morgan on his 1845 visit to Tonawanda, and went
to Onondaga the following year, writing ethnographic reports of these encounters
for the New Confederacy, which are in the Morgan Papers (see Tooker, "Isaac N.
Hurd's ethnographic studies of the Iroquois"). He then became a missionary at the
Madras Mission of the American Board of Commissioners for Foreign Missions,
serving 13 July 1852 to 27 August 1858. Thereafter he returned to New York. He
took a pastorate in Colchester, and in 1864 he moved west, founding a number of
churches in California, Nevada, and Arizona. In India he served (to 1857) at
the Arcot Mission of the American Reformed Church, which was affiliated with
the A.B.C.F.M. in its early years, 1851–57. The Arcot Mission was founded by
H. M. Scudder, Morgan's informant for Tamil and Telugu, and had stations in the
adjoining districts of North Arcot and Cuddapah, whence came the collection of
agricultural implements. Perhaps it was Hurd who arranged for their collection and
shipment to Morgan (see Rufus Anderson, *History of the missions of the American
Board of Commissioners for Foreign Missions in India,* and *General biographical
catalogue of Auburn Theological Seminary 1818–1918,* p. 106).

The title of the AAAS paper, "System of consanguinity of the red race, in its relations to ethnology," tells us that the great change that overtook Morgan's conceptualization of the object of study in his Ojibwa researches the summer previous was now complete. Initially Morgan set out to see whether the Iroquois *code of descent* could be generalized; now, he found, the *system of consanguinity* of the American Indians was unitary. Morgan, to be sure, did not altogether abandon the initial hypothesis of the 1857 AAAS paper, that of the integral connection of the elements of the Iroquois code of descent: tribal organization, descent through the female, degrees of relationship, and exclusion of the son from succession to the sachemship implementing the love of freedom that was the spirit of nomadism. In the perfected schedule he includes, in addition to the schedule of degrees of relationship, seventeen questions bearing on these topics, "the answers to which will have an important bearing upon the full interpretation of the system of relationship, with which they are intimately connected." Nevertheless the system of relationship (or consanguinity) has lost its necessary connection to the other elements of the original theory and has emerged as an object of study in its own right, rather than as an aspect of a code of descent. Additionally, we see that Morgan understands his object of study to be a unitary American Indian system, of which particular tribes offer instances, rather than a number of independent systems that are the same or similar to one another. He believes, moreover, that the identity of cases is more or less directly evident in the synoptic table of kinship terms.

The AAAS paper of 1859 opens with a consideration of the role of nature. Systems of consanguinity, he says, are the necessary result of family relationships, which are as ancient as the human race. To some extent they arise from "the suggestions of an inherent law of generation"; for

> underneath any scheme or code of relationship we may frame, there lies a numerical system which is universal, and unchangeable. All of the descendants of an original pair stand to each other in certain fixed relations, the nearness or remoteness of which, is a mere matter of computation. The link of kindred is never broken, although the separation is measured by centuries of time.[26]

---

[26] "System of consanguinity of the red race, in its relations to ethnology," MS., Morgan Papers, p. 1.

Conversely, Morgan recognizes an element of the arbitrary that makes for variation between systems of consanguinity:[27]

> There is nothing in this, however, which of necessity leads to uniformity in the systems of relationship of the human race; neither does it supply but a small part of the elements requisite for a complete system. Although the descendants of an original pair are consanguinei to the latest generation, yet there is either an intermingling of foreign blood with every generation, or a blending of relationships with every marriage. The blood of the father and of the mother is united in the children. Shall the stream of descent flow in the male, or in the female line? The Hebrews, in founding their Tribes upon the twelve sons of Jacob, decided in favor of the former, some thirty six centuries ago; the Iroquois, on the other hand, while they organised their race in eight Tribes, decided for the latter, and established their descent in the female line.

His conclusion comes down on the side of artifice, not nature: "A classification of these near relationships, with the invention of names with which to distinguish and express the value of each, would be one of the earliest acts of the human mind."[28]

Although artificial, however, a system of relationship is not changeable; once perfected, its nomenclature settled, nothing in the whole range of man's absolute necessities is so little liable to mutation—not even language:[29]

> Language changes its vocabulary, not only, but also modifies its grammatical structure in the progress of ages; thus eluding the inquirings which philologists have pressed it to answer; but a system of relationship once matured, and brought into operation, is, in the nature of things, more unchangeable than language—not in the names employed as a vocabulary of relationships, for these are mutable, but in the ideas which underlie the system itself.

This passage is important, for it is the first formulation of Morgan's conception of his method in its relation to the methods of philology—that is, the comparison of vocabularies and grammars. Americanist philology, as we have seen, asserted that the grammatical structure of a language was more resistant to change than its vocables, hence

---

[27] The same, p. 2.

[28] The same, p. 3.

[29] The same. This passage draws upon ideas that had been presented in the circular letter of January 1859 discussed in note 21.

the superior ability of comparative grammar to yield proofs of genealogical relations between languages. Morgan now asserts that the ideas that underlie a system of relationship—its semantic structure—are more durable than the vocabulary and grammar with which the philologist is concerned and will answer questions the philologist cannot.

He then proceeds to contrast the system of the Indo-European nations with that of the American Indians. The Indo-European nations have a common system, identical in its principal features, that has "an antiquity of thirty five centuries as a fact of actual record." The one idea constant in them all which gives the system its characteristic features is the existence of a lineal and of collateral lines, the latter of which perpetually diverge from the former until after a few generations relationship ceased, terminating in a total dispersion of the blood. The American Indian system is nearly the reverse: collateral lines are not allowed to diverge from the lineal beyond first cousin and are thereafter brought into and merged with the lineal. The 1859 paper illustrates the contrast through the Indo-European and American Indian words for *nephew,* an illustration that did *not* work, as I shall hereinafter relate (chapter 6).

The remainder of the paper consists of a lengthy exposition of the system of relationship of the Red Race, which "is much more special and minute than that of the civilized" and so is analyzed into nine ideas or principal features rather than one. Morgan concludes that the comparison of the fifteen Indian nations establishes that they have one system, whence it follows that they derived it from one another or from a common source; that they are themselves of common origin; and that the system is "coeval with the existence of the oldest of these nations upon the continent."

The ethnological time of the paper is still that of the Protestant biblical chronology. Reference to the thirty-six centuries of the Hebrew tribal organization and the thirty-five centuries over which the Indo-European system of consanguinity is traceable through records takes us back to within a few centuries of the Confusion of Tongues, with which ethnological time commences. And the creation of systems of consanguinity is "one of the earliest acts of the human mind"; hence the Indo-European and American Indian systems are conceived to be parallel and more or less simultaneous inventions near the beginning of ethnological time. It also follows that Morgan thought the peopling of America belonged to an early date in that time frame, again consistent with the biblical frame.

A final point to be made about the 1859 AAAS paper concerns the place of the ancient Hebrews. Speaking of the American Indian distinction of elder and younger siblings, Morgan says that this feature is entirely unlike anything to be found in the Indo-European system; but it is barely possible that a trace of it is found in the system of relationship of the Jews, in which the terms *elder* and *younger brother* are frequently used. The Jewish system may contain a trace of another American Indian feature—namely, that the children of two sisters are brother and sister to each other. For in the Gospel "James is called the brother of our Lord," whereas he was in fact the son of his mother's sister. Morgan insists, however, that he does not mean even to intimate a belief in the derivation of the Indian race from the Jews: "The Indians have dwelt upon this continent too many centuries to have had any connection whatever with the Jewish race, subsequent to their occupation of Judea."[30] Thus the Hebrew people are left unclassified, at this point, as between the Indo-European and the American Indian systems, a piece of unfinished business he must face at a later date, when he would decisively group them with the speakers of Indo-European languages.

Six weeks after receiving the incomplete Tamil and Telugu schedules from H. M. Scudder, and following the delivery of the paper just described at the Springfield meeting of the American Association for the Advancement of Science, Morgan composed the thirteen-page paper contained in the Smithsonian version of the circular letter and schedule. This paper is dated 1 October 1859. Its theoretical stance is much the same as the AAAS paper, although the presentation is somewhat different. It summarizes his findings on the system of the degrees of relationship and consanguinity of the American Indian families, resolving it into radical features, which now number ten. It illustrates the Indian system of relationship, and the manner of filling out the schedule, with a part of the Seneca schedule. The permanence and universality of the system among the Indians could scarcely be understood in any other way "than by the assumption that the system itself was as old as the Indian race upon this continent."[31] Therefore, if the Indians came from Asia, it is probable

---

[30] The same, p. 14. The entire passage is marked for excision; clearly Morgan was sensitive to the possibility that his argument could be appropriated in support of the Ten Lost Tribes theory of Amerindian origins.

[31] "Circular in reference to the degrees of relationship among different nations," p. 8. This is the second circular mentioned in note 21.

that they brought the system with them and that they left it behind in the Asian stock from which they separated.

Morgan then turns to the Asian origin hypothesis and the Tamil and Telugu material, linked to the American Indian via the concept of a Scythian language family. He was, he says, naturally led to extend the inquiry to the Old World, "particularly to those Scythic peoples, with whom it was supposed, on other ethnological grounds, the Red race would affiliate"—on grounds, that is, of Scythian *nomadism.*

> Hence, these schedules have been distributed in some portions of Asia, and in some of the islands of the Pacific, in order to discover whether this system is confined to the American Indians, or is indeed common with them, and the Mongolian, Tungusian, Turkish, and Finnish families, whose languages constitute what is now known as the Scythian group of tongues.[32]

It is under these auspices that the partial schedule of the Tamil and Telugu peoples enters the picture, for they, "with the Canarese, the Malayalam, the Tulu, and a few subordinate Dravidian races, have been recognized as an Ante-Brahmanical people, having their nearest affinities with the Scythian families above mentioned."[33] The source here is almost certainly Caldwell, who did indeed connect the Dravidian language family with the Scythian. Thus, ironically, did the sturdy peasantry of South India enter into relation with the American Indians through the improbable link of nomadism.

There follows an analysis of the Tamil and Telugu systems into seven principal features. The analysis includes some predictions as to classifications that (on the Iroquois analogy) will be found to hold when more complete schedules of Tamil and Telugu are obtained. These predictions proved to be accurate on all but one very significant point, as we shall see in the last chapter. The article concludes with instructions for the accurate completion of the schedule.

Morgan's project had now acquired the overall structure and definition of the object of study that we find in the *Systems.* To a large extent what remained was a matter of filling in the blanks. He believed that the discovery of Tamil and Telugu was an event of great moment and became concerned that he should be forestalled. He

---

[32] The same, p. 9.
[33] The same.

inaugurated a new set of notebooks, bound in two volumes and titled with ponderous humor, "Record of the inquiries concerning the Indian (American and Oriental) system of relationship and the correspondence in relation thereto."[34] This is the *Record of Indian letters*; the first entry, which I have been citing extensively, dated 19 October, relates the history of the project to date and is written with care and finish suggesting that it was to serve, if need be, as a record of his priority. He need not have worried. The circular letter and schedule that the Smithsonian printed for distribution became such a record and was published in the *Smithsonian miscellaneous collections* in 1862.

Even before that appeared, circular and schedule were reprinted in *The Cambrian journal* for 1860 under the unlikely title, "The Welsh Indians." Morgan had sent copies to the U.S. consul at Bristol asking to be furnished with the Welsh system of consanguinity. One D. W. Nash forwarded them to the editor of *The Cambrian journal*. It was, he said, an opportunity to apply a philological test to the question, much discussed in the journal, of the existence among native tribes of North America of descendants of the Welsh emigrants of Prince Madog. (Nearly three centuries previous the tale of the Welsh Prince Madoc, who in 1170 sailed to America and established a colony of Welshmen, had been published as a warrant of Queen Elizabeth's title to a British Empire in the New World claimed by Spain; and from that time to the twentieth century "at least fifteen Indian languages had been identified as Welsh, often by linguists of such uncommon capacity as to be able to recognize the Welsh language without knowing it.")[35] His letter was published with Morgan's circular and schedule, the Welsh terms filled in by the Rev. Mr. J. Williams ab Ithel of Llanymowddwy. It was under these improbable circumstances that Morgan's kinship project came to the notice of John Ferguson McLennan, another pioneer of kinship, who was first to become Morgan's friend and then his chief rival.

---

[34] Manuscript journal in the Morgan Papers.
[35] Gwyn A. Williams, *Madoc, the making of a myth,* p. 43.

6

Nature and Art

On 24 January 1865 a disastrous fire swept through the red sandstone castle that houses the Smithsonian Institution, destroying the upper story of the main segment and the north and south towers. Two days later Morgan wrote to Spencer F. Baird, assistant to Joseph Henry, secretary of the Smithsonian, expressing his concern. The fire might well have consumed the manuscript of *Systems of consanguinity and affinity*. "It is a wonder that my manuscript, which is ready, was not there, and burned with the rest. I expected to have sent it on by the 1ˢᵗ January, at the latest. It is a marvellous escape, as it would be next to impossible to replace it."[1] As it happened, he did not complete the manuscript until 20 January and, fortunately, did not send it immediately. Before it was finished he had been very eager, urging Joseph Henry to appoint a commission to review it, "that the delay between its sending and its acceptance or rejection might be as brief as possible."[2] The fire made him cautious. He kept the manuscript with him and delivered it personally to the Smithsonian in April, when business took him to Washington.[3]

The point of Morgan's letter to Baird was to inquire what effect the fire would have on the publication of his manuscript. If recommended by the commission appointed to review it, he asked, "will the Institution commence printing it, the same as though the fire had not occurred?" But the fire *had* occurred, and there was no insurance. Baird could not be reassuring. "Prof. Henry will I think try to print what is now in press, but will not begin anything new for some time."[4] The review process went forward, but the fire and consequent

---

[1] Morgan to Spencer F. Baird, 1/26/65, Smithsonian Institution Archives.
[2] The same.
[3] Morgan to Joseph Henry, 3/29/65, Smithsonian Institution Archives.
[4] Baird to Morgan, 1/29/65, Smithsonian Institution Archives.

cost of rebuilding directly contributed to the delay in publication of Morgan's book. It did not appear until six years later.

The manuscript Morgan submitted to the Smithsonian in 1865 is significantly different from the published *Systems,* for Morgan re-wrote the work in response to criticisms of Joseph Henry and the review commission and in light of a suggestion made by his friend, J. H. McIlvaine, submitting the revised manuscript for publication in 1867. I shall distinguish these two versions of the *Systems* as the 1865 (or first or original) version and the 1867 (or final or published) version. In this chapter I shall analyze the 1865 version, and in the next I shall identify the sources of the changes Morgan introduced in the final version.

Much of the 1865 version survives among the papers Morgan bequeathed to the University of Rochester; however, it is not always easy to identify its parts. Apparently when the 1865 version was returned to him after it had been reviewed by the commission the Smithsonian had appointed, Morgan used it as the basis for revisions that went into the 1867 version. We find the pages of the 1865 version marked with corrections, deletions, and additions that in many cases are clearly attributable to the recommendations of Henry and/or the commission members. The backs of the pages of the 1865 version, which were invariably left blank at first writing, are often written on, generally in a more rapid hand, indicating a draft rather than a fair copy meant to be read by others. These post-1865 draft revisions are sometimes continued on new pages that are interleaved with the original 1865 version. The successive pages of the 1865 version, therefore, may be separated from one another by one or more pages of material that may or may not be continuous with them, in a hand that is sometimes illegible. Furthermore, early drafts of his subsequent book, *Ancient society,* are written on the backs of drafts of the *Systems.* Finally, in addition to the post-1865 revisions there are pre-1865 drafts.

Fortunately Morgan left a key by which we may sort out this jumble of paper and draw from it the pages of the 1865 version, in the form of a table of contents indicating numbers of manuscript pages against each chapter. As each page of the 1865 version gives the part, chapter, and page numbers at the top (see figure 7), with the guidance of the table of contents we are able to disentangle them from the post-1865 revisions, and also from the pre-1865 drafts with

Preface		9 pp.
General contents		5 pp.
Table of contents		15 pp.
Part I. Natural systems of relationship		
Chapter I.	General observations upon systems of relationship	11 pp.
Chapter II.	Romaic stem of the Aryan family	22 pp.
Chapter III.	Other stems of the Aryan family I. Hellenic, II. Teutonic, III. Sanskritic, IV. Slavonic, V. Celtic, VI. Persic, VII. Armenian	36 pp.
Chapter IV.	Arabic, Hebraic, and Aramaic stems of the Semitic family	13 pp.
Chapter V.	Ugric and Turkic stems of the Uralian family	36 pp.
Chapter VI.	Growth of nomenclatures of relationship	18 pp.
Table of schedules		7 pp.
Appendix to Part I: Table of consanguinity and affinity of the Aryan, Semitic and Uralian families		64 pp. qto.
Part II. Artificial systems of relationship		
Chapter I.	Dravidian stems of the Turanian family	35 pp.
Chapter II.	Gaura stems of the Turanian family	21 pp.
Chapter III.	Other stems of the Turanian family III. Chinese, IV. Japanese	29 pp.
Chapter IV.	Unclassified Asiatic nations	17 pp.
Chapter V.	Stems of the Malayan family I. Hawaiian, II. Micronesian, III. Amazulu, conjecturally	25 pp.
Table of schedules		3 pp.

Fig. 6. Table of contents, 1865 version of the *Systems*. (Morgan Papers, University of Rochester)

Appendix to Part II: Table of consanguinity and affinity of the Turanian and Malayan families		32 pp. qto.
Part III. Artificial systems of relationship continued		
Chapter I.	General observations	27 pp.
Chapter II.	Dakotan stems of the Ganoanian family	27 pp.
Chapter III.	Dakotan stems continued	57 pp.
Chapter IV.	Algonkin stems of the Ganoanian family	56 pp.
Chapter V.	Other stems of the Ganoanian family III. Athapasco-Apache, IV. Salish, V. Sahaptin, VI. Shoshone, VII. Village Indians of New Mexico, IX. Village Indians of South America, conjecturally	41 pp.
Chapter VI.	Other stems of the Ganoanian family continued	17 pp.
Chapter VII.	Eskimo family	21 pp.
Chapter VIII.	General results of a comparison of the several systems of relationship of the families of mankind	71 pp.
Table of schedules		20 pp.
Appendix to Part III: Tables of consanguinity and affinity of the Ganoanian family		128 pp. qto.
Part IV: Evidence of the unity of origin of the American Indian nations		
Chapter I.	Physical geography of the North American continent	
Chapter II.	Migrations of the American Indian nations	
Chapter III.	Domestic institutions of these nations I. The tribal organization, II. Manner of changing and bestowing names, III. The dance, IV. Burial customs	
Chapter IV.	Architecture and agriculture of these nations—The Mound Builders	
Appendix to Part IV		

Fig. 6. *continued*

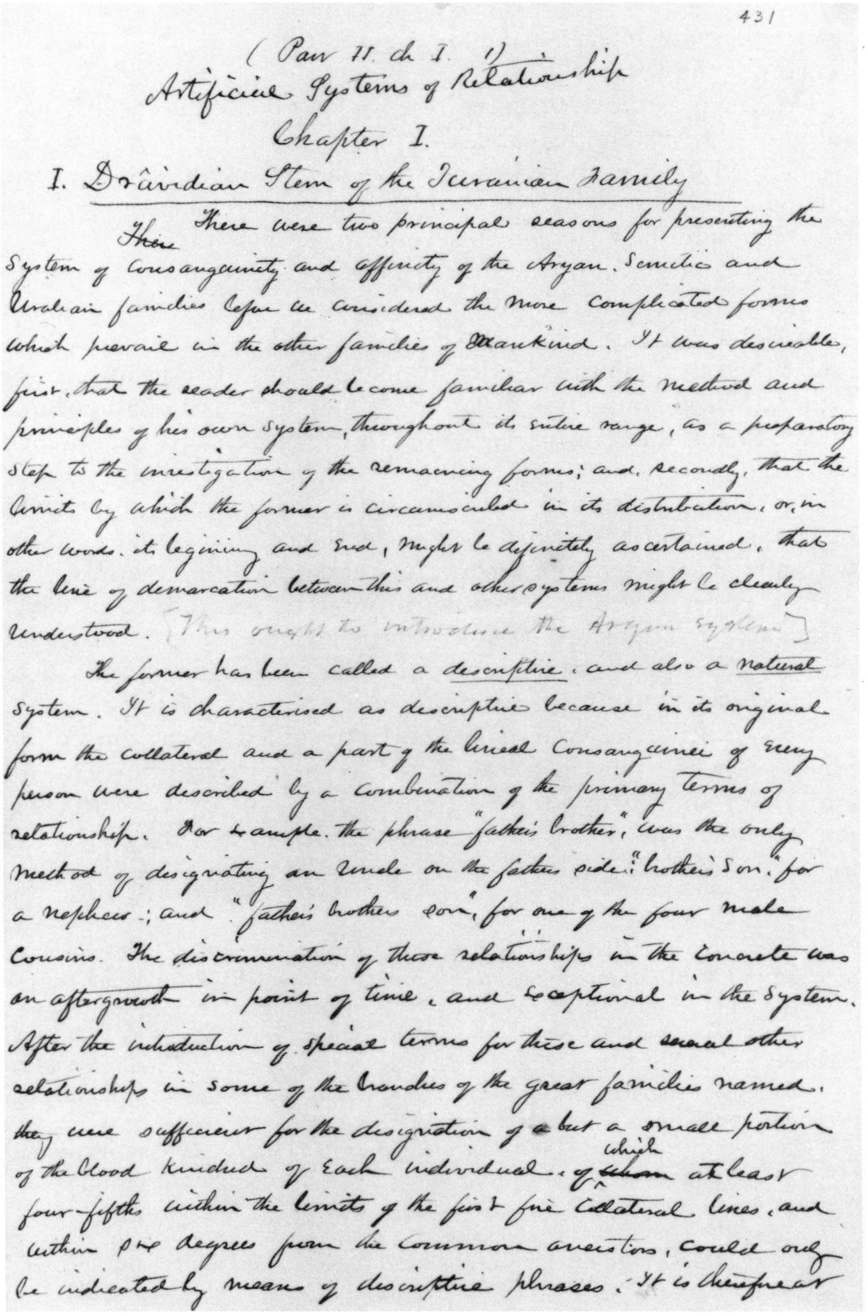

(Part II. ch I.)

Artificial Systems of Relationship

Chapter I.

I. Drâvidian Stem of the Turanian Family

There were two principal reasons for presenting the System of Consanguinity and Affinity of the Aryan, Semitic and Uralian families before we considered the more complicated forms which prevail in the other families of Mankind. It was desirable, first, that the reader should become familiar with the method and principles of his own system, throughout its entire range, as a preparatory step to the investigation of the remaining forms; and, secondly, that the limits by which the former is circumscribed in its distribution, or, in other words, its beginning and end, might be definitely ascertained, that the line of demarcation between this and other systems might be clearly understood. [This ought to introduce the Aryan system]

The former has been called a descriptive, and also a natural System. It is characterised as descriptive because in its original form the collateral and a part of the lineal Consanguinei of every person were described by a combination of the primary terms of relationship. For example, the phrase "father's brother", was the only method of designating an uncle on the father's side; "brother's son," for a nephew; and "father's brother son", for one of the four male Cousins. The discrimination of these relationships in the concrete was an aftergrowth in point of time, and exceptional in the system. After the introduction of special terms for these and several other relationships in some of the branches of the great families named, they were sufficient for the designation of but a small portion of the blood Kindred of Each individual, of which at least four-fifths within the limits of the first five collateral lines, and within five degrees from the Common ancestors, could only be indicated by means of descriptive phrases. It is therefore

Fig. 7. Sample page, 1865 version of the *Systems*.
(Morgan Papers, University of Rochester)

which they are interfiled. Figure 6 gives the contents of the 1865 version of the *Systems*.[5]

This, then, is the *Systems* as Morgan intended it and as originally submitted to the Smithsonian, except that Part IV had not yet been written; Morgan proposed to do so while the commission reviewed the manuscript of Parts I, II, and III. The overall conception differs from the published *Systems* in several significant ways.

In this conception the first three parts are concerned with systems of relationship and Part IV offers further evidence of American Indian unity. Thus whereas in the body of the book Amerindian unity is established through the identity of their systems of relationship—or, rather, their common possession of a single system of relationship—in Part IV this unity is further proved by the universality among them of certain other domestic institutions—namely, the tribal organization (not now presumed to be necessarily matrilineal), the manner of changing and bestowing names, the dance, and burial customs, with a further chapter on architecture and agriculture. Morgan has, then, a larger vision of a bundle of domestic institutions of which systems of relationship are one, which are more conservative and durable than the vocables and grammar of language and which afford proof of historical relations where philology fails. Entries in the notebooks of his western fieldwork are guided by this conception. Henry, however, successfully resisted Morgan's best efforts to add Part IV to an already very long book, and some of its matter was published in other forms on other occasions, so that the conceptual unity of these pieces with the kinship project is not so apparent.[6]

---

[5] Several drafts of the table of contents belonging to different stages in the manuscript's development are filed together in the Morgan Papers; this one consists of the pages numbered 18, 19, 30, 31, and 32 in the library's pagination. Figure 6 gives the substance of these pages, edited for clarity. In the original a number of deletions and additions have been marked; most notably, *natural* and *artificial* are crossed out and replaced by *descriptive* and *classificatory*, probably as the final version of the *Systems* was being written.

[6] On migrations: "Migrations of the Indians" (1862); "Indian migrations" (1869), "Migrations of the American aborigines" (1878). On architecture: "The 'seven cities of Cibola'" (1869), "Architecture of the American aborigines" (1875), "Houses of the mound-builders" (1876), "A study of the houses of the American aborigines" (1880), "On the ruins of the stone pueblo on the Animas River in New Mexico" (1880) and *Houses and house-life of the American aborigines* (1881). An early paper, "The Indian mode of bestowing and changing names" (1859), contains matter that went into the conception of Part IV of the *Systems*. Clearly Morgan did not publish on all the topics he had intended for Part IV.

As to Parts I through III, we see that they deal with the global constructs of *natural* and *artificial systems* (plural) of relationship, whereas in the published *Systems* the rubrics are the *descriptive* and the *classificatory system* (singular) of relationship. The classification of language families here is much as we find it in the published version but in a different order. In Part I the natural systems encompass the Aryan, Semitic, and Uralian families, as in the published version, but of the artificial systems Part II is devoted to the Turanian and Malayan families, and Part III to the "Ganoanian" (Amerindian) family, the reverse of the order of parts found in the published version. These changes will be accounted for in the next chapter.

Even without Part IV the 1865 manuscript was very long: 640 pages of text and 224 quarto pages of tables. Morgan estimated that in the type and format of the *Smithsonian contributions to knowledge* series for which it was intended, it would take 394 pages of print for the text and the massive quarto pages of tables would require 448 pages. At the equivalent of 842 printed pages altogether, the *Systems* submitted in 1865 was some 200 pages longer than the *Systems* as eventually published.

In attempting to characterize this huge manuscript I shall take advantage of the fact that over half of its matter consists of tables of kinship terms and the bulk of the narrative consists of elucidation of the terms that, apart from some alterations in the way in which the material was presented in the interests of economy, were carried over into the published *Systems* and have thereby entered the public domain. I will therefore concentrate my treatment of the 1865 version on those interpretive parts of it that draw conclusions from the data very different from the published version, rather than dwelling on the data themselves. Because the *Systems* is in a real sense built around the tables, however, we must first see how they were constructed.

The program of collecting data on degrees of relationship by circular letter and schedule that Morgan inaugurated in January 1859 was very much in the style of Smithsonian research, which enlisted the collaboration of amateurs in the collection and processing of data as a matter of policy; meteorological and zoological data especially commended themselves to this kind of collection.[7] It was natural, therefore, for Joseph Henry to offer Smithsonian assistance

[7] See Curtis M. Hinsley, Jr., *Savages and scientists, the Smithsonian Institution and the development of American anthropology 1846–1910.*

to Morgan in the printing and dissemination of the schedules at the Springfield meeting of the American Association for the Advancement of Science in August 1859. Morgan did not at first accept, but in February of the following year, having nearly exhausted his second printing of 700 schedules, he accepted the offer.[8] From then on his correspondence with Henry and Henry's assistant, Spencer F. Baird, has many references to the schedules. It will require, Morgan writes, 150 schedules to furnish U.S. military posts west of the Mississippi.[9] Could Baird take a schedule on the expedition to Labrador which he is to accompany, and procure the Eskimo system?[10] Would Henry procure the Japanese system through the [Perry] embassy?[11] Could Henry write Sir George Simpson, governor of the Hudson's Bay Company, asking him to have our schedule distributed to agents at its posts from Hudson's Bay to the Pacific and Arctic Oceans? Schedules sent out to Mexico, Central and South America nearly a year ago have not been returned—could the circular and schedule be translated and printed in Spanish?[12] Please write to Baron Osten Saken, requesting him to fill out a schedule for Russian.[13] I enclose a letter for overland mail to Rev. James L. Scott, acknowledging Tamil and Canarese schedules, and applying for a Malay; I wrote you about a Swedish schedule some time ago—if it is done I should be glad to receive it; if you have a correspondent in Persia, I should be extremely glad to have you send him a schedule for the system of relationship of that nation.[14] Will you send me two more packages of schedules?—the American Board of Comrs. for Foreign Missions are to meet here Oct. 6th and it will give me an opportunity to see a good many missionaries and to send out a number of schedules.[15] Will Dr. Henry send these letters overland to India?—they are the last so far as I know I shall have occasion to send.[16]

In addition, Morgan distributed many of the circular letters and

---

[8] Morgan to Henry, 2/21/60, hand copy in Morgan Papers, *Record of Indian letters*.

[9] The same.

[10] Morgan to Baird, 5/7/60, Smithsonian Institution Archives.

[11] Morgan to Baird, 5/17/60, Smithsonian Institution Archives.

[12] Morgan to Henry, 8/11/60, hand copy in Morgan Papers, *Record of Indian letters*.

[13] Morgan to Henry, 1/14/62, Smithsonian Institution Archives.

[14] Morgan to Baird, 3/26/63, Smithsonian Institution Archives.

[15] Morgan to Henry, 9/25/63, Smithsonian Institution Archives.

[16] Morgan to Baird (?), 1/12/64, Smithsonian Institution Archives.

schedules himself; his two-volume manuscript *Record of Indian letters* logs this correspondence and serves as an address book.

As had been the case in the first year of collection, the gathering of data by correspondence was of limited success, and personal inquiry brought Morgan the greater part of his results. We can see this in the uneven distribution of data published in the *Systems*. Africa, Australia, and Spanish-speaking America are practically blank. The table for Indians and Eskimos of America north of the Rio Grande cover the schedules of 80 peoples, the majority of them directly collected by Morgan during his field trips or as opportunities presented themselves. This is more than the other two tables put together, representing Europe and the Near East (39) and the rest of Asia plus Oceania (18), for which Morgan largely depended on correspondents.

Morgan made four field trips to the West in successive summers from 1859 to 1862 and kept notebook records of the journeys, which he later bound. The principal purpose of these field trips was to collect systems of relationships from the many different tribes thrown together in the Indian territory and points beyond; but the contents of the notebooks show that it was the larger bundle of Indian domestic institutions of the unpublished Part IV that governed his inquiries. On the first two trips he went to Kansas and Nebraska. The third trip, in 1861, took him up the Red River of the North to Fort Garry on Lake Winnipeg in Canada. These were rather brief excursions of little more than a month each. The last trip, in 1862, was the longest and most far reaching, taking him by steam the length of the Missouri River to Fort Benton in Dakota territory. On this last trip personal tragedy overtook him. On the return journey, at Sioux City, Iowa, a telegram awaited him telling of the death of his older daughter Mary, several weeks earlier. His younger daughter Helen was to die two weeks later. "Thus ends my last expedition," he wrote. "I go home to my stricken and mourning wife a miserable and destroyed man."[17] He planned to dedicate the *Systems* to his daughters and to illustrate it with a vignette depicting the brown sandstone family mausoleum he built for them in Mount Hope Cemetery, Rochester. The kinship project took on the character of an intellectual memorial to his grief.

---

[17] Entry for 3 July 1862. See *Lewis Henry Morgan, the Indian journals 1859–62*, edited by Leslie A. White, p. 200. The originals are in the Morgan Papers. White's edition is a selection, omitting kinship terminologies.

The many schedules of relationships Morgan acquired personally or through correspondents were entered into one of three synoptic tables of systems of consanguinity and affinity. The construction of these tables was exacting and time-consuming work. A letter to Joseph Henry shows that the making of the tables commenced in January of 1863—in other words, after the last of the western field trips. The letter tells us that Henry had appropriated $100 of Smithsonian funds to assist this work and that the wages of Morgan's amanuensis had exhausted the grant in April. By that time only the "Eastern Asiatic and Polynesian" schedules needed tabulation—that is, Table II (Turanian and Malayan) of the 1865 version—which Morgan did himself.[18] We may assume that the task was completed at some date thereafter, but certainly before the year was out.

These manuscript tables are preserved in the Morgan Papers. There are two sets: a preliminary set that is presumably the one on which Morgan and his amanuensis first tabulated the schedules, and a final set that appears to be in Morgan's hand. The captions of the latter agree with the 1865 table of contents (Table I), so that they clearly belong to the first version. They bear printers' inky fingerprints, however, showing that they were carried over into the 1867 version. Corrections in this set show significant changes in Morgan's classification of languages.

The problem of classification is central to Morgan's project; indeed, it can be said that the *Systems* is a work of classification. Morgan's classification scheme is, in the first instance, a philological one, a classification of languages into families. The philological design of his work affected the classification of kinship systems at many levels. No philologist himself, and conceiving his own project to be the continuation of philology by other means, he looks to the experts to define the baseline of his work, the point to which philology had succeeded in showing the genealogical interconnections of peoples. He particularly looked to Friedrich Max Müller.

Müller's *Lectures on the science of language* had been immensely popular when first delivered at the Royal Institution of Great Britain in 1861, and their publication shortly thereafter made Müller the leading purveyor of philological knowledge to the reading public in England and America. Morgan purchased the book in December 1862, just as he was about to form the synoptic tables of consanguinity and affinity.[19]

---

[18] Morgan to Henry, 4/21/63, Smithsonian Institution Archives.
[19] "Inventory of books of L H Morgan & wife," MS., Morgan Papers.

Müller's influence can be seen in a change in the names for language families that overtakes Morgan's work around this time. In his earlier writings Morgan used the name *Indo-European*; for example, on 17 January 1860 he gave a talk before the Club titled "The Indo-European system of consanguinity and relationship." In the 1865 version of the *Systems* text and tables, however, we regularly find *Aryan*. Again, when speaking of Central Asian nomads as supposed congeners of the American Indians, Morgan's earlier usage is to call them *Tartars* (as in Jefferson) and later *Scythians*, under the influence of Caldwell's theory of the connection of Dravidian with the Scythian language family. In the 1865 version text and tables Morgan adopts the name *Turanian*. This name derives from *Turān* in Old Persian, indicating the outland inhabited by barbarians, coordinate with and opposed to Irān, the land of the Aryans. Müller and Baron Bunsen had created the name *Turanian* for a language category embracing the greater part of Asia in the 1840s.[20] What must have appealed to Morgan in Müller's choice of names was the theory of civilization versus nomadism that motivated it, so congenial to Americanist thinking on the relations of Euroamericans to Native Americans, and the Central Asian origin of the latter. For Müller, with great show of science (which in point of fact is probably wrong in both etymologies) derives *Aryan* from a root *AR*, to plow (e.g., Latin *arare*); the Aryans seem to have chosen for themselves a name meaning "one who plows or tills," he says, "as opposed to the nomadic races, *the Turanians*, whose original name *Tura* implies the swiftness of the horseman."[21] It is an interpretation and generalization of the Irān/Turān distinction.

It is owing to the appeal of this kind of meaningful naming, as Morgan directly states in the *Systems*, that the third change overtakes Morgan's nomenclature.[22] Hitherto, and up to the completion of the 1865 tables, Morgan had spoken of *American Indians*. In the captions of the 1865 tables we find *American Indian Family* changed to *Ganoánian Family*. This name, later rendered Ganowánian (which spelling I shall use throughout), is Morgan's own coinage, from the Seneca words *gä⸍no*, "arrow," and *wä-ä⸍no*, "bow," he tells us,

---

[20] See *Oxford English dictionary*, s.v. Turanian. See also the Bunsen *Outlines of the philosophy of universal history, applied to language and religion* (1854), and Max Müller entries therein; also Ernst Herzfeld, *Zoroaster and his world*, vol. 2, pp. 717–718.

[21] Müller, *Lectures on the science of language*, p. 248.

[22] *Systems*, p. 131.

signifying "the family of the bow and arrow." Thus the critical elements of Morgan's classification problem bear names that encode different subsistence types: the hunter state (Ganowánian), nomadism (Turanian), plow agriculture (Aryan).

Morgan's classification of nations in the first instance is a classification of languages, taken more or less as he finds it in contemporary philology. "The achievements of comparative philology have been so brilliant and so remarkable, as to justify the expectation, that with its augmented means and improved methods it will yet be able to solve the great problem of the linguistic unity of mankind, of which, as a science, she has assumed the charge," he says. "In this great work, philology will welcome any assistance, however slight, which may be offered from any source," by which he means the comparative study of systems of relationship. These words come from the closing chapter of the 1865 version, wherein we also find a clear statement of the relation of Morgan's subject to the philologist's.[23]

Systems of relationship, or at any rate the classificatory system that is the subject of this passage,[24]

> once established, finds in the diverging streams of the blood an instrument and a means for its transmission through periods of indefinite duration. As we ascend these innumerable lines through the ages of the past they converge continually until they finally meet in a common point; and whatever was in the original blood, and capable of flowing with its currents, was as certain to be transmitted as the blood itself. Language has rolled along the same diverging lines, first breaking up into dialects, which, in the course of time, become distinct, and each the fountain of still other dialects, until, by repeated subdivision, this not less wonderful attendant of the blood, has become worn down, under the friction of time, into indurated forms which interpose serious obstacles to the reascent of its converging streams beyond certain points of demarcation.

The grammatical structure of a language is more durable and resistant to the friction of time and may remain to show genetic connection between languages when comparison of vocables fails before the fact of the inexorable divergence of vocabularies. The ideas deposited in the grammatical structure of a language are analogous to the ideas

---

[23] *Systems* draft, Part III, Chap. VIII, "General results," MS., Morgan Papers, p. 60 in Morgan's pagination for this chapter, p. 1595 in the library's continuous pagination for the *Systems* draft.

[24] The same, p. 59/1594.

contained in a system of consanguinity, and analogous laws govern the development of each. For a variety of reasons, however, the former is much less able to hold and transmit its original indicative features. Just as language consists of vocables and grammatical structure, the second being more resistant to the friction of time than the first, a system of relationship (or, at any rate, the classificatory system of which the passage speaks) consists of terms of relationship and its more durable ideas and conceptions.

> The terms of relationship have passed through the same ordeal as the vocables of language, and have lost themselves as completely; but the ideas and conceptions which they represent are each independent of the mutations of language; and they have lived without essential modification, because they were defined and made perfect at the beginning once for all, both separately, and in their relations to each other.[25]

These ideas of Morgan build upon his understanding of Americanist philology, in whose discourse the *vocabulary/grammar* distinction played a central role, as we have seen. Comparison of Native American vocabularies had established a certain number of groups of genealogically related languages but not the hoped-for proof of Indian unity. It had, however, been Du Ponceau's thesis, restated as an orthodoxy of the science by Gallatin and others, that among all American languages there was a commonality of grammar or structure even when vocabularies differed. Du Ponceau characterized the Amerindian languages as polysynthetic. The vocabulary/grammar distinction refers to different phases within the same project of the genetic classification of American languages, corresponding to a notion of differing rates of change affecting the two aspects of language.[26] These levels (more durable ideas of grammar, less durable vocables) are reflected in the composition of Morgan's Ganowánian group. The Ganowánian *family,* corresponding to the level of grammar, is composed of several *stems* or nations corresponding to the level of vocabulary in Americanist philology, these in turn consisting of *stock languages* and *dialects.* Thus the overall conception is that the sound strings that make up a vocabulary are the most vulnerable to the friction of time, the ideas of grammatical structure less so, and

---

[25] The same, pp. 59–60/1594–1595.
[26] See Haas, "Grammar or lexicon?" and her articles on the history of Americanist philology in her book, *Language, culture, and history.*

the ideas of systems of relationship the least of all. Although Morgan acknowledges that philology has assumed the charge of the ethnolinguistic program, the unmistakable implication of his conceptions is that the lead in the common project must pass from philology to ethnology.

Morgan's classification problem may be simply put. Its baseline was provided by philology's genetic classification of languages. At the highest level of integration this yielded six families: Aryan, Semitic, Uralian, Turanian, Malayan, and Ganowánian. Then through a comparison of systems of relationship he must further integrate these six families into two and only two taxa. This would supply the proof of Indian unity and Asian origin if one of the taxa, representing a common system of relationship, included all Indians and some Asians and if the other taxon included Europeans and others from whom the American Indians were *not* derived. In the solution of this problem Morgan constructs a class around what he calls the descriptive or natural system of relationship, containing the Aryan, Semitic, and Uralian families, and another class representing what he calls the classificatory or artificial system of relationship, consisting of the Turanian, Malayan, and Ganowánian families.

The more difficult and, for us, more interesting aspects of Morgan's classification problem appear not among the Amerindian systems of relationship that were the main focus of his research efforts but in the systems of the Old World. Leaving aside the myriad details of the lower reaches of the classification scheme upon which he settles, two gross features of his Old World classifications require comment: the position of the Semitic family in the overall scheme, and Morgan's departures from philological authority, in the person of Max Müller, in the composition of the Uralian and Turanian families.

The position of Semitic side by side with Aryan is motivated in many ways, most immediately by the negative side of Morgan's project. Morgan does not make the negative side of his project explicit, but the history of the question of Indian origins makes it apparent that the unnamed rival to Morgan's Asian origin thesis is the thesis that the Amerindians derived from European peoples or the Lost Tribes of Israel.[27] We have already seen in his 1859 AAAS paper how gingerly he handles structural similarities between

---

[27] See Retzius in Smithsonian *Annual report* for 1863.

Hebrew and Seneca systems of relationship, and how careful he is to dissociate himself from the Hebrew origin thesis, although he does not yet put the Indo-European and Semitic systems in a single class.[28] (I suspect he had done so by 31 March 1863, when he gave a talk before the Club, which has not survived, on "The system of consanguinity and affinity of the Semitic nations.") The association of Aryan and Semitic comes about through the logic of his classification scheme. Of the division of the human family into two great branches on the basis of their systems of relationship—Aryan, Semitic, and Uralian on one side, and Turanian, Malayan, and Ganowánian on the other—he says, "It gives very nearly the line of demarcation between the civilized and uncivilized nations."[29] It was a traditional Christian position, shaped by the short chronology, that the authors of civilization were the ancient Greeks, Romans, and Hebrews, probably reinforced for Morgan both by McIlvaine's belief in the historical exceptionalism of the ancient Hebrews and by Max Müller's belief in the common origin and evolutionary parity of the Aryan and Semitic languages. It is well known that comparative philologists of the nineteenth century made important contributions to the formation of ideologies that were not only Eurocentric but also racist and anti-Semitic. It is important, therefore, to recognize that those possibilities were not inherent in the science and that philo-Semitic readings of its findings were adopted by some, especially in a Christian interest.

If the deep logic of Morgan's classification scheme is a distinction of the civilized from the uncivilized nations, what will be unintelligible to us at first blush is not the placement of Semitic on the civilized side but the placement of, among others, the civilizations of India and China on the other side of the line of demarcation. Müller's scheme of language evolution was perhaps Morgan's starting point for Old World classifications.

In Müller's book the "genealogical classification of languages" establishes the Aryan and Semitic language families through the study of cognates, but we must resort to morphological classification for a comprehensive historical scheme that unites these two families and opposes them to the "nomad" languages of the Turanian family

---

[28] "Systems of consanguinity of the red race, in its relations to ethnology," MS. of a paper delivered before the American Association for the Advancement of Science in August 1859, Morgan Papers; see chapter 5 of this book.

[29] Morgan, *Systems* draft, "General results," p. 4/1496.

and Chinese and its cognate dialects. In brief, his scheme incorporates three evolutionary stages in language history, as follows:[30]

1. Radical Stage	Each root preserves its independence, and there is no formal distinction between a root and a word. Also called Monosyllabic or Isolating.	Ancient Chinese
2. Terminational Stage	Two or more roots coalesce to form a word, the one retaining its radical independence, the other sinking down to a mere termination. Also called Agglutinative.	Turanian family
3. Inflectional Stage	Roots coalesce so that neither the one nor the other retains its substantive independence. Also called Amalgamating or Organic.	Aryan and Semitic families

As to the Turanian family, Müller frankly admits that it is the creature of morphological comparison, not that of vocables; that some scholars would deny it the name of a family, as its constituents were not so closely interconnected as the Aryan or Semitic; and that genealogical comparison (i.e., the comparison of vocables) would fail to reveal a family likeness.[31] The *genealogical/morphological* distinction is effectively the same as the vocabulary/grammar distinction of Americanist philology.

Morgan seems to have taken Müller's admission of the merely morphological character of the Turanian family as license to redesign it accordingly as the evidence of his schedules of the degrees of relationship should require. However that may be, the fact is that he changed Müller's Turanian family beyond recognition. The changes were essentially two: the formation of a Uralian family out of constituents of Müller's Turanian, and certain additions to the Turanian

---

[30] Müller, *Science of language*, pp. 298–299.
[31] The same, p. 301.

family, notably the Sanskritic (that is, Aryan) languages of North India.

Müller's classification, in outline, is as follows:[32]

Turanian family

Northern division (Ural-Altaic or Ugro-Tataric)

Tungusic
Mongolic
Turkic
Finnic
Samoyedic

Southern division

Tamulic
Bhotiya
Taïc
Malaic

Of the five classes of Müller's northern division, Morgan had failed to obtain reliable data for three—the Tungusic, Mongolic, and Samoyedic. Those of this division he did acquire he classified as follows:

Uralian

Turkic

Osmanli-Turk
Kuzulbashi

Ugric

Magyar
Esthonian
Finn

The striking fact that comes to light from examination of the manuscript tables is that these Uralian systems are at first classified with Turanian, but then Morgan changes his mind and classes them with

[32] The same.

Aryan and Semitic. Thus Table II is originally titled "Table of consanguinity and affinity of the Turanian, Uralian and Malayan families." At some later point the entries on this table for Finn, Esthonian, Magyar, and Osmanli-Turk are crossed out, along with the title, which is now changed to "Systems of consanguinity and affinity of the Turanian and Malayan families" (as may be seen in figure 8). Similarly, Table I is changed from "Tables of consanguinity and affinity of the Semitic and Aryan families" to "Systems of consanguinity and affinity of the Semitic, Aryan and Uralian families."[33] Thus a reclassification of some moment overtook these tables some time after 1863, when compilation began, and before the 1865 version—with which the corrected titles agree—took shape.

The motivation for the creation of Uralian and its classification with Aryan and Semitic, though unstated, is nevertheless clear from the composition of this family. It consists of Europeans and Muslim peoples of the biblical lands of the Near East. The detachment of the Ottoman Turks from their Central Asian linguistic cousins and their classification among the civilized nations evidently conformed to the opinions of McIlvaine, who, on a later occasion, gave it his blessing, calling the Ottomans the one really great and historic race that the Turanian portion of mankind had produced.[34] We may say that the descriptive or natural system of relationship is found among the "Peoples of the Book": Christians, Jews, and Muslims.

Beyond the removal of Uralian, other digressions from Müller are equally striking, as may be seen by comparing the composition of Morgan's Turanian family:

Turanian

    Dravidic

      Tamil
      Telugu
      Canarese

----

[33] "Final drafts of tables for *Systems of Consanguinity*," MS., Morgan Papers.

[34] McIlvaine, "The organisation of society," paper delivered before The Club of Rochester, 20 November 1866, MS., Morgan Papers, p. 28/32: "It is worthy of remark, that the Turanean portion of mankind has produced but one really great & historic race, namely the Turks: among whom no trace of this [classificatory] system is found. In consequence of which Mr. Morgan removes them out of this class." McIlvaine's paper is a comment upon the 1865 version of the *Systems*, of which he was a reader for the Smithsonian Institution. See chapter 7 of this book.

Gauraic

> Bengali
> Marathi
> Gujerati
> Chinese
> Japanese

Unclassified

> Burmese
> Karen

Thus Morgan's Turanian excludes Malayan, as a separate family, but absorbs Chinese and Japanese. Although Sanskrit is of the Aryan family, its modern descendants in North India (here Gauraic or Gaura) are absorbed by Turanian, perhaps under the influence of some of Caldwell's statements about the Dravidian element in the languages of North India; at any rate, a Dravidianizing theory of Indian history, from whatever source, is implied by Morgan's taxonomy. In general Morgan seems to have felt that in Asia and Oceania he was in territory that philology had scarcely begun to explore and that he was therefore free to form such families of systems of consanguinity and affinity as his own data suggested. In the reworking of Müller's classification scheme, however, he was working to much the same end as had Müller: to define the outer boundaries of biblically based civilization and its relation to the other. The geography of kinship unites the great civilizations of Europe and the Near East and opposes them to nations that even now bear the marks of nomadism.

These two great taxa Morgan calls the *descriptive* or *natural* system of consanguinity and affinity, comprising Aryan, Semitic, and Uralian, and the *classificatory* or *artificial* system, comprising the Turanian, Malayan, and American Indian families. These alternative designations are present in the 1865 version, and Morgan emphasizes the *natural/artificial* contrast; in the 1867 version this contrast will be all but eliminated. As Morgan originally conceived it, the text of the *Systems* was a disquisition upon Nature and Art.

Morgan opens his manuscript with an overview of the two systems and the different relations in which they stand to nature and natural suggestion. Family relationships are as ancient as the family—that

Fig. 8. Table of systems of consanguinity and affinity of the Turanian,
(Uralian) and Malayan families. (Morgan Papers, University of Rochester)

is, they are primeval. "They exist in the nature of descents," being the result of sexual reproduction, and are therefore "independent of human creation, and unaffected by any devices which may be adopted for their discrimination or classification."[35] Systems of consanguinity merely recognize and express these naturally occurring family relationships. Morgan then paints a word picture of these natural relationships, and the picture shows a remarkable resemblance to the figure he found in *Coke upon Littleton* (see figure 9).

---

[35] *Systems* draft, Part I, Chap. I, "General observations upon systems of relationship," MS., Morgan Papers, p. 1/87. This corresponds to Chap. II of the published *Systems*.

Around every person there is a circle or group of kindred, of which each person is the centre, the *Ego,* from whom the degree of the relationship is reckoned and to whom the relationship itself returns. Above him are his father and his mother, and their ascendants; below him are his children and their descendants; while upon either side are his brothers and sisters and their descendants, and the brothers and sisters of his father and of his mother and their descendants, as well as a much greater number of collateral relatives descended from common ancestors still more remote. To him they are nearer in degree than other individuals of the nation at large. A formal arrangement of their more immediate blood kindred into lines of descent, with the adoption of some method to distinguish one relative from another, and to express the value of the relationship, would be one of the earliest acts of human intelligence.[36]

---

[36] The same.

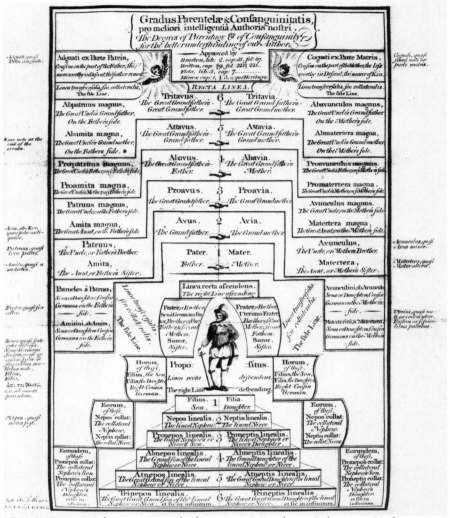

Fig. 9. Degrees of parentage and of consanguinity, from *Coke upon Littleton*.

Underneath any system of consanguinity which man may contrive there is already one self-existing, by an ordinance of nature, which is both universal and unchangeable. All of the descendants of an original pair stand to each other in fixed degrees of proximity, the nearness or remoteness of which is a mere matter of computation.[37]

---

[37] The same, pp. 1–2/87–88.

Ascending to the common ancestor, and descending the collateral line, the circle of kindred bound to the *Ego* by a chain of consanguinity encompasses millions of the living and the dead; and the precise degree in which they stand to him can be ascertained and numbered wherever the connection can be traced. The links of kindred are never broken, but the streams of descent perpetually diverge from one another; the collateral lines spring out from the lineal and depart from it one degree every generation. "This self-existing system, which may be called the numerical, is theoretically the system of nature; and, as such, is taught to all the families of mankind by natural suggestion. It specializes each relationship, and indicates, with more or less distinctness, a generalization into classes of all such persons as stand in the same degree of nearness to the central *Ego*," he says, thinking perhaps of English terms such as *aunt, uncle,* and *cousin,* "with a further discrimination of the difference in value of these several classes, according as they are ascendants or descendants, lineal or collateral."[38]

Every system of consanguinity, therefore, that distinguishes the lineal from the collateral and recognizes the constant divergence of the latter with decreases of nearness and value of the relationship with every remove in degree from *Ego* is a natural system, "since it follows the actual streams of blood." It is "obvious to the most simple intelligence" and is in fact the primitive system of the Aryan and other families; but as the existence of the artificial or classificatory system shows, the numerical or natural system does not necessarily impose itself on a primitive society. It is, however, "the one to which all nations must inevitably gravitate if they seek to conform their respective systems to the ultimate standard prescribed by the nature of descents."[39]

Consulting the tables, we find only two radically distinct forms of consanguinity: the descriptive or natural, and the classificatory or artificial.[40]

---

[38] The same, p. 2/88.

[39] The same, p. 3/89.

[40] The same, pp. 4–5/90–91. The passage bears several significant later emendations that bring it into line with the "conjectural history of the family" interpretation of the 1867 version subsequently published. For example, the "arbitrary generalizations" of the classificatory system become "apparently arbitrary generalizations," and the words "or natural" and "or artificial" that qualify the two systems are crossed out. Compare the wording in the published *Systems,* pp. 11–12.

The first, rejecting the classification of kindred except so far as it is in accordance with natural suggestion, and depending chiefly upon the primary terms, describes the remaining consanguinei by an augmentation or combination of these terms, with slight assistance, in some cases, from the language at large. Each relationship is thus made independent and distinct from every other; and the primary terms are employed in strict accordance with their original signification. . . . The second form, rejecting descriptive phrases in every instance, and reducing consanguinei to great classes by a series of arbitrary generalizations, applies the same term to all the members of the same class. It thus confounds relationships which, in their nature, are independent and distinct from each other, and enlarges the signification of the primary terms beyond their appropriate sense.

The system of relationship of the Aryan, Semitic, and Uralian families is a descriptive or natural system. That of the Turanian, Malayan, and American Indian or Ganowánian families is a classificatory or artificial one. The chapter closes with illustrations of differences between the two, and arguments for the great antiquity of both: a system once matured, its nomenclature invented, its method of description or of classification determined upon would be slow to change, being universal to the community, necessary to each individual, existing by usage rather than enactment; moreover, "their channel of transmission is the blood."[41]

Thus in a few pages Morgan sketches the circuit of his thought. Starting from the "degrees of relationship" in *Coke upon Littleton* and in Blackstone on title by descent, these in turn resting on canon law and the civil law of Justinian, he finds therein a true representation of nature "independent of human creation." If it is true, however, it must also be natural, springing from that great source of knowledge for the Common Sense school, the promptings or suggestions of nature herself. Thus the "degrees of relationship" constitute a system existing in nature, which suggests a system of consanguinity of the natural or descriptive type we find among civilized nations. This system is both primeval (following the suggestions of nature) and progressive or scientific ("the one to which all nations must inevitably gravitate if they seek to conform their respective systems to the nature of descents"). The argument returns to Coke and Blackstone, its source. Starting, that is, from the scientific representation of descent in the European tradition, he finds that the scientific

---

[41] The same, p. 11/98.

representation is a copy of nature and "obvious to the most simple intelligence"; and examining the European and cognate systems of consanguinity through that scientific tradition, he finds that they too are natural and follow the suggestions of the natural or numerical system that the jurists expound. Thus the descriptive system is natural in a manifold sense that combines the notions of primitiveness and science, being "obvious to the most simple intelligence" and being "true to the nature of descents."

This formulation is not without difficulties, and Morgan addresses two of them at length. In the first place, in the system of the Aryan, Semitic, and Uralian families there are what appear to be classificatory tendencies, which must be accounted for in some way. Morgan discusses these under the rubric of "the growth of nomenclatures of relationship," to which he devotes an entire chapter. In the second place, non-Western systems are put in the anomalous position of being both precivilized and nonnatural, in the dual sense of not having conformed themselves to the numerical system that is universal and unchangeable in the period of its origin, and of constituting obstacles to the present recognition of the numerical or natural system, "to which all nations must inevitably gravitate if they seek to conform their respective systems to the ultimate standard prescribed by the nature of descents." The classificatory system is both artificial and nonscientific, or even antiscientific. How, then, did it arise? Morgan devotes much of the long concluding chapter to this question. I shall summarize his treatment of both issues.

The "growth of nomenclatures of relationship" concerns the historical development of secondary terms of relationship. Morgan conceives that the eight primary terms—those for husband and wife, father and mother, son and daughter, and brother and sister—are universally necessary and are the first to be invented. "They are as old as the Family organization."[42] A nomenclature, for purposes of this discussion, is a vocabulary, a set of simplex terms such as *father* but excluding descriptive phrases such as *father's brother*; it is, in short, the philologist's vocabulary list set against the natural categories expressed in English. The primary terms, then, constitute the

---

[42] *Systems* draft, Part I, Chap. VI, "Nomenclatures of relationship," MS., Morgan Papers, p. 2/82. This chapter, because of later writing on the backs of its pages, is filed in reverse order, from p. 86 to p. 54 (with omissions) in the library's pagination. The chapter was cut in the final version, and its matter is reduced to two footnotes in the published *Systems*, pp. 35 and 37.

first nomenclature for any and every people; and although the different names or vocables separate the languages of different peoples, the underlying relationships are identical.

It is beyond this nomenclature of primary terms that the differentiation of systems begins. Descriptive and classificatory systems differ as to whether they use descriptive phrasal terms to indicate secondary relationships or merge them with primary ones; or whether relations that are collateral are described or merged with lineal ones. Within the descriptive system, however, are secondary terms that are simplex ones, not descriptive phrases. Morgan sets himself the task of showing "the natural growth of nomenclatures of relationship in a system originally purely descriptive," insofar as this can be ascertained from the facts disclosed in the tables.

After the invention of the primary terms had answered the initial necessities imposed by the family organization, "the further growth of the nomenclature might be arrested for an indefinite period of time, since with these terms, and slight aid from the body of the language, all of the remaining relatives are readily described by the Celtic method."[43] The Erse and Gaelic have no terms for uncle, aunt, nephew, niece, or cousin, using instead descriptive phrases such as father's brother, mother's brother, brother's son, and so forth. The Celtic forms, then, are purely descriptive.[44] Not all nations that follow the descriptive system are purely descriptive in the treatment of secondary relatives, however.

Any progress beyond the state exemplified by the Celtic languages would involve generalization and classification. The first and lowest form of classifications involves use of the plural or primary terms, which would reduce several sons, or several brothers, to one class. Beyond this point, to express the collateral relationships three alternatives offer themselves: (1) to invent special (simplex) terms or, in other words, "the growth of nomenclatures of relationship"; (2) to describe each relative, resorting to the Celtic method; and (3) the classificatory solution: "by a false generalization, as under the Turanian system in part, to classify the collateral with the primary relatives, as uncles with the father, aunts with the mother, & cousins with the brother."[45] The inconvenience of the Celtic method leads

---

[43] The same.
[44] Chap. I, "General observations," pp. 5–6/91–92.
[45] Chap. VI, "Nomenclatures," p. 2/82.

those nations that do not choose the classificatory solution to take the first alternative, that of inventing special terms.

This nomenclature of special terms would grow in a particular way. Because creating special terms for every relationship would be even more inconvenient than descriptive phrases, new terms would be limited to the nearest degrees of collateral kindred, and they would be used in a general sense until restricted in scope by the introduction of yet more terms. The nomenclature of relationships, then, would grow outward from a central *Ego* "to ascendants, descendants, and collaterals; or generally from the primary terms, to the secondary which are applied to the collaterals."[46] Morgan then examines the materials of Table I in light of this historical theory, concentrating attention on the Aryan languages, but with some remarks on Semitic and Uralian ones as well.

In the Aryan family the only terms of relationship that are constant are the primary (because we find cognates for these terms in the several languages) but also the Latin *nepos* and its cognates. The variability of this word between the Indo-European languages is notorious, and Morgan's analysis is one of the first to recognize and grapple with this fact. At the outset, he argues, *nepos* was used indiscriminately for nephew, grandson, and cousin (see, for example, the use of *nepos, neptis, nephew,* and *niece* in figure 9). Because the terms for grandfather and grandmother, grandson and granddaughter, uncle and aunt, nephew and niece, and male and female cousin, as now discriminated from each other, are not constant in these languages, they probably did not exist in the primitive speech. Assuming a purely descriptive system for the three great families of Table I, it is probable that a term (such as *nepos*) for nephew and grandson would be the first to be invented "in the natural order of development of the nomenclature,"[47] growing outward from the primary terms. *Nepos* and its cognates in the Aryan languages illustrate the case. It is universal in them, hence primitive; its original signification (that is, the "translation" of Morgan's schedule) is lost; as it is older than terms for grandfather, grandmother, uncle and aunt, it must have first existed without a correlative special term. That it designated both grandson and nephew in several Aryan languages is undoubted, and Morgan gives many illustrations of the fact; indeed, in the

---

[46] The same, p. 3/81.
[47] The same.

beginning it was "a general term of relationship applied to a nephew, a grandson, a cousin, and possibly to the descendants of each."[48] He concludes that it was the first special term introduced into the Aryan family to indicate relationships beyond those expressed by primary terms, and that at first it was used in a more comprehensive sense than at present—until, that is, its scope was reduced by the introduction of further special terms. "Nepos did not originally signify a son's son, or a brother's son, but . . . it was a general term of relationship used promiscuously to designate a class of persons next without the primary relationships (except ascendants), who were related to *Ego* in several different ways."[49] With the invention of new terms it became restricted to grandson in Sanskrit, Latin, Spanish, and Portuguese, and to the son of a brother and sister in English, "Belgian," Norman, French, and German, while it continued to stand for both in Anglo-Saxon, Italian, and "Holland Dutch," and in the latter for cousin also, and in its feminine form for female cousin in "Platt Dutch" and "Belgian" in addition to "Holland Dutch."

The next required would be special terms for grandfather and grandmother, and uncle and aunt, correlatives of *nepos* and its cognates. Here the same terms do not run through the several branches of the Aryan family, leading us to infer that descriptive phrases were applied at the period of separation of these languages from one another. A term for cousin would be the last invented "on the supposition of the growth of the nomenclature from *Ego* outward." English *cousin* is a generalization of four different classes of persons each in the same degree of nearness to *Ego* into one class; and because of its complexity as well as its remoteness it is a more difficult generalization than the previous one. The Aryan relationship seems to have been reached by accident, through a previous generalization of the children of sisters under Latin *consobrinus, -a* afterward extended to the children of all siblings by the Roman people, whence it was adopted by most of the Aryan nations. That is to say, it is a later borrowing from Latin. In Semitic the relationship of cousin "in the concrete"—that is, under a simplex term—is unknown, and so too for Uralian, with the exception of the Finns.

Thus, in brief, the growth of nomenclatures of relationship among the families that have the descriptive system of relationship. Again and again Morgan states that this growth is a natural process, follow-

---

[48] The same, p. 6/78.
[49] The same, p. 7/76.

ing a natural order; a kind of imminent law of growth guides it. He recognizes the existence of generalization or classification within the descriptive system, but he distinguishes it from the "false generalizations" of the classificatory system, which are not natural. But if not of nature, how then do we explain them?

Morgan considers the question of the origin of the classificatory system at length in the concluding "General results" chapter. In the version under discussion (that of 1865) Morgan gives an artificialist interpretation of the classificatory system; in the published version (that of 1867) the interpretation is entirely changed to a naturalistic one governed by what I shall call Morgan's "conjectural history of the family." The published *Systems,* however, carries over substantial blocks of material from the 1865 version, and the artificialist interpretation still clings to bits of that original material, which accounts for the slightly mixed character of the interpretation we find in the book. It is important, therefore, to identify the artificialist interpretation in its integrity, presenting as briefly as I can the original argument of the very long, repetitious concluding chapter in the 1865 version.

The argument that there are only two systems of consanguinity and affinity, the descriptive and the classificatory, and that only the first is a natural system was not without difficulty. If the descriptive system were purely and exclusively natural, Morgan says, the argument for the unity of origin of the Aryan, Semitic, and Uralian families would be without force, as it would be "the form to which all nations must gravitate under the exercise of ordinary intelligence."[50] It is evident, however, that man, whether in a primitive or a civilized condition, would not unavoidably discover and adopt this form, as the tables of systems of relationship show its rejection by the majority of mankind.[51] Intelligence and choice entered into its adoption and maintenance. Because he chooses to interpret the classificatory system of the human majority as nonnatural, Morgan cannot entirely eliminate elements of the free exercise of will in the formation, from the suggestions of nature, of the descriptive system.

---

[50] *Systems* draft, Part III, Chap. VIII, "General results," MS., Morgan Papers, p. 5/1497. Many later draft pages are interfiled with this chapter, and much of it is corrected in accordance with the later "conjectural history of the family" interpretation.

[51] The same, p. 11/1507.

This problem will be relieved by the conjectural history interpretation in the final version.

As to the classificatory system, it is vital to Morgan's purpose that it be shown to be "arbitrary, artificial and complicated" and "a work of intelligence and design."[52]

> The number of definite conceptions embodied in this system of relationships, is such as to excite astonishment at the fertility of invention which it exhibits, and the ingenuity of discriminations which it displays. While it violates our more correct perceptions of the true relations which consanguinei sustain to each other, it possesses a high degree of merit for the recognition of the obligations and the sacredness of the ties of blood, which it enforced to their widest limits.[53]

The classificatory system, to give it its due, is "complicated without obscurity, and diversified without confusion."[54] It is a work of Art.

In light of the fact that Morgan, in accounting for the descriptive system, had argued that "nature teaches an affirmative system of relationship, and reveals a natural method of classification"[55] upon which the descriptive system builds, it is now necessary to show that natural suggestion is not the source of the classificatory system. In doing so he clarifies the workings of this most important force for us in a paragraph that deserves quotation in full.[56]

> "Natural suggestion" must be understood to indicate what nature may be supposed to teach to all alike, and which man might discover as truth by the exercise of slight intelligence. Such suggestions might spring from internal sources, or from the subject; and also from external sources, or from the object, or from both united. Thus, in the formation of a plan of consanguinity, reflection upon the nature of descents would reveal the method of nature in the evolution of generations of mankind from common ancestors; and this would develop the suggestions of nature from the internal source, or the subject. On the other hand, the uses which the system, when formed, should be made to subserve, would reach

---

[52] The same, p. 4/1496.

[53] The same, p. 9/1503. The passage was heavily corrected at a later date to bring it into line with the "conjectural history of the family" interpretation of the 1867 version. In particular, a clause is added to the second sentence that reads: "on the assumption that mankind lived in single pairs in the married state."

[54] The same.

[55] The same, p. 10/1505.

[56] The same, p. 13/1511.

outward upon their condition and wants, and induce reflection upon the supposed teachings of nature from external sources, or from the object to be gained. It must be observed that suggestions which spring from the subject, arise spontaneously in the mind upon slight reflection. As deliverances from nature they are necessarily uniform to all men and in all times. If they arise from the subject, they are uniform, irrespective of the conditions of society; but if from the object, uniformity of suggestion would require similarity of condition. The teachings of nature from the latter sources, which are complex, and liable to modify each other, must, for these reasons, be uncertain and indefinite.

As it is perfectly evident that the classificatory system was not drawn from the nature of descents—a point upon which Morgan would reverse himself in the 1867 version—that is, from the suggestions of nature acting uniformly upon the individual human mind, we must look to sources of natural suggestion external to the individual in the objective conditions of society. Morgan specifies three possible external sources of natural suggestion: (1) the use of the bond of kindred for the mutual protection of related persons; (2) the influence of the tribal system (that is, exogamous clans); and (3) the influence of polygamy and polyandria. The first of these amounts to the deliberate merger of collaterals with lineals to extend and maintain a large network of kin relations. Such considerations may well have influenced the foundation of the system but do not necessarily suggest this or any other particular plan of consanguinity and so cannot account for its origin. The tribal organization may also have been an influence but is similarly unable to account for the specific mergers of the classificatory system. In his treatment of this question Morgan's careful analysis shows in effect why he now abandons the line of explanation of the Seneca system of relationship he had first essayed in the *League of the Iroquois*. Finally, although polygamy and polyandria can explain some of the mergers of relationships that are features of the system, they cannot account for all of them and cannot have been practiced by the majority of any society in any age; whence the supposed reason fails for want of universality. Against these hypothetical causes the inescapable fact remains: "natural descents are traversed over and over again in the fundamental frame work of the system, and, therefore, nature could not have taught that part of it which is in derogation of herself."[57]

---

[57] The same, p. 23/1528. This page was later marked for excision as it did not conform to the "conjectural history of the family" interpretation. In the published

Had the great teacher remained silent upon the domestic relationships, and furnished neither guide nor intimation for the instruction of mankind, then she might be supposed to teach whatever human fancy may suggest; but she was not able to remain concealed, and was forced to develop an affirmative system of consanguinity in the method by which the species is perpetuated.[58]

The classificatory system rejects the promptings of the great teacher; its artificial and arbitrary character is apparent from the tables; it is "purely a product of human contrivance, and not the result of accidental or spontaneous growth." How it began is unknown and may never be explained.[59] It is exactly its artificiality, however, that gives it great value and importance for ethnology. The classificatory system's value for ethnology, of course, is that it is a proof of the Asiatic origin of the Indians.

How may we account for the possession of this system by the Turanian family of Asia and the Ganowánian of America? Morgan considers four possibilities, of which the last is the mechanism of choice: (1) by borrowing from one another; (2) by accidental invention in disconnected areas; (3) by spontaneous growth in disconnected areas under the influence of natural suggestions springing from similar wants in similar conditions of society; and (4) by transmission with the blood from a common, original source. I need not recite the arguments with which Morgan eliminates the first three alternatives, but it is important to note that of the third Morgan says, "From the commencement of this research it has appeared to the author to be the essential, the manifest and the only difficulty which stood in the pathway between this extraordinary system of relationship, and the important testimony it might otherwise deliver upon ethnological questions."[60] Once the difficulty was surmounted, Morgan could conclude that the classificatory system is found both among American Indians and in the Asia whence they came because it must have been invented only once, for all time. And the invention of this kinship system was unique precisely because it was a product of human intelligence, unaided by nature's promptings.

Systems the corresponding discussion of the three possible external causes of the classificatory system occurs at pp. 474–479.

[58] The same, pp. 23–24/1528–1529.

[59] The same, p. 25/1530.

[60] The same, p. 54/1582.

Ethnology may be said to be a program of elucidating the relationship of the cultural other to the collective self; but it is also, first, a
program of the definition of the collective self, of the other, and of
the boundary between the two. It is, to begin with, a work of
classification. In Morgan's 1865 ethnology the collective self com-
prehends the Christians, Jews, and Muslims of Europe and the biblical Near East, opposed to the uncivilized other. This construct was
largely motivated, I believe, by what I should like to call (borrowing
words from Herbert Butterfield) "the Whig or Protestant interpretation of ethnology." By this I mean that view of the cultural other in
relation to the civilized, Protestant Christian collective self that was
expressed not only in the works of doxological science such as Max
Müller's book but also and in a more popular way in those memoirs
of American missionaries abroad found in Morgan's and so many
Americans' libraries at mid-century, books such as Hiram Bingham's
Twenty-one years in the Sandwich Islands and Wayland's *Life of
Judson.* Consistent with the general tendencies of this tradition, however, Morgan's ethnology ended not with the six families of philology
(as interpreted by himself) or the two systems of consanguinity and
affinity but with the unitary human family. At the highest level of
integration the opposition of self and other vanished.

The nature of Morgan's project obliged him to stop short of that
ultimate, however, and to dwell upon the gulf between the civilized
and the uncivilized. The peculiar requirements of his project led him
to join to this opposition a distinction between the natural and the
artificial. At the end of his strange journey Morgan comes upon a
startling creature: the savage intellectual who creates a system of
wonderful complexity, for reasons no one knows and in contradiction to the teachings of Nature.

7

Conjectural History

++

Between the completion of the first version of the *Systems* in 1865 and its publication in 1871, Morgan's kinship project was exposed to critical examination by the Smithsonian Institution's readers and to delays occasioned by the Smithsonian's strained finances. Under pressure of these forces Morgan's manuscript was reshaped and resubmitted in 1867; it is essentially the *Systems* as published. In this chapter I shall examine the changes that Morgan introduced into the final version and their causes. It will be especially useful to elucidate the review process, for through it the kinship project was first brought before the gaze of the community of scholars, albeit in small. We shall see that Morgan responded to the criticisms by making a number of revisions. The most important of these concerned the overall interpretation of the "classificatory or artificial" system of relationship. In the first version he had seen it as a wonderfully complex, logically integrated creature of pure intellection unaided by nature, opposed to the naturalistic descriptive system. He now naturalized his interpretation of the classificatory system, making it, like the descriptive, a product of natural suggestion. Why and how he did so we must now discover.

Central to this question is the role of Joseph Henry, secretary of the Smithsonian Institution. Morgan's relationship with Henry went back at least to 1854, and although the long delays in the acceptance and publication of the *Systems* was to strain their friendship (if we may use the word for a relationship so formal, between persons so reserved) nearly to the breaking point, it continued to Henry's death in 1878. Henry was the senior of Morgan by some twenty years. He was, like Morgan, a New Yorker and a Presbyterian. He was the country's leading physicist, a practicing scientist of international repute. Morgan knew him through the Smithsonian, whose annual reports he read regularly, and the American Association for the

Advancement of Science, of which Henry was a past president and leading light.[1]

Henry was an austere man, whose public life was dedicated to raising the level of American science and ridding it of chicanery and amateurism by bringing its results under professional review. At the American Association for the Advancement of Science, for example, he was involved in the decision to publish only those papers that received the approval of the publication committee. At the Smithsonian a similar sense of discrimination decided which of its public lectures were published in the annual reports, and it guided the series he inaugurated, called *Contributions to knowledge,* of which the *Systems* would comprise the seventeenth volume. He took a very active stance in his role as publisher, although he also sought the opinion of experts, and he was an interventionist editor. The *Systems* bears the impress of those qualities.

When Morgan brought the 1865 version to Washington in April, Henry's position was awkward. He had encouraged Morgan in his researches and materially aided them over the previous five years. The result of those researches, however, was a manuscript that promised to take up some 800 of the large quarto pages of the *Contributions to knowledge* series. At the best of times a project of this size would be a major undertaking. The cost of printing and paper had nearly doubled since before the Civil War, and he estimated that the *Systems* as submitted would cost at least $7,000 to publish.[2] To undertake a project of this size would absorb the entire publishing budget for a year, crowding out everything else. And it was not the best of times; the Smithsonian fire, for which there had been no insurance coverage, would require extensive rebuilding, and Congress proved unwilling to provide the needed funds. The cost of rebuilding would have to be met out of the endowment income, and publications would have to suffer.

Henry had been a professor at Princeton, and it was to Princeton that he turned for the members of a commission to pass judgment on Morgan's manuscript. Professor J. H. McIlvaine, Morgan's old

---

[1] See Thomas Coulson, *Joseph Henry, his life and work;* Arthur P. Molella et al., eds., *A Scientist in American life: essays and lectures of Joseph Henry;* Nathan Reingold, ed., *The papers of Joseph Henry;* and Leslie A. White, "The correspondence between Lewis Henry Morgan and Joseph Henry."

[2] Joseph Henry to Joshua Hall McIlvaine, 5/26/65, Smithsonian Institution Archives. Smithsonian budgets are published in the *Annual reports.*

friend and former pastor, was an obvious choice; his Smithsonian lectures had concerned themselves with the two preoccupations of Morgan's work—philology and ethnology. The other member was Professor William Henry Green, a Semiticist, who was especially to examine the materials that had been derived from the Orient.[3]

Henry was anxious that the value of Morgan's manuscript be fully established by a commission of experts before undertaking the heavy responsibility of publishing so expensive a work. He also wished the commission to recommend revisions, however, and to that end he laid out his own plan for the revision of the manuscript in a letter to McIlvaine.[4] The nub of his critique was that as it stood the 1865 version was not in the form of the *Contributions to knowledge,* in which the author confined his exposition of the subject to that part of it for which he had new findings to report; rather, it was like "systematic treatises or monographs of an entire subject." This was a constant theme of his, and he addressed it to Green and to Morgan on other occasions. For Henry, Morgan's contribution to knowledge lay in his American Indian material, and the Old World material was of interest not in itself but strictly as background and insofar as it subserved the question of Asiatic origin. The manuscript would require a major reorganization of the material, and leaving nothing to the imagination, Henry outlined his conception of a suitable form:

> *First* A brief statement of the causes which led to the investigation & the accidental discovery of the peculiar system of consanguinity of a particular Indian tribe & the inquiry whether it was adopted by others— the discovery of its general use by all the tribes on this continent, and the subsequent investigation as to whether anything of a similar character is to be found in other parts of the world. Under this head also a full account should be given of all the materials collected with an explanation of the tables.

> *Second* As introductory to the general subject of systems of consanguinity an account may be given of the Roman System, and that used by civilized nations of the present day, but since this is known matter it should be given with as much brevity as is compatible with clearness.

> *Third* A critical exposition in full of the American Indian System should next be given.

---

[3] Henry to William Henry Green, 12/6/65, Smithsonian Institution Archives.
[4] Henry to McIlvaine, 4/26/65, Smithsonian Institution Archives.

Fourth The systems adopted in other parts of the world should follow and,

Fifth A careful comparison should be presented of the whole—care being taken to avoid unnecessary repetition and undue prolixity.

Henry seems to have believed that the organization of the 1865 version, putting the American Indian matter last and giving equal treatment to Old World matter, displaced its true subject to the back of the book and filled the exposition with information that was not new and did not advance the object. He proposed, therefore, a major reordering of the core:

	1865 version	Henry's proposal
Part I:	Aryan, Semitic, Uralian	Roman, "that used by the civilized nations at the present day"
Part II:	Turanian, Malayan	American Indian
Part III:	American Indian	Systems adopted in other parts of the world

In December Henry again wrote McIlvaine to say that a visit from Morgan had shown him disposed to agree to changes in the manuscript that might reduce its bulk or improve its character, and asking him to consult with Green and report on the changes they thought desirable.[5] Having been so well prompted by Henry, the commissioners obliged by recommending, in effect, the changes Henry had originally proposed. Their report took the form of two letters to Henry in March 1866, one of them by Green and countersigned by McIlvaine, the other by McIlvaine, countersigned by Green.[6] Green's letter essentially endorses Morgan's claim to have found a method superior to philology in showing ancient genealogical relations among peoples and in having proved the unity and Asiatic origin of the American Indians. McIlvaine's letter is supplementary to Green's, with numbered points in respect of the problem of revision. McIlvaine says that all the various departments of the subject found in the 1865 version should be retained, especially the Turanian sys-

---

[5] Henry to McIlvaine, 12/6/65, Smithsonian Institution Archives.

[6] Green to Henry, 3/14/66; McIlvaine to Henry, 3/29/66, Smithsonian Institution Archives.

tems, which "are hardly less important contributions to the science of Ethnology than that of the American Indians." The tables should be published as they are, without abridgment. The arrangement, however, should very nearly follow that which Henry had sketched. McIlvaine's proposed order for the *Systems,* in essence, is as follows:

1. Statement of the causes which led to the investigation
2. Indo-European system, taking the Roman as the typical system
3. Ganowánian or American Indian System
4. The Turanian System, taking the Tamil as typical
5. The Malayan System, taking the Hawaiian as typical
6. General results and conclusions
7. Other evidence of the unity of race and migrations of the American Indians

Thus McIlvaine endorsed the reorganization of the core that Henry had proposed, putting American Indians before the Turanian and Malayan part. He did not endorse reducing the Indo-European material to a single, Roman case, but he did propose a "type case" method of exposition that would reduce the length of the text. The purpose was to abbreviate the elaborate method of "description by lines" that Morgan employed throughout the 1865 version. This involved exposition of the terms constituting the "lineal line" passing through *Ego,* followed by exposition of five collateral lines in turn: the first collateral line commencing with the brother and sister and composed of them and their lineal descendants; the second collateral line commencing with the parent's siblings; the third collateral line commencing with the grandparents' siblings; and the fourth and fifth collateral lines commencing with the siblings of the great-grand-parents and of the great-great-grandparents. This stategy of exposition was modeled on that of the Roman jurists. It was also very lengthy, not to say tedious. McIlvaine's proposal was to confine this method of exposition to select typical cases (and a few exceptional ones), other cases to be "exhibited in those particulars only in which they differ from the typical form."

Henry concurred in these suggested changes—as well he might, considering that he had inspired most of them.[7] On 21 April 1866

---

[7] Henry to McIlvaine, 4/21/66, Smithsonian Institution Archives.

he wrote Morgan, forwarding copies of Green and McIlvaine's reports and commending to him the suggested changes in the manuscript Morgan had submitted almost exactly one year previous.[8]

Morgan responded at length in a letter of 12 May.[9] He was gratified with Professor Green's report, that "this new instrument for Ethnological investigation possesses 'more penetrative power than the grammatical structure of language.'" He reluctantly agreed to place the American Indian system in Part II: "It violates the natural order of the subject, but has undoubtedly compensating advantages." He agreed to make the suggested introductory explanation, though this would be an additional chapter. In order to reduce the first part, "on our own system," he proposed to rewrite the whole, except the first two chapters. He adopted the type case method of exposition, using Roman as typical; the description by lines would be reserved for type cases and a few exceptional cases, the descriptions of other cases being confined to divergences from the typical.

Morgan completed the revision of Part I and posted it to Henry on 29 October. He explains the changes he had made:[10]

> The first Chapter is new, and consequently additional; the second has been rewritten and reduced; the third, on the Roman system, I found I could neither reduce nor improve, and it is therefore the same as before, with the exception of a few erasures; the fourth, fifth and sixth have been rewritten, and reduced as much as they could be consistently with a statement of the necessary facts to sustain the conclusions I wished to draw from identity of forms. The last chapter, on "the growth of nomenclatures of Relationship" has been suppressed, except the most material portions, which have been condensed into two notes and transferred to chapter fourth.

The changes in Part I may be diagrammed thus:

---

[8] Henry to Morgan, 4/21/66, Smithsonian Institution Archives. "I regret that I am unable to say, in the present state of our finance, when the work can be put to press; but as the publication of such contributions as that which you have presented, is in my opinion one of the most important features of the establishment, an effort will constantly be made to provide means for carrying on this part of our active operations." Morgan appears to have taken this as a commitment to publish the manuscript, after the required changes had been made, when finances permitted. He was mistaken.

[9] Morgan to Henry, 5/12/66, Smithsonian Institution Archives.

[10] Morgan to Henry, 10/29/66, Smithsonian Institution Archives.

	1865 Version		1867 Version
Chap. I.	General observations upon systems of relationship	Chap. I.	Introduction
Chap. II.	Roman	Chap. II.	General observations upon systems of relationship
Chap. III.	Other stems of the Aryan family	Chap. III.	Roman
Chap. IV.	Semitic family	Chap. IV.	Other stems of the Aryan family (including notes on growth of nomenclatures of relationship)
Chap. V.	Uralian family	Chap. V.	Semitic family
Chap. VI.	Growth of nomenclatures of relationship	Chap. VI.	Uralian family

He had not found it possible to follow Henry's recommendations fully:

> It was a part of your original suggestion that after the Roman form was presented I should pass at once to the American Indians, and afterwards return to, and present the system of the remaining Aryan, Semitic and Uralian nations. I have tried to devise some arrangement by which this could be done, but cannot find any natural and proper way to do it. The descriptive system is subordinate, and chiefly important to fix the ethnic boundaries between it and the classificatory. It is also important to show the permanence of systems of relationship considered as domestic institutions. A preliminary knowledge of the descriptive system is further useful, and, to some extent, indispensable to the appreciation of the classificatory. The time spent upon it is an excellent preparation for understanding what follows. As the preponderating amount of the materials relate to the classificatory system, and as this when taken up will hold uninterruptedly to the end of the work, there can be no recurrence to the descriptive form without violating the order of the subject, and compressing the materials to be discussed.

Morgan had completed the revision of Parts II and III by 21 February 1867, though (for reasons that will shortly be explained) he did not send them to Henry until 25 July.[11] In his letter of that date he states that he has rewritten the whole of Part II except portions of Chapters I and III, and the whole of Part III except the chapter on the Unclassified Asiatic nations. This rewriting did not, on the whole, change the order of presentation except for the inversion of Parts II and III between the manuscript of 1865 and the final version. Comparison of the two—indeed, of the 1865 table of contents given in the previous chapter with the published *Systems*— shows that the number, substance, and order of chapters is the same, except that the order of Parts II and III has been inverted, putting the American Indian systems in the second place, the Turanian and Malayan after them. The extensive rewriting of which Morgan speaks, therefore, touches only the manner of presentation. He specifies that in accordance with the suggestion of the committee, he found it better "to take out the description by lines and substitute the indicative relationships." He did so willingly: "This method will have the great advantage of showing the positive elements of the system. It is done, in each case, on less than half a page of M.S. and is more effective than a description by lines."

To sum up, the changes described represent a compromise between the conflicting visions of Henry and Morgan, in which conflict the commission—that is, McIlvaine's letter—served as a mediator rather than a distinct third force. Henry's conception of scientific writing was that of a physicist, for whom contributions to knowledge were made within the context of a paradigm that was well understood and that might be taken as given, and for whom the comprehensive treatise was an inferior species. For kinship no such paradigm existed, however; Morgan was in fact inventing it, building it from the ground up. In so doing his project was, in fact, larger than its ostensible theme, that of Indian unity and Asiatic origin. It needed the global reach and philosophical character he gave it even though, as Henry's critique acutely observes, its supposed central theme is pushed to the

---

[11] Morgan to Henry, 2/21/67 and 7/25/67, Smithsonian Institution Archives. In the first of these letters he voiced his impatience and apprehension of being forestalled by McLennan: "I must now make it my constant effort to see this work published until it is accomplished. It is absolutely necessary that I should be relieved from it, and turn my attention to other matters. For nearly nine years I have given to this subject almost my entire time: and it will demand more or less of my time until it is printed. It is also necessary for another reason, lest I should be forestalled in some of its conclusions. This has already occurred, as to one or two points, by McLennan's work on Primitive Marriages." See chapter 10, this book.

back of the book. In order to be able to make kinship visible, Morgan had to view it as a whole. We have seen how difficult it was even to perceive Iroquois kinship and how necessary to that first perception an explicit comparison with familiar kinship categories had been. After the *Systems* it would be possible to write contributions to knowledge in the newly defined field, and indeed Fison and Howitt would do so shortly; but the *Systems* itself had to have a wider scope in order to define the field for the first time, a scope that comprehended the systems of consanguinity both of the anthropologist and the savage whose relation to himself he sought to understand.

Thus Henry's fears that Morgan's book was a mere treatise "unnecessarily increased by old matter" were misplaced, and Morgan was right to compromise their differences by conceding what did not touch his central purpose, such as inverting the order of Parts II and III to put the American Indians in the middle of the book, but standing fast on essentials, such as the need for a full treatment of Aryan, Semitic, and Uralian systems in Part I rather than a brief exposition of the Roman system as baseline for the exposition of the American Indian system. It is tempting to say that Morgan responded to Henry's criticisms with changes that affected only the manner of presentation but protected his original vision of the work. That, however, would put the outcome of their conflict far too negatively. For in responding to the demand to shorten the manuscript Morgan was forced to become more analytical and to resort to the analysis of kinship terminologies into "indicative features" that he had already had to devise for his circular letters rather than the "description by lines." Morgan was something of a naive empiricist, believing that his tables spoke for themselves and that he had only to describe his data for the reader to see in them the truths that were apparent to him. The requirement to abridge forced him in the direction of abstraction of features from the data. It was the beginning, in fact, of kinship analysis. Both Morgan and his readers are indebted to Henry's insistence on this point.

This is not the sum of Henry's effect upon the *Systems,* for he had then to edit the 1867 version for press, and we find in the manuscript considerable crossings-out that are certainly his doing. More particularly, he forced three further changes on Morgan. The first of these was the vetoing of the dedication. Morgan wished to dedicate the book to the memory of his daughters, who had died while he was on his last field trip, and to include a vignette of the family mausoleum he had built to inter their remains in Mount Hope Cemetery. This was an issue of great delicacy, and Henry handled it tactfully but firmly: "Though your feelings are natural and do honor to your heart, yet the work itself is one exclusively of the intellect, and would suffer in reputation by being connected with anything of an emotional character."[12] "It would not be consistent with the usages of Scientific Institutions to introduce anything of the kind in a Memoir of its Transactions."[13]

The second change Henry imposed concerned the rendering of diagrams. In one of these Morgan had superimposed a genealogical chart upon the figure of a Corinthian column. For Henry, "the diagram is not the illustration of a physical structure, but of an ideal system. I never have myself fancied the 'genealogical trees,' in which relationships are exhibited by gnarled oaks and crooked branches."[14] On another occasion Morgan submitted a genealogical diagram in which the lines were tied up in a bow at the top, similar to a diagram in Blackstone. Henry responded with a lecture on the aesthetics of science:[15]

> We do not agree with you as to the propriety of a loop at the top of the diagram which will involve the necessity of a special woodcut. The illustration is not a picture supposed to be hung against the wall, but a simple conventional diagram on the page of the book to assist in a ready conception of the system of relationship and any idea foreign to this in regard to it is irrelevant. Adventitious ornament is, we think, a vice of our country. While writing this there are now before us, two maps, one published in Germany and the other in the United States: the first is surrounded with a plain trim border in which the degrees of latitude and longitude alone are conspicuous; the other is bordered with a broad decorated meretricious embellishment having no relation to the map and tending to distract the attention.

The third point of some moment concerned the projected Part IV. The original conception may be seen in the 1865 table of contents given in the previous chapter (figure 6). It was to open with chapters devoted to the geography of North America and Morgan's theory, based on that geography, of the migration route of the American

---

[12] Henry to Morgan, 3/21/68, Smithsonian Institution Archives.
[13] Henry to Morgan, 12/6/67; see also 5/27/70, Smithsonian Institution Archives.
[14] Henry to Morgan, 4/29/68, Smithsonian Institution Archives.
[15] Henry to Morgan, 6/11/68, Smithsonian Institution Archives.

Indians. This theory, in brief, was that the Indian tribes had spread across the continent from the valley of the Columbia River in the Pacific Northwest, which was the principal point of diffusion, and that they had come to the Columbia from the Amur River basin in east Asia via the Aleutian chain. Part IV continued with chapters on Indian "domestic institutions" that, by virtue of their universality among the Indians, were further proofs of Indian unity parallel with the existence of a single system of relationship, and a chapter on architecture and agriculture. These matters had not been written up and submitted with the 1865 version, but drafts of the various chapters are preserved in the Morgan Papers and the correspondence makes it clear that Morgan intended to add something along these lines up to the last minute. In April 1870 Henry definitively ended his hopes that a last, shrunken vestige of Part IV, now reduced to a proposal to include an appendix on Indian migrations, could be included in the book.[16] Henry was able to decline on grounds that Morgan by that time had already published his theory in the *North American review,* among other venues. This was surely the right decision, and elements of the Part IV that was to have been were published elsewhere. It is well to know, however, that for Morgan there was an essential continuity between his work on systems of relationship on the one hand and his interests in Indian naming practices, dance, architecture, and the like on the other. All of them, he believed, were parallel proofs of the essential sameness of Indian life and hence of their historical unity. For Morgan, indeed, the whole of the ethnological venture was a continuation of philology by other means.

More profound by far than the effect of Joseph Henry upon the *Systems* was that of what we may call "McIlvaine's suggestion." For although Henry's demands wrought changes in presentation and promoted the use of analytic devices, they did not touch the interpretation of the data. McIlvaine's suggestion, on the contrary, caused Morgan to rethink his interpretation of the descriptive/classificatory dichotomy completely.

Morgan acknowledges McIlvaine's contribution in a note: "I am indebted to my learned friend, Rev. Dr. J. H. McIlvaine, Prof. of

---

[16] Morgan to Henry, 3/21/70 and 4/2/70, describe the material as an appendix of three sections and a map; Henry to Morgan, 4/8/70, declines to publish. Smithsonian Institution Archives.

Political Science in the College of New Jersey, for the suggestion of a probable solution of the origin of the classificatory system upon the basis of the Hawaiian custom."[17] This "probable solution" and the global interpretation to which it gives rise is what I have called the "conjectural history of the family" interpretation. Morgan exactly, if briefly, specifies McIlvaine's suggestion, but a certain amount of confusion has come about as to its precise nature owing to an error in Resek's biography. Much recent scholarship takes Resek's treatment of this question as authoritative; thus it will be necessary to examine it in some detail.

Resek identified McIlvaine's suggestion with the substance of a letter he wrote Morgan on 3 March 1864.[18] It is important to note that this was well before the 1865 version—of which McIlvaine was a reader for the Smithsonian—was completed.

> I have just lighted upon certain references, which throw some light upon the origin of your Tamilian or Indian system of relationship; at least of some parts of it. You remember we were talking about whether it did not point back to a state of promiscuous intercourse. You will find in Aristotle's Politics, Book II chap 3, where he is refuting Platos doctrine of a community of wives, this sentence, "Some tribes in upper Africa have their wives in common;["] and in a note in Bohn's Translation of it, the following references, "For example, the Nasimanes (Herodotus IV, 172) and the Aysenses (Ib. iv,180) and the Agathyrsi (Ib. iv,104); also the Garamantes (Pom. Mela I,8, and Pliny Nat. Hist. v.8)
> With respect to the Agathyrsi Herodotus says, "They have their wives in common, that so they may be all brothers (kasignetoi) and being all akin, may be free from envy & mutual enmities."
> I am inclined to think that this state of society might, upon a full & minute investigation of the remains of antiquity, be found more extensively to have prevailed than is commonly supposed.

According to Resek, Morgan pondered McIlvaine's suggestion for three years, and had not McLennan been establishing his priority in the field he might have withheld it longer. Then, in May 1867, "Morgan accomplished his most startling intellectual feat."[19] He hurriedly wrote a paper, "A conjectural solution of the origin of the

---

[17] *Systems*, p. 479 fn.
[18] Resek, *Morgan, American scholar*, pp. 93–97. McIlvaine to Morgan, 3/3/64, Morgan Papers.
[19] Resek, *Morgan, American scholar*, p. 97.

classificatory system of relationship," which was thereafter delivered before the American Academy of Arts and Sciences in Boston (11 February 1868) and, with Joseph Henry's blessing, published in its proceedings.[20] The paper constituted a conjectural history of family types from the sexual promiscuity of the primitive horde—the zero of the case—through fifteen stages of evolution to the modern monogamous family. These different family types were taken to be the causes of the different systems of relationship, and their existence was inferred from the structuring of those systems—that is, from the mergers of kin. The final manuscript version of the *Systems* included a disquisition on the evolution of the family in the concluding chapter.

In addition to its inherent implausibility, this reconstruction does not accord with the facts. Morgan makes it clear that McIlvaine's suggestion concerned not the "state of promiscuous intercourse" of the 1864 letter but of what he calls "the Hawaiian custom." Other testimony of both parties (as I shall hereinafter relate) further shows that McIlvaine's knowledge of "the Hawaiian custom" came from reading the last chapter of Part II of Morgan's 1865 version while he was reviewing the manuscript for the Smithsonian. His "suggestion" consisted of showing how the Hawaiian custom might explain the origin of the classificatory system—the unresolved puzzle of Morgan's last chapter. He subsequently wrote Morgan offering his suggestion, and, on 20 November 1866 during a visit to Rochester, he made his interpretation of the causes of the classificatory system the subject of a lecture before the Club. The letter has not survived but the paper for the Club has, and it bears close examination. Morgan took up his friend's suggestion and elaborated it into the "conjectural history of the family" interpretation which he worked into the 1867 version of the *Systems*. There is nothing to the theory of a three-year delay between McIlvaine's suggestion and Morgan's response.

Nevertheless, Resek's view has the merit of drawing attention to the fairly early point at which McIlvaine took an active interest in Morgan's problem of accounting for the existence of the classificatory system. This interest begins in the earlier discussions of a state of promiscuous intercourse as possible origin, to which the 3 March 1864 letter refers, and continues as late as McIlvaine's 20 November 1866 talk before the Club, in which "the Hawaiian custom" is the

---

[20] Morgan, "A conjectural solution of the origin of the classificatory system of relationship"; Henry to Morgan, 3/24/68, Smithsonian Institution Archives.

interpretive nutcracker, a good three years and, moreover, the very period in which the two versions of the *Systems* were being formulated. Furthermore, a penciled note of Morgan's in the Morgan Papers indicates a third intervention of McIlvaine upon the problem of the origin of the classificatory system, that of polygamy and polyandria, a proposal that is logically and chronologically intermediate between the other two. Thus we can distinguish at least three phases in McIlvaine's contribution to Morgan's interpretation of the classificatory system.

In order to elucidate these different proposals and Morgan's reaction to them it will be useful to resort to a diagram (figure 10). The classificatory system was composed of three families and their type cases: Ganowánian (Iroquois), Turanian (Tamil), and Malayan (Hawaiian). All three showed a tendency to merge collateral with lineal relationships; but for the Iroquois and Tamil, only some of the collaterals were so merged, whereas in the Hawaiian all or nearly all were merged. The diagram illustrates the classifications for relatives of the parents' generation as Morgan conceived them. (Comparable classifications are made in ego's and in the children's generations.) It was the similarity and oddity of the semantic patterning in the Iroquois and Tamil cases that was the hub around which Morgan's great project turned. We have no record of Morgan's response to McIlvaine's 1864 letter, but the absence of reference in the 1865 version to its substance or to the "state of promiscuous intercourse" hypothesis the two had discussed requires us to suppose that Morgan did not believe that the answer to the problem of origins lay here. Promiscuity or "community of wives" at best could be thought to lead to a situation in which all parents' generation kin would be mothers and fathers. This would explain only the Malayan pattern, but the peculiarities of the central pattern represented by the agreement of Tamil and Iroquois would be untouched. Promiscuity would be revived as a first stage to account for the Malayan pattern, but only later, after Morgan had adopted a different explanation for the Turanian and American Indian pattern. This, then, was the first of McIlvaine's three contributions (although we do not know whose suggestion—McIlvaine's or Morgan's—primitive promiscuity originally was); and although it was ultimately adopted by Morgan and integrated into his conjectural history of the family, it was at first (that is, in the 1865 version) without effect.

The second of McIlvaine's contributions, however, did show up in the 1865 version. In a series of penciled notes to himself, in which

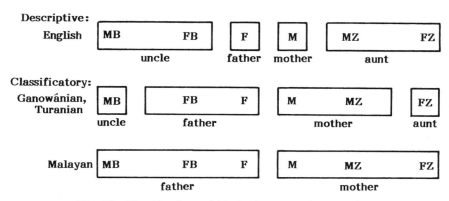

Fig. 10. Classifications of kin in the parents' generation.

Morgan recorded a numbered list of improvements to be implemented in the 1865 version, the third item reads, "III. Polygamy &
polyandria D^r M thinks if these could be made a probable explanation of the origin of the system it would be better thus to account
for it."[21] This hypothesis—or, rather, a special case of it—made up
the deficiencies of the "state of promiscuity" case. If as a result of
my father's having married two or more *sisters* I called these women
my mothers, the merger typical of the Iroquois and Tamil cases
would be accounted for by a cause that did not also affect the father's
sister. Similarly, "polyandria" among *brothers* could account for
the fact of my father and his brothers being equally fathers, without
also merging the relationship of the mother's brother. Thus the
specific character of Iroquois and Tamil, and not Hawaiian, mergers
was accounted for by the hypothesis so modified. Morgan discussed
it in the 1865 version (that is, the hypothesis of sororal polygyny
and fraternal polyandry as we would say) but dismissed it as an
originating cause for want of universality, as we have seen; the
argument is carried over into the published version. McIlvaine's third
contribution was similar in formal properties but plowed the same
furrow more deeply.

It was after McIlvaine had read the 1865 version, containing the
critique of the polygamy and polyandria theory just mentioned, that
he came up with the suggestion that was to be decisive for Morgan.
It is probable that he alludes to it in a letter to Joseph Henry of 28
April 1865, written shortly after Morgan had submitted the manu-

---

[21] *Ancient society* drafts, Morgan Papers, pp. 1023–1025. Other items on the list
are clearly implemented in the 1865 version.

script and the Smithsonian had referred it to McIlvaine for review. McIlvaine says,[22]

> I am already nearly, or quite, half through the M.S.; and will try to perform the duty you have assigned me in a thorough & consciencious manner. Having been acquainted with Mr. Morgan's labors from the beginning & through out their progress, I have no doubt but that the work contains a valuable contribution to knowledge. Indeed his results lead to new ethnological conclusions, which even he has not anticipated; and which will, I think, afford a more satisfactory explanation of the superior life of the Aryan & Semitic families, and of the inferiority of the Turanean, than any before known. I am in correspondence with him upon some of these.

Half the 1865 manuscript would take McIlvaine through Part II— that is, through the Tamil and Hawaiian material that provide elements of his suggested solution. The correspondence with Morgan of which he speaks here has not survived, but in the Morgan Papers we do have McIlvaine's paper delivered before the Club on 20 November 1866, which gives a full-blown exposition of his solution.[23]

McIlvaine's paper draws attention to information on the Hawaiian relationship of *punalua* in Morgan's 1865 manuscript. This relationship obtains between the spouses of a pair of brothers or of a pair of sisters; that is, for ego a male, my wife's sister's husband is my *punalua,* and for ego a female, my husband's brother's wife is my *punalua* (the term being self-reciprocal). Judge Lorrin Andrews, one of Morgan's informants on the Hawaiian terminology, explained that the relationship arose from the former custom of brothers and their wives, or sisters and their husbands, being inclined "to possess each other in common." Another correspondent, the Rev. Mr. Bishop, a missionary, confirmed the theory: "This confusion of relationships is the result of the ancient custom among relations of the living together of husbands and wives in common."[24] Thus the sup-

---

[22] McIlvaine to Henry, 4/28/65, Smithsonian Institution Archives.

[23] McIlvaine, "The organisation of society," MS. (The Club, 11/20/66), Morgan Papers. Elisabeth Tooker was the first to draw attention to the significance of this paper: Comment on "The mind of Lewis H. Morgan" by Elman R. Service in *Current Anthropology* (1981). See also Trautmann, "Decoding Dravidian kinship: Morgan and McIlvaine."

[24] See *Systems*, p. 453 fn., item 26, quoting Judge Andrews: "The relationship of *pinalua* [*sic*] is rather amphibious. It arose from the fact that two or more brothers, with their wives, or two or more sisters with their husbands, were inclined

posed "Hawaiian custom" that brothers had their wives in common and sisters, their husbands.

McIlvaine then considered "what would actually be the result upon relationships of this social custom," and he looked to the "Turanean System, that which Mr. Morgan discovered first among the American Indians"; in fact his type case is the Tamil, representing the Turanian family, and the classificatory system generally.

Upon the hypothesis that such a social custom (McIlvaine does not call it a form of marriage but "a promiscuous intercourse") prevailed in the Turanian group, many features of the (Tamil) kinship terminology can be accounted for. It would explain, for example, the fact that the brothers of a father are fathers to all his children, and he a father to the children of all his brothers, as "all these brothers cohabit with all the mothers of these children; hence are indiscriminately fathers to them all." Conversely, all the brothers of a mother are uncles to her children, and she is an aunt to the children of all her brothers. "The reason of this is that brothers & sisters do not cohabit together; consequently, they cannot be fathers & mothers to each others children." Nevertheless, McIlvaine does recognize that within the classificatory system there are a number of cases (falling in Morgan's Malayan family, which, *nota bene,* includes Hawaiian) in which this latter characteristic does not appear; that is, the relationships of uncle and aunt are absent (so that *all* ones parents' siblings are fathers and mothers). "This would seem to indicate that in these cases, even brothers and sisters cohabited together, the same as brothers with their sisters-in-law, according to the unmodified Turanean System." This exception aside, McIlvaine extends the argument from the "Hawaiian custom" to most of the numbered "indicative features" that Morgan has specified for Tamil, features of a kind that are now often called "bifurcate-merging." By McIlvaine's reckoning, thirty-one of Morgan's forty-four features of Turanian (that is, Tamil) are explained by the hypothesis of this kind of intercourse—presumably in the past, because it is not directly attested.

Of the remaining thirteen traits, three or four are explained "by a slight extension of the hypothesis i.e. the cohabitation of cousins." These cousins are cross cousins within the meaning of the act; they

---

to possess each other in common; but the modern use of the word is that of *dear friend,* an intimate companion." See also *Systems,* p. 457. Alexander Spoehr has written about these informants in "Lewis Henry Morgan and his Pacific collaborators."

are those Tamil or Dravidian kinship categories for which Morgan asserts that *cousin* is the correct English translation, and they include the mother's brother's and the father's sister's children. The Hawaiian custom explains the fact that for ego male, the children of my brothers are my children, since brothers "cohabit with each others wives," and that for ego female, the children of my sisters are my children, since "all the children have the same fathers." So, too, "all the children of several brothers are brothers and sisters to each other, because these brothers cohabit with each others wives, and the children have the same fathers indistinguishably." What of cross cousins, however, and their children? The supposition that "promiscuous intercourse may be extended to that between cousins . . . would give a full explanation of the reason why ego male, I call the children of my female cousins my children, and why ego female, I call the children of my male cousin, my children"—features in which the Tamil classifications differ from those of the Iroquois, and which Morgan in the 1865 manuscript of the *Systems* had found odd and inexplicable.[25] Other peculiarities of the Dravidian system are similarly explained by McIlvaine, who explicitly regards them as irregularities or modifications of the system (whose norm is Morgan's Seneca example).

McIlvaine's suggestion was, in effect, two separate putative causes of the Tamil system, the supposed Hawaiian custom and cross cousin marriage which he considered a "slight extension" of the former. The Hawaiian custom is a very doubtful piece of goods, and there is reason to question whether such a thing ever existed. Morgan's sources speak of it as a former custom, reporting it not as something they have observed in the present but as an interpretation of the causes of, as we might say, the equivalence of same-sex siblings' spouses under the self-reciprocal term *punalua*. It may be the creature of pure theorizing; in any case modern authorities deny it.[26] Cross

---

[25] See *Systems*, p. 391: "It is a little singular that the children of my male cousin, *Ego* a male, should be my nephews and nieces, instead of my sons and daughters, and that the children of my female cousins should be my sons and daughters instead of my nephews and nieces, as required by the analogies of the system. It is the only particular in which it differs materially from the Seneca-Iroquois form; and in this the Seneca is more in logical accordance with the principles of the system than the Tamilian. It is difficult to find any explanation of the variance."

[26] Mary Kawena Pukui and Samuel H. Elvert, *Hawaiian dictionary*, s.v. *punalua*; E. S. Craighill Handy and Mary Kawena Pukui, *The Polynesian family system in Ka'u, Hawai'i*, pp. 60–65.

cousin marriage, by contrast, very definitely does exist among Dravidians and is crucial to the understanding of their kinship terminology. McIlvaine found substantiation of its existence in Morgan's manuscript, which refers to the marriage of cousins among the Karen; but for all practical purposes he made it up out of thin air, years before it even had a name.[27] Lévi-Strauss has said that if cross cousin marriage did not exist, anthropologists would have invented it;[28] McIlvaine had indeed done so nearly a century previous. One cannot but regret that Morgan's reaction was to embrace the first of McIlvaine's suggestions and all but bury the second.

Morgan adopted McIlvaine's partial recognition of the cross cousin rule in such a manner as to minimize and obscure its significance in relation to the terminology as a whole. The sole passage of the *Systems* that recalls McIlvaine's argument on this point is as follows:[29]

All the children of my male cousins, myself a male, are my nephews and nieces; and all the children of my female cousins are my sons and daughters.

Such is the classification amongst the Dravidian nations of South India. Unless I cohabit with all my female cousins, and am excluded from cohabitation with the wives of all my male cousins, these relationships cannot be explained from the nature of descents. In the Ganowánian family this classification is reversed; the children of my male cousins, myself a male, are my sons and daughters, and of my female cousins are my nephews and nieces. These are explainable from the principles, and from the analogy of the systems. It is a singular fact that the deviation upon these relationships is the only one of any importance between the Tamil and the Seneca-Iroquois, which in all probability has a logical explanation of some kind. If it is attributable to the slight variation upon the privilege of barbarism above indicated [that is, the cohabitation of

---

[27] On the Karen, McIlvaine refers to material from Francis Mason quoted in *Systems* (see pp. 443–444, n.): "In the matter of marriages the rule among the Karens is diametrically opposite to that among the American Indians. Marriages must always, among the Karens, be contracted by relations. First cousins marry, but that is deemed undesirably near. Second cousins are considered the most suitable matches, but third cousins may marry without impropriety, though that is considered undesirably remote. Beyond third cousins marriages are forbidden. These rules are not carried out very strictly, but sufficiently so to produce a weakly people, owing to the intermarriages of near relations."

[28] Claude Lévi-Strauss, *The elementary structures of kinship*, p. 144.

[29] *Systems*, p. 486.

cross cousins as a variation upon the Hawaiian custom] a singular solution of the difference in the two systems is thereby afforded.

Here as in McIlvaine it is a question of cohabitation and not of marriage; it is additionally a wholesale cohabitation. It is also an explanation of the *difference* of Tamil from the Seneca-Iroquois pattern, taken to be the norm, in respect of a *single* feature. And the point is so tentatively and ambiguously put as to make scarcely any impression upon the reader.

It was, rather, upon the Hawaiian custom that Morgan raised the edifice of his conjectural history of the family.

Resek suggests that Morgan did not work up his conjectural history of the family until May 1867—shortly before he submitted the final version of Parts II and III to Joseph Henry, as he states in his letter to Henry of 25 July. An implication of this theory is that Part I, which had been submitted the previous October, was innocent of the conjectural history interpretation. We are led to think, indeed, that the conjectural history interpretation of the data was a more or less self-contained bit added to the 1867 version at the last minute. My reading of the evidence is quite different. McIlvaine's paper delivered before the Club in November 1866 was not Morgan's first knowledge of his friend's theory; Morgan's narrative of these events in a letter to Henry speaks of McIlvaine having corresponded with Morgan about the solution of the classificatory system, and the context leads us to conclude that he did so at the time of his first reading of the 1865 version, as McIlvaine's letter to Henry, cited earlier, tends to confirm.[30] Morgan's account of the effect of McIlvaine's suggestion is so revealing that I quote it at length:[31]

> In the final chapter I have added a conjectural solution of the origin of the classificatory system. It is founded upon the assumption of the existence, in the primitive ages, of a series of customs and institutions, commencing with Promiscuous Intercourse, and followed by the Intermarriage or Cohabitation of Brothers & Sisters, the Communal Family, and the Tribal Organization. These together furnish the solution. Afterwards, as the growth of the ages, and of mans experience, came marriage between single pairs, then the Patriarchal Family through Polygamy, and

---

[30] See note 22.
[31] Morgan to Henry, 7/25/67, Smithsonian Institution Archives.

last of all the true family through Property and the establishment of lineal succession to estates. In the same chapter, as originally sent, I considered the probable influence upon the formation of the system of the Bond of Kin, as a means of mutual protection, of the tribal relationships, and of polygamy and polyandria, all of which I found insufficient to explain the origin of the system from the nature of descents; although I found that the last two would explain, more or less directly, several of the indicative relationships.

After Dr McIlvaine had read this chapter he took it up on the basis of the Hawaiian custom described in the previous chapter, which is a broad form of polygynia and polyandria united, and sent me a solution of the origin of the system on the basis of this custom. While this custom alone is insufficient to do this, it enabled me to find the remainder of the causes, which, if assumed, would afford a complete solution of the origin of the system from the nature of descents, showing the relationships to be those which actually existed. These are 1. Promiscuous Intercourse & 2. the Intermarriage of Brothers and Sisters. Together, or rather the last, explains the origin of the Malayan system, as the first state of the classificatory. After this the tribal organization, which broke up the cohabitation of brothers and sisters proved sufficient to explain the origin of that part of the system which is distinctively Turanian. Although the series is in part hypothetical, if it will explain the origin of the system in its two great stages of development, the Malayan and the Turanian, given the Turanian system the antecedent existence of these customs and institutions may be inferred with a strong degree of probability. This solution is given in full under proposition IV. in the final chapter, commencing with sheet 11. Dr. McIlvaine's suggestions proved to be of great value. It is by far the most important result yet reached by this investigation.

McIlvaine had taken the Hawaiian custom as an explanation for the Turanian system; but he could not then use it to explain the features in which the Hawaiian (Malayan) system differed from the Turanian, and suggested the cohabitation of brothers and sisters as cause on those points. There were none of the supposed effects of the Hawaiian custom in the Malayan system itself, however, and no evidence of its practice among the Turanians whose system of relationship was supposed to show its effects. This was hardly satisfactory, and that being so Morgan could not simply adopt McIlvaine's argument as it stood. But he thought he saw in it the key to a different solution if one read the argument backwards, finding in the Hawaiian custom one of the causes of the Malayan rather than the Turanian

system. We see this in the evolutionary stages he gives in the concluding chapter of *Systems*:[32]

    I. Promiscuous Intercourse.
    II. The Intermarriage or Cohabitation of Brothers and Sisters.
    III. The Communal Family. (First Stage of the Family.)
    IV. The Hawaiian Custom. Giving
    V. The Malayan form of the Classificatory System of
        Relationship.
    VI. The Tribal Organization. Giving
    VII. The Turanian and Ganowánian System of Relationship.
    VIII. Marriage between Single Pairs. Giving
    IX. The Barbarian Family. (Second Stage of the Family.)
    X. Polygamy. Giving
    XI. The Patriarchal Family. (Third Stage of the Family.)
    XII. Polyandria.
    XIII. The Rise of Property with the Settlement of Lineal Suc-
        cession to Estates. Giving
    XIV. The Civilized Family. (Fourth and Ultimate Stage of the
        Family.) Producing
    XV. The Overthrow of the Classificatory System of Relationship,
        and the Substitution of the Descriptive.

The whole process is one of a series of moral reforms, which put
increasingly narrow restraints upon the promiscuous intercourse of
the primitive state. In Morgan's argument the critical causative institutions are two: first "the intermarriage or cohabitation of brothers
and sisters" that accounts for the features of the Malayan system,
such as the unlimited scope of terms for father and mother (rather
than, as in McIlvaine's paper, accounting for only those features in
which Malayan departs from a Turanian norm), and second the
imposition upon this regime of the tribal organization (clan exogamy)
having the effect of bringing down a barrier against brother-sister
marriage but leaving intact the existing solidarity of brothers among
themselves and of sisters among themselves. Thus under brother-
sister marriage the father's brother is a father and so is the mother's
brother; but introduce the tribal organization and the mother's
brother can no longer be a father, because he may not marry the

---

[32] *Systems*, p. 480.

mother. Morgan here brings back under new auspices the "tribal" explanation he had attempted to give for the Seneca system of relationship long ago in the *League of the Iroquois*.

Where does the Hawaiian custom come into this apparently self-sufficient scheme? Its role is decidedly secondary in the *Systems*. Its importance is simply this: "The existence of this custom necessarily implies an antecedent condition of promiscuous intercourse, involving the cohabitation of brothers and sisters, and perhaps of parent and child," yet unlike these earlier evolutionary stages whose universal prevalence "rests upon an assumption," "The Hawaiian custom is neither a matter of conjecture nor of assumption. Traces of its prevalence were found by the American missionaries in the Sandwich Islands when they established their missions, and its antecedent universal prevalence amongst this people is unquestionable."[33] The Hawaiian custom is not an actor in these events but a witness.

Once this much of the evolutionary scheme was decided upon, the rest was more or less determined. The finished conjectural history of the family would have as many distinct stages as there were distinct systems of relationship to account for, and from which to decode them, the whole framed by the zero of primitive promiscuity and the zenith of monogamy. It was not Morgan's "most startling intellectual feat"; it was an intellectual house of cards. He had taken a bad idea and made it worse. The real question is not his source but his motivation. What attracted him to McIlvaine's suggestion in spite of all the bells and whistles he was obliged to add in order to make it work?

We see that motivation in the way in which the conjectural history of the family reworked Morgan's interpretation of the descriptive/ classificatory dichotomy. As we have seen, these categories were not just morphological types, they referred to the historic culture areas delimited by philology; they referred, in Morgan's intent, to the civilized and noncivilized peoples. The first "followed the nature of descents" and was a natural system; but the second did not and was artificial. The 1865 version made a virtue of this artificiality in its argument about the Asiatic origin of the Indians; but it was scarcely satisfactory to say, in effect, that savages were guided in this not by nature but by a kind of perverse intellection—in effect, by whim. McIlvaine's suggestion offered Morgan a way to renaturalize the savage. The origin of the classificatory system of the noncivilized was

---

[33] The same, pp. 480–481.

now "explained on the principle of natural suggestion, and the relationships proved to be in accordance with the nature of descents."[34]
The classificatory system was as natural as the descriptive. The difference lay elsewhere, in different family types.

As the conjectural history of the family returned the classificatory
system to nature, it temporalized the relation between the descriptive
and classificatory systems. In the 1865 version the descriptive system
represented the future for uncivilized peoples, the system "to which
all nations must inevitably gravitate if they seek to conform their
respective systems to the ultimate standard prescribed by the nature
of descents." Now a new dimension was added, and the classificatory
system became the past of the civilized nations, their prehistory. This
turning was no part of McIlvaine's original intent. Quite the contrary; for him the revolting Hawaiian custom explains "the permanent type of degradation and inferiority" characteristic of the peoples
whose system of relationship was classificatory, which is caused by
"breeding in & in," and likewise explains "the elevation and power
of the two great historic families of mankind, the Semitic and the
Aryan, among whom this system is not found."[35] Morgan rejected
the permanent degradation and inferiority of the cultural other;
contrary to McIlvaine's interpretation, he put the classificatory system in the Aryan, Semitic, and Uralian past. What had been in the
1865 version a kind of *tableau vivant* representation of civilization
versus nomadism is now turned into a story of progress.

The 1865 manuscript, returned to Morgan and used by him as the
basis for the draft of a revised version, bears the marks of the change
that had come over his thinking. The erasures and additions are not
many, but the change they implement is great. The names *natural*
and *artificial* systems of relationship in the titles of the three parts
are changed to *descriptive* and *classificatory*. The natural versus
artificial contrast in the text is downplayed or eliminated; *artificial*
is changed to *complicated*. The "arbitrary generalizations" of the
classificatory system is corrected to "seemingly arbitrary generalizations"—arbitrariness demoted to the rank of first impression. The
descriptive system, Morgan now recognizes, "proceeds upon the
assumption of the existence of the marriage relation," and the classi-

---

[34] The same, p. 480.

[35] McIlvaine, "The organisation of society," MS., Morgan Papers. McIlvaine's
funeral address makes it clear that finding the classificatory system to be *ancestral*
to the descriptive was purely Morgan's doing, one of his Newtonian achievements.

ficatory system "violates our more correct perceptions of the true
relations which consanginei sustain to each other," as Morgan said
in the 1865 version, adding above the line, "on the assumption that
mankind lived in single pairs in the married state."[36] It had been this
assumption, he now sees, that led him wrongly to think that the
classificatory system was artificial and the product of human intelligence rather than natural suggestion. In revising his text he need
only insert that proviso at each discussion of what is now an *apparent*
departure from nature of the classificatory system; at the conclusion
he would show, through the conjectural history of the family, that
that assumption was false. Thus much of the language of the 1865
version could be carried over into the 1867 revision with a very
small number of changes—which, nevertheless, profoundly altered
the interpretation.

The finding that savage sexuality lay in the past of the civilized
nations had about it the bitter taste of modern science in the age of
Darwin, and it is only natural that one should look to the *Origin of
species* (1859) for the source of the evolutionism that overtakes
Morgan's interpretation of the classificatory system. Indeed, in a
letter to Lorimer Fison of 30 September 1872 Morgan himself seems
to encourage us to do so. Fison had written, as to the cause of man's
cultural development, "where sceptical philosophers see only man's
power, I see and reverently acknowledge the finger of God." Morgan
replied,[37]

> I noticed your remarks upon the religious bearing of these investigations
> and respect your views. When Darwin's great work on the origin of
> species appeared I resisted his theory, and was inclined to adopt Agassiz's
> views of the permanence of species. For some years I stood in this
> position. After working up the results from consanguinity, I was com-
> pelled to change them, and to adopt the conclusion that "Man com-
> menced at the bottom of the scale," from which he worked himself up
> to his present status.

Nevertheless, on closer inspection the passage says quite the reverse:
the Darwinian theory was not the cause of Morgan's new interpreta-

[36] See especially *Systems* draft, Morgan Papers, Part III, Chap. VIII, "General
results," pp. 3–4/1495–1496.

[37] Fison to Morgan 5/27/72; Morgan to Fison 9/20/72, Morgan Papers. Quoted
in White, "Morgan's attitude toward religion and science," p. 224.

tion of kinship (the conjectural history of the family); rather, it was the study of kinship that overcame his resistance to Darwin. The letter contains an echo of the draft of his great work of social evolution, *Ancient society,* not published until 1877 but begun a couple of months before the Fison letter. A draft of the first chapter dated 18 July 1872 begins,

> Those who adopt the Darwinian theory of the descent of man from a quadruped, and those who, stopping short of this, adopt the theory of evolution, equally recognise the fact that man commenced at the bottom of the scale and worked his way up to civilization through the slow accumulations of experimental knowledge. That early state of man, on either alternative, was one of extreme rudeness and savagism, the precise conditions of which, though not wholly inconceivable, are difficult of apprehension.[38]

The reference to Darwin does not appear in the published version, and there is surely something in White's thesis that Morgan was inhibited from expressing allegiance to Darwin publicly by his friendship with McIlvaine. In any event the passage makes it clear that in Morgan's conception the Darwinian theory was but a special case of the theory of evolution. In his own view again the intellectual charter of the work he had just undertaken was the invention not of Darwin but of Horace and Lucretius, the latter above all, and he devoted the second chapter of the draft of *Ancient society* to an appreciation of the "Roman genesis of human development" as precursor of modern evolutionism.

The fact is that there is no evidence of the direct influence of Darwin on the *Systems,* and one must conclude that at best the influence was indirect. Morgan read and admired Darwin, certainly. He made a point of meeting him on his European travels (they lunched, very briefly, at Down) and the two were on terms of distant amiability thereafter, Morgan offering hospitality to Darwin's sons during a visit to the United States, Darwin mentioning Morgan's

---

[38] "Genesis of human development, original draft, July 18, 1872." *Ancient society* drafts, Morgan Papers. There are several versions of this statement, dated 1872 and 1873. Compare the opening paragraph of the published version (1877): "The latest investigations respecting the early condition of the human race, are tending to the conclusion that mankind commenced their career at the bottom of the scale and worked their way up from savagery to civilization through the slow accumulations of experimental knowledge," p. 3.

beaver book and his "Conjectural solution of the origin of the classificatory system of relationship" paper in the *Descent of man*.[39] None
of the ideas in the *Systems*—or in *Ancient society*, for that matter—is
distinctly Darwinian. There are no specific linkages between Darwin's ideas and Morgan's.

The vast scope of the changes wrought by the Darwinian revolution tends to obscure for us the other sources of evolutionism in the
1860s. Social evolution was not, in fact, a new element in Morgan's
thought arising now for the first time and for which we must find a
contemporary source. Morgan's thought had had a strong evolutionary theme in it—the "scale of mind" theme—all along, which was a
variant of a pre-Darwinian structure of thought that included the
scale of nature and scale of civilization ideas. The scale of mind
theme is present, though in a very restrained form, in the 1865
version with its underlying dichotomy of civilization and nomadism,
with its agricultural Aryans representing the future of the nomadic
Turanians and bow-and-arrow-wielding Ganowánians. And when
this evolutionism is elaborated in the 1867 version, Morgan's language deliberately locates his ideas within the tradition of the social
evolutionism of the Scottish Enlightenment.

In the chapter on the Iroquois language in the *League of the
Iroquois,* Morgan repeatedly refers to ideas, sometimes in direct
quotation, from a source that, because he does not name it, must
have been very well known to his readers. As we saw in chapter 3,
it is in fact Adam Smith's essay, "Considerations concerning the first
formation of languages, and the different genius of original and
compounded languages." In the nineteenth century, editions of
Smith's *Theory of the moral sentiments* included this essay as an
appendix and opened with a biographical sketch of Smith by Dugald
Stewart. In this sketch he gives the name "theoretical or conjectural
history" to the kind of reasoning contained in Smith's dissertation
on the formation of languages. It consists, in the "want of direct
evidence" on a particular question, of considering in what manner

---

[39] "Extracts from the European travel journal of Lewis Henry Morgan," edited
by Leslie A. White, entry for 9 June 1871 (pp. 338–339), describes the meeting.
Darwin's letter of invitation instructs him to take the 11:15 train for Orpington,
reaching Down a little after 12:30, lunch to be served at one o'clock in time to catch
the 2:40 train back to London. "It grieves me to propose so short a visit, but my
health has been very indifferent during the last week, & I am really incapable of
conversing with any one except for a short time." (Facsimile in the same, opposite
p. 341.)

men "are likely to have proceeded, from the principles of their nature, and in the circumstances of their external situation," a method he particularly commends for the study of the question "by what gradual steps the transition has been made from the first simple efforts of uncultivated nature, to a state of things so wonderfully artificial and complicated" as the "period of society in which we live."[40] It is to this idea of theoretical or conjectural history that Morgan alludes when he calls the scheme of evolution he worked up from McIlvaine's suggestion a *conjectural* solution of the classificatory system.

If, then, Morgan's thought had a social-evolutionary structure all along, the differences that separate the 1865 and the 1867 versions, which could be characterized as an intensification of its underlying evolutionism, will require a different explanation than has hitherto been ventured. I suggest the explanation lies in that other intellectual revolution that occurred more or less simultaneously with the Darwinian—namely, the revolution in what I have called ethnological time.

Years later, in *Ancient society* (1877), Morgan identified the time revolution, not Darwinism, as the most profound intellectual change his generation had undergone. Some thirty years before, in his "Essay on geology" (1841), he had favorably noticed the interpretation of Genesis that permitted a believer to accept a great antiquity for the earth, but the antiquity of man remained cramped within the short chronology of the Bible.[41] At what point did he abandon the short chronology? There is evidence to show that he did so between the writing of the 1865 and the 1867 versions of the *Systems*.

According to the table of contents (figure 9), the final chapter of the 1865 version has 71 manuscript pages, and indeed the text of the chapter in the Morgan Papers ends in the middle of the manuscript page numbered (by Morgan) 71. There are, however, three additional pages, numbered 72, 73, and 74, which must have been added after the manuscript was returned to Morgan by the Smithsonian. These additional pages concern the time revolution.[42]

---

[40] Dugald Stewart in Adam Smith, *Theory of the moral sentiments*, p. xxxiv–xxxv. On the Scottish tradition of social evolutionism see Ronald L. Meek, *Social science and the ignoble savage*.

[41] See chapter 2.

[42] *Systems* draft, Morgan Papers, Part III, Chap. VIII, "General results," pp. 72–74/1609–1611.

"The final results of this investigation," Morgan writes, "have some bearing upon the question of the Antiquity of man upon the earth."

> Upon this great and important question the most eminent scientific men of the present age have formed an opinion, which, from the weight of its authority, is destined to exercise a commanding influence in the future. It recognises a period of occupation by man much longer than any formerly entertained. Without establishing any precise epoch for mans first appearance upon the earth, he is made contemporaneous with the mastodon, and thus the present geological age is opened for him indefinitely backwards in the past. The time when his existence commenced may be measured by thousands, or tens of thousands, or hundreds of thousands of years, not to use the still higher measurements which more properly define geological ages. Each person is at liberty to adopt for himself such a scale of antiquity for man, as the evidence may lead him to adopt. This opinion assumes, on the part of most of those who entertain it, the unity of origin of the human family, and explains the varieties of the species, by the gradual operation of physical causes.

The passage goes on to argue that the age of the Aryan family, whose languages are closely related through "identity of vocables," must be more recent than others in the tables (a necessary step to the view that the classificatory system is also to be found in the Aryan past). Enough is known of the rate of divergence of unwritten languages to show that a moderate number of centuries would account for the present relative condition of these dialects before they were arrested in their development by writing. It is impossible to presume a history measured by "thousands upon thousands of years." The same goes for the Semitic family.

Contrarily, "upon the Asiatic continent the evidence from language indicates a higher antiquity of man." The Asiatic languages are more remotely related, through "grammatical affinities" rather than "identity of vocables," exceeding the antiquity of the Aryan or Semitic separately. Upon the North American continent the great number of stock-languages based on identity of vocables equals or exceeds that of the Asian languages. "They undoubtedly indicate the occupation of this continent by the Ganoánian family for several thousands of years, upon any scale of progress in the formation of dialects and stock-languages, which might reasonably be adopted." He concludes, "The real argument for the great antiquity of man upon the Earth rests upon the numbers of these stock-languages."

These pages of draft did not make it into the published version, and the *Systems* does not directly speak of the time revolution. Even in the early 1870s Morgan seems to have regarded the issue as a sensitive one. A draft passage of *Ancient society* written at that time is very telling: "Neither the ancients nor the moderns," he says, "until after geology had familiarized the mind with the prolonged existence of animal life upon the earth, and with the Aeons of Time consumed in the formation of the geological record, took any note of the necessarily great antiquity of man *which even yet must be mentioned with bated breath, and in cautious language.*"[43] Neverthe-less in this period he could confidently say, "the evidence of the antiquity of man is accumulating from year to year, and has already become overwhelming and decisive. Since the publication of Lyells conscientious and carefully prepared work on this subject the ac-quiescence has become general among all classes of scholars."[44] Lyell's high standing before the Victorian reading public as the pre-mier authority in geology together with his evident lack of ill-will toward religion made *The antiquity of man* the seal of approval on the new chronology for Morgan and many like him. At about the same time, in another passage from a draft for *Ancient society,* Morgan wrote: "Evidence has now accumulated nearly to the point of certainty, that man was contemporaneous with the mammoth, the mastodon and the rhinocerous, with the cave lion, cave bear and cave hyena, now extinct, as well as with the existing species." Then, in pencil, he crossed out the word "nearly."[45]

Here, then, is the root change that overtakes Morgan in the period between the two versions of the *Systems.* The history of the civilized portion of mankind no longer begins with Homer and the Bible but opens out indefinitely backward; the bottom drops out of history. Morgan makes use of McIlvaine's suggestion not as McIlvaine had intended, to show the permanent degradation and inferiority of the savage, but to integrate the story of savagery into the story of civili-zation. As he would put it later:[46]

We owe our present condition, with its multiplied means of safety and of happiness, to the struggles, the sufferings, the heroic exertions and the

---

[43] *Ancient society* draft, Morgan Papers, Chap. II, "Roman genesis of human development," p. 126, emphasis added.

[44] *Ancient society* draft, Chap. I, p. 9/37.

[45] The same, Chap. II, p. 4/86–87.

[46] *Ancient society*, p. 554.

patient toil of our barbarous, and more remotely, of our savage ancestors. Their labors, their trials and their successes were a part of the plan of the Supreme Intelligence to develop a barbarian out of a savage and a civilized man out of this barbarian.

Or, more succinctly, "the history of the human race is one in source, one in experience, and one in progress."[47]

---

[47] *Ancient society*, p. xxx.

8

Kinship's Other Inventors

In 1867, as Morgan yielded up the final version of his manuscript to the Smithsonian, the kinship project reached its culmination. In the interval since the circular letter of 1859, which was a kind of *Systems* in miniature, there had come into existence a colloquy on descent, marriage, and family through which kinship began to take on coherence and definition as an object of study. We shall see that Morgan's circular letter played a role in this colloquy, but it was a minor one. The leading voices belonged to the four books previously identified: Henry Sumner Maine's *Ancient law* (1861), Johann Jakob Bachofen's *Das Mutterrecht* (1861), Numa Denis Fustel de Coulanges' *La cité antique* (1864), and John Ferguson McLennan's *Primitive marriage* (1865). Morgan felt a mounting frustration and fears of being forestalled as this discourse unfolded; he would have to endure the agony of four years' wait before he would see his book in print, as I shall relate in chapter 10. In this chapter I shall step outside the private history of the *Systems* to examine the public kinship discourse of the 1860s and, in the next chapter, the time revolution that irrevocably altered its terms of debate, before returning to Morgan's manuscript to see it through press and into the public domain.

My treatment of kinship's other inventors will inescapably be cursory. I shall not attempt to expound their books in all fullness, but will concentrate on the relations among them. For it was in their interactions or, more bluntly, their quarrels, that the discourse of kinship was created. McLennan, more than any other, was the one who drew their originally disparate voices into one debate. Kinship came into being not so much as a thing or a body of knowledge as a running argument.

In the middle of Maine's *Ancient law* we find the following thesis:[1]

The movement of the progressive societies has been uniform in one respect. Through all its course it has been distinguished by the gradual dissolution of family dependency and the growth of individual obligation in its place. The individual is steadily substituted for the Family, as the unit of which civil laws take account. The advance has been accomplished at varying rates of celerity, and there are societies not absolutely stationary in which the collapse of the ancient organisation can only be perceived by careful study of the phenomena they present. But, whatever its pace, the change has not been subject to reaction or recoil, and apparent retardations will be found to have been occasioned through the absorption of archaic ideas and customs from some entirely foreign source. Nor is it difficult to see what is the tie between man and man which replaces by degrees those forms of reciprocity in rights and duties which have their origin in the Family. It is Contract. Starting, as from one terminus of history, from a condition of society in which all the relations of Persons are summed up in the relations of Family, we seem to have steadily moved towards a phase of social order in which all these relations arise from the free agreement of individuals. . . .

The word Status may be usefully employed to construct a formula expressing the law of progress thus indicated, which, whatever be its value, seems to me to be sufficiently ascertained. All the forms of Status taken notice of in the Law of Persons were derived from, and to some extent are still coloured by, the powers and privileges anciently residing in the Family. If then we employ Status, agreeably with the usage of the best writers, to signify these personal conditions only, and avoid applying the term to such conditions as are the immediate or remote result of agreement, we may say that the movement of the progressive societies has hitherto been a movement *from Status to Contract.*

These words might serve as a charter for kinship as object of study. Every anthropological investigation of kinship sets out from one variant or another of the idea that kinship is somehow more important to the working of simple societies than of complex ones, and that in the course of their development complex societies have substituted something else for kinship. If Maine was not the first to come up with the idea, he gave it its motto. "From status to contract" might well adorn the family crest of anthropology.

---

[1] Henry Sumner Maine, *Ancient law, its connection with the early history of society and its relation to modern ideas,* pp. 163–165. On the life see George Feaver, *From status to contract, a biography of Sir Henry Maine 1822–1888.*

It is characteristic of Maine's tortuous line of reasoning that it should have deposited this, the true conclusion of the book, in its middle. *Ancient law* is an asymmetrical masterpiece, full of odd turnings that lead to unexpected treasures. It is left unfinished. It does not close the subject; it opens it up for exploration. One might have thought that the study of Roman law had nothing new in it, and that a fresh beginning was, after centuries of scrutiny, no longer possible. Maine shows otherwise. His book, published in 1861, was immediately successful and exercised an influence upon the reading public well beyond the confines of its ostensible subject.

Part of its wide appeal is attributable to its polemical character. For Maine does not confine his vision to the immediate materials of ancient law. He devotes considerable attention to conceptualization and approach, in which he argues fundamental change is needed. The discussion of conceptualization and approach is the outcome, in fact, of a wide-ranging attack upon the prevailing legal theories of John Austin and his intellectual forebear, Jeremy Bentham; in a word, an attack upon utilitarianism.

Benthamite discussions of law proceed upon the basis of a human nature that is universal, changeless, and untouched in its essence by the diversities of language, custom, and history which divide peoples. Maine's critique has essentially two parts. One of them is to show that the sociological conditions that Benthamite thinking about law takes for granted are historically specific to modern English society and are not, therefore, universal. This is especially true of the competitive individualism that Bentham takes as his universal starting point. The "status to contract" thesis asserts that utilitarianism is true—if true—only for the progressive societies, in their latest stages.

The other part of the critique is to show that the conception of nature as it participates in such ideas as those of the "state of nature," the "law of nations," and the "law of nature" is itself a product of history, an artifact of human devising, which therefore may not be taken as given in nature. He does so by tracing the history of this broad current of Western thought from the Stoics, through whose philosophy of nature Roman law acquired its theory of the law of nations, through the law of nature of French jurists, to the state of nature in Rousseau:

> Now, in all the speculations of Rousseau, the central figure, whether arrayed in an English dress as the signatory of a social compact, or simply stripped naked of all historical qualities, is uniformly Man, in a supposed

state of nature. Every law or institution which would misbeseem this imaginary being under these ideal circumstances is to be condemned as having lapsed from an original perfection; every transformation of society which would give it a closer resemblance to the world over which the creature of Nature reigned, is admirable and worthy to be effected at any apparent cost.

The theory of Rousseau "is still that of the Roman lawyers, for in the phantasmagoria with which the Natural Condition is peopled, every feature and characteristic eludes the mind except the simplicity and harmony which possessed such charms for the jurisconsult,"[2] and one cannot but suppose that in criticizing the mind of the jurisconsult he is thinking of Bentham as well.

The currency of this idea and the speculative errors of which it is the parent were promoted by the demotion of the Bible by the French philosophers:[3]

> One of the few characteristics which the school of Rousseau had in common with the school of Voltaire was an utter disdain of all religious antiquities; and, more than all, of those of the Hebrew race. It is well known that it was a point of honour with the reasoners of that day to assume not merely that the institutions called after Moses were not divinely dictated, nor even that they were codified at a later date than that attributed to them, but that they and the entire Pentateuch were a gratuitous forgery, executed after the return from the Captivity. Debarred, therefore, from one chief security against speculative delusion, the philosophers of France, in their eagerness to escape from what they deemed a superstition of the priests, flung themselves headlong into a superstition of the lawyers.

Maine goes on to attribute the "grosser disappointments of which the first French revolution was fertile"[4] to the theory of the state of nature. Maine does not explicitly connect utilitarianism with these doleful developments—he leaves that to the reader's imagination. It becomes quite clear that the political cast of Maine's critique is Tory and antireformist.

This superstition of the lawyers is the antagonist of what Maine calls "the historical method" or, elsewhere, "the comparative method." Maine's overall approach is cultural—a fastening upon the

---

[2] *Ancient law,* pp. 84–85.
[3] The same, pp. 86–87.
[4] The same, p. 88.

particularities of custom and local circumstance. Montesquieu's *Esprit des lois,* which "with all its defects, still proceeded on that Historical Method before which the Law of Nature has never maintained its footing for an instant,"[5] was an intellectual ancestor, but the method had more recent refinements. "Comparative jurisprudence" is the more precise name he uses to characterize his own work, and it is a child of comparative philology.

This comparative jurisprudence is, on his own showing, modeled upon the study of the Indo-European languages by comparative philology. Maine's principal interest is Roman law; by analogy with comparative philology, he looks not only to the laws of ancient Greece but to ancient Hindu law as well to illuminate his Roman materials under the assumption that these bodies of law are codescendants of the law of an ancestral society. This conception gives Maine a principle of source criticism: common features of these related but distant legal cultures are archaic, whereas features peculiar to one of them are likely to be recent innovations. It discriminates among societies to be compared, drawing them from a single language family, in this case the Indo-European, but not from ancient peoples indiscriminately. In *Ancient law* comparison is largely confined to the Roman, Greek, and Hindu law, with a few references to other Indo-European speakers such as Germans and "Sclavonians." After the success of *Ancient law,* Maine continues to work the vein of comparative Indo-European law, writing a series of books in which more Indo-European groups are brought into the picture.

What comparative jurisprudence supplies that existing theories of jurisprudence lacked is an account of "what law has actually been" in place of the conjectural histories of the state-of-nature type. When investigating the laws of the material universe one commences with the particles that are its simplest ingredients, Maine reasons. Just so, theories of jurisprudence must commence from knowledge of "the simplest social forms in a state as near as possible to their rudimentary condition. In other words, if we followed the course usual in such inquiries, we should penetrate as far up as we could in the history of primitive societies."[6] The rudimentary jural conceptions thus revealed are to the student of law what the primary crusts

---

[5] The same, p. 83.

[6] The same, p. 115. J. W. Burrow, *Evolution and society,* and "The uses of philology in Victorian Britain" are very useful on the philological dimension in Maine.

(earliest strata) of the earth are to the geologist. Theorizing on the Law of Nature or the Social Compact makes the inquiries of the jurist similar to inquiry in physics and physiology before observation took the place of assumption.[7] Maine's method holds out the bright promise of raising the field to the level of the empirical sciences.

It becomes clear in the course of this argument that Maine is working within the traditional framework of the short biblical chronology. No one believes, now or then, that the comparison of Indo-European languages, laws, and so on allows us to form reconstructions that take us back more than a few thousand years. What allows Maine to propose comparative jurisprudence to replace speculations upon the state of nature as a source of knowledge of ancient law—of earliest law, in fact—is the short chronology. In the perspective of the long chronology, however, which was shortly to break in upon the consciousness of the reading public to which Maine addresses his book, the reach of comparative jurisprudence extends over only the most recent part of human history.

Maine's historical or comparative method was compounded with another element—evolutionism. Maine seems to regard his evolutionism as a result of the comparative method, as the findings of empirical study, not as a separate theoretical component of his views. Law itself is the object of a law of progress or development, of which the early states are royal judgments inspired by the gods (*themistes*), customary law in the custody of a privileged order, and written codes of law; to these must be added the "movement of progressive societies" from status to contract. At several points Maine makes explicit the difference between the relative time of evolutionary stages and absolute time. He says, for example, "in Greece, in Italy, or the Hellenised sea-board of Western Asia," law codes "all made their appearance at periods much the same everywhere, not, I mean, at periods identical in point of time, but similar in point of the relative progress of each community."[8] It is another example of the scale of civilization kind of thinking that is so prominent in Morgan's work.

The combination of evolutionism with the comparative method and its philological way of conceptualizing the object of study had the effect, within the short chronology, of giving the particular historical stages one might find in the legal history of Indo-European speaking people a claim to universal significance. Or perhaps we

---

[7] The same, p. 3.
[8] The same, p. 13.

should say that this conceptual and methodological package is a way of preserving, in scientific dress, the traditional sense of the universal significance of classical antiquity. Much as Morgan's work is an exercise in generalizing Iroquois, Maine's *Ancient law* is Roman law generalized.

The provisions of the earliest historical stratum therein to be discerned with the help of the comparative method are those of the family under the power of the father. Thus at the end of his project of sifting out the layers of Indo-European legal literature, Maine arrives at a vision of ancient law that is radically different from that of Rousseau, intellectual forebear and surrogate for Bentham in Maine's argument. Rousseau finds man in the state of nature to be innocent of the family, of the domination of one sex or class over the other, living scattered and alone. In place of the state of nature Maine gives us "the patriarchal theory":[9]

> The effect of the evidence derived from comparative jurisprudence is to establish that view of the primeval condition of the human race which is known as the Patriarchal Theory. There is no doubt, of course, that this theory was originally based on the Scriptural history of the Hebrew patriarchs in Lower Asia; but, as has been explained already, its connexion with Scripture rather militated than otherwise against its reception as complete theory, since the majority of the inquirers who till recently addressed themselves with most earnestness to the colligation of social phenomena, were either influenced by the strongest prejudice against Hebrew antiquities or by the strongest desire to construct their system without the assistance of religious records. Even now there is perhaps a disposition to undervalue these accounts, or rather to decline generalising from them, as forming part of the traditions of a Semitic people. It is to be noted, however, that the legal testimony comes nearly exclusively from the institutions of societies belonging to the Indo-European stock, the Romans, Hindoos, and Sclavonians, supplying the greater part of it; and indeed the difficulty, at the present stage of the inquiry, is to know where to stop, to say of what races of men it is *not* allowable to lay down that the society in which they are united was originally organised on the patriarchal model.

Shortly after the publication of *Ancient law,* however, the short chronology exploded and with it the sufficiency of Maine's argument. His claim to have found the original condition of man collapsed, and the patriarchal theory suffered a serious setback. He would have

---

[9] The same, pp. 118–119.

reason to be glad of the caution with which he put the case for the universality of the patriarchal model.[10]

Leaving behind the convoluted line of argument of Maine's treatise—so learned but so lacking in system—we come to the bell-like clarity of Fustel de Coulanges' *La cité antique* (1864). The book is an outgrowth of lectures on ancient history delivered at the University of Strassbourg. It has all the virtues of a popular university lecture course: a lucid exposition, which delivers the material in manageable increments; a distinct thesis strongly underscored; little reference to primary sources and none to the opinions of contemporaries. The force of the thesis is undiminished by doubts, hesitations, or the recognition of merit in opposing views. On the few occasions when Fustel debates an issue, his victories are always decisive and his opponents anonymous. It is a wonderful read but somewhat difficult to locate in relation to the work of others.

We would particularly like to know whether Fustel had read Maine (his biographer, Guiraud, says he had not),[11] for the two books have a great deal in common. *The ancient city*—to call it by the title it has borne in the English-speaking world since the translation of Willard Small appeared in 1873—has a larger reach than *Ancient law,* taking the story of Greek and Roman religion, laws, and institutions from an "Aryan" antiquity to the coming of Christianity. The first third, roughly, is devoted to family law in earliest Greece and Rome and its cult of the ancestors, prior to the rise of the city-state; and here the convergence with Maine is pronounced.

---

[10] I disagree, then, with Kenneth E. Bock ("Comparison of histories: the contribution of Henry Maine") when he says that Maine was not a social evolutionist. "His objectives, we shall see, were more specific and limited. He abhorred universals. His attention was confined to a particular group of Indo-European peoples" (p. 236). (Burrow, "The uses of philology," p. 188, makes the same point.) "On occasion he used the intemperate language of universalism and designated the patriarchal family as *the primeval* form of social organization, but he later withdrew from that position" (p. 254). Bock misses the expansion of ethnological time that separates *Ancient law* with its universalist pretensions from Maine's later work and its more modest, specifically Indo-European scope.

[11] Paul Guiraud, *Fustel de Coulanges* (1896), p. 37 fn.: *Ancient law* was translated into French only in 1874, and in a letter of 15 April 1864 Fustel states that he does not know English. The more recent biography by J.-M. Tourneur-Aumont (1931) cannot be recommended. Fustel's inaugural lecture ("Une leçon d'ouverture") explains the development of *La cité antique.*

Fustel sets out to cure his countrymen of the habit of regarding the Greeks and Romans as ancient Frenchmen. He resolves, as against that tendency, to treat the ancients as foreign nations, "with the same disinterestedness, and the mind as free, as if we were studying ancient India or Arabia."[12] The source of the resolve to ethnologize the ancients is, as in Maine, a political conservatism. The moderns, he believes, have misunderstood the meaning of liberty among the ancients, "and on this very account liberty among the moderns has been put in peril. The last eighty years have clearly shown that one of the great difficulties which impede the march of modern society is the habit which it has of always keeping Greek and Roman antiquities before its eyes."[13] Like Maine, he writes to undo the French Revolution.

From this vantage, "Greece and Rome appear to us in a character absolutely inimitable" and cannot be models for man now or at any future time. Wherefore?[14]

If the laws of human association are no longer the same as in antiquity, it is because there has been a change in man. There is, in fact, a part of our being which is modified from age to age; this is our intelligence. It is always in movement; almost always progressing; and on this account, our institutions and our laws are subject to change. Man has not, in our

---

[12] Fustel de Coulanges, *The ancient city,* pp. 3–4.

[13] The same, p. 3. See Edouard Champion, *Les idées politiques et religieuses de Fustel de Coulanges.* Arnaldo Momigliano, in the foreword to the recent edition of *The ancient city* (pp. xi–xii) says, "Throughout his career Fustel was involved in a polemic against socialist and generally egalitarian ideas. He defended the institution of private property against French and German socialists by making private property one of the original institutions of mankind. . . . He maintained with equal firmness that the revolutionaries of 1789 had deceived their followers by presenting the ancient republics of Athens, Sparta, and Rome (more especially Sparta) as models of liberty. In agreement with B. Constant and indeed with a whole line of anti-Jacobin thinkers Fustel believed that there was no respect for individual liberty in ancient Greece and Rome (not even in Athens). Individual liberty was to him the product of Christianity, which in its turn he considered unthinkable without the universality of the Roman Empire. Here is the root of Fustel's ambiguity about ancient values. On the one hand he admires, and feels nostalgia for, the ancestral traditions that ensured private property and family solidarity in the days of old. On the other hand he feels that without Christianity there would be no respect for the individual or even separation between state and religion; therefore, though a confessed unbeliever, he chooses to remain within the Catholic Church and avoids discussing the Bible."

[14] The same, p. 4.

day, the way of thinking that he had twenty-five centuries ago; and this
is why he is no longer governed as he was governed then.

It is in their religious ideas that those institutions of the ancients that
we find obscure, whimsical, and bizarre have their explanation. For
Fustel history is a series of revolutions in religious ideas followed by
periods of social upheaval that bring institutions into harmony with
the new ideas.

Fustel employs the comparative method in his treatment of the
family, using Greek, Latin, and a few Sanskrit materials in translation (the *Ṛg Veda,* Manu, the *Bhagavadgītā,* the *Mitākṣarā*) in what
amounts to an attempt to reconstruct the earliest "Aryan" (Indo-
European) institutions and religious beliefs. Comparison is especially
necessary because, although "we know what the Aryans of the East
thought thirty-five centuries ago" from the ancient Vedic literature
of India, in Greek and Latin literatures the ancient ideas persist only
as vestiges of a system that was defunct at the time those works were
written. This is exactly Maine's "comparative jurisprudence" of
Indo-European legal traditions.

Fustel insists that we are not to naturalize the ancient family. It is
based neither upon birth nor upon natural affection, nor upon the
superior strength of the husband over the wife. It is based instead
on the worship of the dead, of the patrilineal ancestors. Fustel first
expounds that cult of the ancestors, then the provisions of family
law and structure as if they were so many logical resultants of beliefs
about the dead.

The deceased ancestors are the only divinities of the earliest
Aryans, and they have the peculiarity of being objects of worship for
their living patrilineal descendants exclusively, depending upon them
for offerings of food. It is a further peculiarity that these dead are
immortal but unable to feed themselves. The family is organized on
the principle of what the Romans called *agnation* to secure the
perpetual worship of the dead; and to that end family law encodes
several of what we might call legal fictions to ensure the perpetuation
of the patrilineal family, such as adoption and the institution of the
heiress, to create sons where nature will not. It is along these lines
that Fustel's unforgettable exposition (over the details of which we
must not linger) develops the causal relation he finds between religion
and family institutions. The end point of this argument is a vision
of the earliest Aryan family as a large, extended family, isolated,

self-sufficient, and entering into relations with other families as sovereign states through treaty relations:[15]

> From all this we see that the family, in the earliest times, with its oldest branch and its younger branches, its servants and its clients, might comprise a very numerous body of men. A family that by its religion maintained its unity, by its private law rendered itself indivisible, and through the laws of clientship retained its servants, came to form, in the course of time, a very extensive organization, having its hereditary chief. The Aryan race appears to have been composed of an indefinite number of societies of this nature, during a long succession of ages. These thousands of little groups lived isolated, having little to do with each other, having no need of one another, united by no bond religious or political, having each its domain, each its internal government, each its gods.

Fustel's book was immensely popular in the English-speaking world as well as the French and has remained in print more or less continuously for almost a century and a quarter. To the English-speaking readership, at least, who saw it in relation to Maine's book, it appeared to be another instance of the patriarchal theory. That was the reading of the Rev. T. Childe Barker, whose *Aryan civilization* first presented Fustel's work in English and for whom its accomplishments included "the revival of the patriarchal theory for at least a portion of the Aryan race."[16] Fustel's book shares with *Ancient law* both the patriarchal theory of mankind's primitive state and the traditional time frame, which makes it possible for him to think that in reconstructing earliest Indo-European religion we reach the very first religious conceptions of the human race:[17]

> This religion of the dead appears to be the oldest that has existed among this race of men. Before men had any notion of Indra or of Zeus, they adored the dead; they feared them, and addressed them prayers. It seems that the religious sentiment commenced in this way. It was perhaps while looking upon the dead that man first conceived the idea of the

---

[15] The same, p. 108.

[16] T. Childe Barker, *Aryan civilization: its religious origin and its progress, with an account of the religion, laws, and institutions, of Greece and Rome, based on the work of De Coulanges* [*sic*] (1871), part translation, part condensation, part reinterpretation of Fustel (p. iii). Maine calls Fustel's "a very brilliant work," citing it in support of the patriarchal theory ("The patriarchal theory," p. 189).

[17] *The ancient city*, pp. 16–17.

supernatural, and began to have a hope beyond what he saw. Death was the first mystery, and it placed man on the track of other mysteries. It raised his thoughts from the visible to the invisible, from the transitory to the eternal, from the human to the divine.

As S. C. Humphreys rightly says, speaking of Maine and Fustel, "For a brief period—until discoveries of stone age archaeological sites and stone age aborigines brought a shift in perspective—the Indo-Europeans represented Primitive Man."[18]

The patriarchal theory of Maine and Fustel was the inversion of that of the seventeenth-century apologist for the divine right of kings, Sir Robert Filmer, to whom Maine alludes in his discussion of it.[19] For Filmer the true original and model of all government is the government of a family by the father. Government, in short, is the family writ large, the king a patriarch who derives his authority from the God-given authority of Adam, passed down through Noah and his three sons to the various kingships of the three continents over which they severally ruled. Maine and Fustel reverse the perspective of Filmer: the family, in its primitive condition, is the state writ small, the father a little king.

The revolution in ethnographic time that was breaking just as Fustel's book was published would deal unkindly with this view, and in its aftermath *The ancient city* would lose the universalist resonance it had held for its first readers. The real failing of Fustel's argument, for all its power, lies in its logic, not in its factual base. Perhaps the most interesting of his ideas is that of a relation among different religious cults and different structural levels of social organization. The cult of the ancestors is the source of *family* structure, whereas the "national gods"—Jupiter, Zeus, Indra—govern inter- or extra-familial social relations that make a *national* institution, the city-state, possible. The value of this insight gets lost when Fustel temporalizes the relation between the two levels: for him the development of the national gods comes later and is in the nature of a religious revolution, leading to the new institution of the city. But this can hardly stand. It happens that a Sky Father (Jupiter, Zeus Pater, Dyaus Pitṛ) is one of the few Indo-European gods that can readily be reconstructed, as indeed the very notion of a god (*deus*,

[18] S. C. Humphreys, "Fustel de Coulanges and the Greek 'genos,'" pp. 36–37.

[19] Filmer, *Patriarcha and other political works of Sir Robert Filmer*, edited by Peter Laslett.

theos, deva) itself. We therefore have no evidence of a period at which Indo-European speakers had no national gods, contrary to what Fustel says. More serious perhaps is the faulty concept of the isolation and self-sufficiency of the family that his evolutionary scheme requires. The families of which Fustel speaks cannot have been self-sufficient in one respect—namely, marriage: they must have acquired brides from one another. Indeed, the existence of a common language and a shared religious and domestic culture among inter-marrying lineages informs against Fustel's isolated, self-sufficient families. For Fustel, and for Maine, the family-as-little-kingdom conception is a master idea beyond which they cannot go. Their subject remains the family, not that broader conception of kinship through which in simpler societies the domestic sphere is brought into relation to the public.[20]

Using the same materials—the literature of classical antiquity, the short, biblical time frame, a conservative (not to say reactionary) temperament—the Swiss scholar Johann Jakob Bachofen arrived at a reading of the past that was radically different from that of Maine and Fustel de Coulanges—or, indeed, from any previous reading. *Das Mutterrecht* (1861) is a most original book.[21]

---

[20] The contemporary critique of Louis Ménard was very acute. "M. Fustel de Coulanges suppose que le culte des morts a précédé le culte des dieux chez les populations indo-européenes. . . . Cette opinion n'a pour elle aucune espèce de preuve. Dès qu'ils ont levé leurs regards vers le ciel, les Aryas ont dû adorer les puissances de la lumière, les *Devas,* les Dieux. Les morts, accueillis dans le monde invisible par ces Dieux qu'ils avaient invoqués pendant leur vie, ont dû être regardés comme des protecteurs naturels par leurs parents et leurs amis, et c'est ainsi sans doute qu'à côté du culte public rendu aux énergies universelles, il y eut une religion particulière pour chaque famille; mais pour admettre que cette religion ait pu exister seule, il faut supposer des familles isolées les unes des autres, et cette supposition, tout à fait arbitraire, a entraîné M. Fustel de Coulanges à méconnaître la morale sociale des anciens." Quoted in Edouard Champion, *Les idées politiques et religieuses de Fustel de Coulanges,* pp. 13–14.

[21] The critical edition of *Das Mutterrecht* appears as volumes 2 and 3 of *Johann Jakob Bachofens gesammelte Werke,* edited by Karl Meuli. In English we have only selections of *Mutterrecht* and other of Bachofen's books in *Myth, religion and mother right,* a translation of the 1926 volume of selections, *Mutterrecht und Urreligion.* A complete translation of Bachofen's very long work—over a thousand pages in the Meuli edition—has never been made. The selections do, however, include the "Vorrede und Einleitung" to Mutterrecht in full, which contains the overview, the remainder of the book consisting of case-by-case studies of mother right.

Bachofen's conservatism is explicit and unrepentant. Scion of a wealthy commercial family of Basel, he expresses his disdain for democracy and his admiration for the Roman empire. Nevertheless, he is by no means politically inclined, and his conservatism is rather an attitude toward the intellectual, not the political, climate of the day. The unnamed antagonist in *Das Mutterrecht* is Theodor Mommsen and what he stands for: history that is built upon a skeptical criticism of the ancient sources.[22] This source criticism proceeded to delimit a body of reliable sources by ruthlessly discarding myth and legend. Bachofen's philology opposes the skeptical, positivist spirit of the scholarship of his day. Mythology, he believed, was in fact a faithful reflection of the past; but what it reflected was a stage of society before that of the Greeks and Romans of history and a way of thinking that was as obscure to the Greeks and Romans as it is to modern skeptical scholarship. The principle around which this earlier stage is organized is that of which the *Vaterprinzip* of historical antiquity is the inversion: the principle of "mother-right."

Mother-right or *gynaikocracy*—we would use the word *matriarchy*—is above all a form of family organization, and to assert that the family has gone through such a stage prior to the stage of father-right directly challenges the sense that the patriarchal, monogamous family is given in nature.[23] In point of fact, Bachofen has relatively little to say about mother-right as a principle of kinship. For him it is much more than that; it is an entire way of thinking. Its religion is maternal-Tellurian as opposed to the paternal-Uranian one of later times that replaces it, its cult that of Demeter rather than that of the paternal Apollo. It attaches great importance to the moon, not the sun; earth, not the sea; night rather than day; left over right—and so forth through a dictionary of symbols, so to say, in which Bachofen assigns things their natural gender. Mother-right is a material or corporeal kind of thinking based on the physical connections of things and persons; paternity, in which physical connection is not apparent to the senses, gives rise to a higher, spiritual kind of thought.

Mother-right so described is itself a major advance over the earlier stage of hetaerism, or (to adopt Morgan's language) promiscuity.

---

[22] See Lionel Gossman, "Orpheus philologus: Bachofen versus Mommsen on the study of antiquity."

[23] Bachofen, *Mutterrecht,* p. 16 (*Myth, religion and mother right,* p. 75). Karl Meuli, "Nachwort" (*Ges. Werke,* vol. 3), p. 1101. Johannes Dörmann, "War Johann Jakob Bachofen Evolutionist?" p. 4.

The marks of this stage are the cult of Aphrodite, the wild lowland vegetation of the swamp as opposed to the cereals that belong to the Demeter cult, and so forth. The lower matriarchy is the sensual life of nature itself, and the nobler matriarchy is humanity's first school of morality and the arts of civilization, bringing marital chastity and the invention of agriculture. It is Bachofen's purpose to recover that lost worldview and pay tribute to its civilizing role.

The stage of matriarchy is represented by the prehistoric nations, so to say, of classical antiquity: the Etruscans and Sabines in Rome and the pre-Hellenic Pelasgians; but it persists in Egypt, India, the Orient—in short, "static Africa and Asia." The victory of patriarchy is gradual and late in completing itself; its political expressions are Alexander's conquest of the Orient and the Roman empire. Even then there remain vestiges in religion and myth of the older, matri-archal worldview. There are also regressionary movements: Pytha-goras, for example, renews the mystery of the chthonian-maternal cults, and the cult of Dionysus restores the sensuality of an earlier stage.

This much and more may be learned from the long preface and introduction with which *Das Mutterrecht* opens. The body of the book is divided into chapters, each of which is devoted to a particular nation, presenting and commenting upon the surviving evidence of mother-right: Lycia, Crete, Athens, Lemnos, Egypt, India and Central Asia, Orchomenus and the Minyae, Elis, the Epizephyrean Locrians, Lesbos, Mantinea. The Lycian case is, of course, the clearest, most unequivocal instance of matrilineal descent attested in classical liter-ature, and one has the feeling that Bachofen proceeded by generaliz-ing the Lycian case, using it as a lens through which he viewed less promising material, much as Morgan proceeded by generalizing Iroquois and Maine, the Romans. In this way the genuine evidence of matrilineal descent was universalized into a matriarchal stage of evolutionary development.

For all its bold originality, *Das Mutterrecht* must seem, at the distance of over a century, as a very unconventional book constructed of very conventional materials. As Dörmann shows, its time frame is that of the short chronology of the Bible, and its author an adherent of the conventional Protestant Christianity of his time and place.[24]

---

[24] Dörmann, "War Johann Jakob Bachofen Evolutionist?" pp. 22–23. He cites Christian Beck's as the generally known chronology of that period, giving for the repopulation of the earth after the Flood a date of 1657 Aera Mundi or 2544 B.C., which puts the Creation at 4201 B.C. Dörmann's research on the relation of Bachofen

One need not delve deeply into Bachofen's personal affairs to discover the obvious fact that his matriarchal theory is the expression
of attitudes toward gender, sexuality, and the relation of Africa and
Asia to Europe that were commonplace and by no means peculiar
to him. Bachofen's evolutionism was of the traditional, scale-of-
civilization kind and owed nothing to Darwin or to kinds of advanced
scholarship on man that affected a scientific or positivist image.

Bachofen intended his work as a contribution to the study of
classical antiquity, not an emergent ethnology. At first it made very
little impression on the former and none on the latter. It was through
Alexis Giraud-Teulon of Geneva that Bachofen's massive, difficult
work was introduced into the beginnings of an ethnological dialogue,
and ethnology was brought to Bachofen's attention. Giraud-Teulon
called his *La mère chez certains peuples de l'antiquité* (1867) an
extract from *Mutterrecht,* although it is much more than that and
by no means simply a digest of Bachofen. McLennan did not know
of Bachofen's work when he published the first edition of *Primitive
marriage* in 1865, although he reviews it in the second edition of
1876 (*Studies in ancient history, comprising a reprint of primitive
marriage*); and Morgan became aware of his work only in 1872.[25]
Bachofen himself, having become sensible of the importance of
ethnology for his theory of mother-right, embarked in 1870 upon a
program of study of ethnological literature with a view to a thorough
revision of *Das Mutterrecht,* one that would comprehend "the rest
of the maternity-systems of all peoples of the world."[26] The inlet of
ethnology into antiquarian research resulted in ten thousand pages
of notes, but Bachofen died before he could complete the work.

McLennan was the first of our four authors to develop an ethnographic method resting upon a conception of the field of study that
was postphilological, and to embrace a chronology that, if of unstated duration, was in any case much longer than the traditional
chronology of Archbishop Ussher. The two features of the argument
of *Primitive marriage* are intimately related. For if the dispersal of

---

to other ethnologists is indispensable. In addition to the article mentioned, there is
his "Bachofen-Morgan" and a long Nachwort to the eighth volume of the *Gesammelte Werke,* "Bachofens 'Antiquarische Briefe' und die zweite Bearbeitung des
'Mutterrechts.'"

[25] Dörmann, "Bachofen-Morgan," and Nachwort, p. 525 ff. (Giraud-Teulon), p.
538 ff. (McLennan), and p. 551 ff. (Morgan).

[26] Dörmann, Nachwort, p. 524.

mankind begins long before the traditional date of the Flood (McLennan gives 2348 B.C. in a later article), then philological reconstructions of earliest Indo-European social institutions are far removed in time from the primitive condition of man and the Indo-European speakers far advanced from that primitive condition. Whereas Maine, Fustel, Bachofen, and Morgan in the first version of the *Systems* worked within the confines of the traditional ethnological time, McLennan was beginning to try out the implications of the long chronology for ethnographic theory and method. It gave him a decided critical advantage, especially vis-à-vis Maine and the patriarchal theory of which he was to become the leading opponent.

The word *primitive* in the title of the book is carefully chosen. It may now mean structurally simple, or serve as a replacement for *savage*; but for McLennan, and for his contemporaries generally, *primitive* always referred to the earliest condition of the human race, even when applied to the customs of contemporary savages. For him, the *ancient* nations are far from *primitive*. The kind of marriage that is primitive in this sense is specified in the book's subtitle: *An inquiry into the origin and form of capture in marriage ceremonies.*

The inquiry into the origin of the widespread custom of giving to the marriage rite the form of a (mock) capture of the bride by the groom—of the "symbol of capture"—is, he tells us in the opening paragraph of the preface, "an exercise in scientific history." The symbol in question throws new light on the primitive state. "For it will be seen that the symbol is not peculiar to any one of the families of mankind. It is at once Indo-European, Tauranian [*sic*], and Semitic; and the frequency of its occurrence is such as strongly to suggest—what I incline to believe—that the phase of society in which it originated existed, at some time or other, almost everywhere."[27]

In the opening pages of the introductory chapter McLennan elaborates his methodological principles very clearly. "The chief sources of information regarding the early history of civil society," he says, "are, first, the study of races in their primitive condition; and, second, the study of the symbols employed by advanced nations in the constitution or exercise of civil rights."[28] The usual methods of historical inquiry—geology and philology—do not conduct us back to forms

---

[27] John Ferguson McLennan, *Primitive marriage, an inquiry into the origin of the form of capture in marriage ceremonies,* p. 3. The introduction by the editor of the reprint, Peter Rivière, is excellent.

[28] The same, p. 5.

of life so nearly primitive as those of many savages of today. Geology (or archeology, as we would say) is summarily disposed of. "The geological record, of course, exhibits races as rude as any now living," but it is limited to material remains; it cannot preserve "any memorials of those aspects of human life in which the philosopher is chiefly interested—of the family or tribal groupings, the domestic and political organisation."[29] Then it is the turn of philology, specifically of Indo-European philology. It is shown to have a limited reach back into evolutionary time:[30]

> Again, the facts disclosed by philology as to the civil condition of the Indo-European race before its dispersion from its original head-quarters—the earliest, chronologically considered, which we possess respecting the *social* state of mankind—cannot be said to tell us anything of the origin or early progress of civilization. Assuming the correctness of the generalization by which philologers have attempted to reconstruct the social economy of the Aryans, we find that people, at an unknown date before the dawn of tradition, occupying nearly the same point of advancement as that now occupied by the pastoral hordes of Kirghiz Tartary, and leading much the same sort of life. They had marriage laws regulating the rights and obligations of husbands and wives, of parents and children; they recognised the ties of blood through both parents; they had great flocks and herds, in defence of which they often did battle, and they lived under a patriarchal government with monarchical features. It is interesting—a short time ago we should have said surprising—to find that such progress has been so early made. But in all other respects this so-called revelation of philology is void of instruction. Those Aryan institutions are—to use the language of geology—postpliocene, separated by a long interval from the foundations of civil society, and throwing back upon them no light. Marriage laws, agnatic relationship, and kingly government, belong, in the order of development, to recent times.

The passage speaks directly in criticism of the patriarchal theory; it seems to have Maine's *Ancient law* in mind.

Thus ethnology must steer its own course, reconstructing the past from the study of contemporary savages. "For the features of primitive life, we must look, not to tribes of the Kirghiz type, but to those of Central Africa, the wilds of America, the hills of India, and the islands of the Pacific; with some of them we find marriage laws

---

[29] The same.
[30] The same, pp. 5–6.

unknown, the family system undeveloped, and even the only acknowledged blood-relationship that through mothers." He continues, "These facts of to-day are, in a sense, the most ancient
history."[31] Belief in an immanent law of progress informs the conception of the primitiveness of contemporary savages and makes the
sciences of law and society possible. "In the sciences of law and
society, old means not old in chronology, but in structure: that is
most archaic which lies nearest to the beginning of human progress
considered as a development, and that is most modern which is
farthest removed from that beginning."[32]

The revolution in ethnographic time has, for McLennan, altered
the relation of philology to ethnology. Ethnology is no longer the
continuation of philology by other means; it puts itself in charge and
makes philology its assistant. The abundance and variety of primitive
forms among contemporary savages make up for the limited historical reach of philology:

> And since the historical nations were so far advanced at the earliest dates
> to which even philology can lead us back, the scientific investigation of
> the progress of mankind must not deal with them, in the first instance,
> but with the very rude forms of life still existing, and the rudest of which
> we have accounts. The preface of general history must be compiled from
> the materials presented by barbarism. Happily, if we may say so, these
> materials are abundant. So unequally has the species been developed,
> that almost every conceivable phase of progress may be studied, as
> somewhere observed and recorded. And thus the philosopher, fenced
> from mistake, as to the order of development, by the interconnection of
> the stages of their shading into one another by gentle gradations, may
> draw a clear and decided outline of the course of human progress in
> times long antecedent to those to which even philology can make refer-
> ence. All honour to philology; but in the task of reconstructing the past,
> to which its professors declare themselves to be devoted, they must be
> contented to act as assistants rather than as principals.[33]

The thesis McLennan advances in *Primitive marriage* can hardly
be said to fulfill the promise of its bold methodological manifesto;
indeed, a century of ethnology later it seems hopelessly distant

---

[31] The same, p. 6.
[32] The same.
[33] The same, pp. 6–7.

from the real life of the savages of whom he speaks but of whom he knows only through books. It is difficult at this late date to recapture the sense of how daring and advanced was this first attempt to reorient ethnology to the long chronology.

Briefly put, it is McLennan's thesis that the form of capture in marriage is a legal symbol of what in the past was substance. The primitive condition of man was one in which wives were regularly obtained by capture from hostile foreign tribes. This was so because there existed a rule against marriage between members of the same tribe—for which rule McLennan invents the name *exogamy*. This is more archaic in an evolutionary sense than its opposite, for which he coins the term *endogamy*. The cause of exogamy was the imbalance of the sexes—that is, a relative scarcity of women within the tribe—which was due to the practice of female infanticide. This in turn was the result of the harsh struggle for food and security in the initiatory stage of progress, which placed a premium on male children as "braves and hunters."[34] The imbalance of the sexes also brought about polyandry as an evolutionarily early marriage form. This custom is in fact a form of modified promiscuity, McLennan avers, testifying to the general promiscuity that he posits as mankind's initial condition, not yet extinct: "the sin of great cities shows that there are no natural restraints sufficient to hold men back from grosser copartneries" than those of polyandrous savages.[35] These early marriage forms take their place within the first of a developmental series of descent systems: kinship through females only as the earliest (to which, in McLennan's view, polyandry is necessarily connected), succeeding to kinship through males and females, before the stage of kinship through males only, which Maine and other proponents of the patriarchal theory wrongly take to be man's earliest estate. Thus McLennan's curious argument. Bachofen and Fustel were unknown to him at this time, but he cites both Morgan and Maine. His relation to each is worth exploring.

Morgan's circular letter of 1 October 1859 and schedule of degrees of relationship as printed by the Smithsonian Institution had been reprinted in *The Cambrian journal* for 1860, as we have seen, through which McLennan came to know of it. He quotes a long passage from it "as the most recent and authoritative statement regarding the tribal divisions of the red men."[36] The quotation in-

---

[34] The same, p. 68.
[35] The same, p. 69.
[36] The same, p. 51, n. 19.

cludes a single sentence representing a vestige of the matrilineal theory that Morgan had abandoned in the course of his Ojibwa researches, or, in light of his subsequent resumption of it, we should perhaps say he tabled. Speaking of the Iroquois, he says, "the children are of the tribe of the *mother,* in a majority of the [Indian] nations; but the rule, if anciently universal, is not so at the present day." Elsewhere McLennan refers to this passage as evidence that the system of kinship through females only prevails "among the majority of the nations of the American Red-men," [37] on which in fact Morgan was quite mistaken, as he would subsequently discover through his western field trips. In another place McLennan cites Morgan on radical features of the American Indian system of relationship: [38]

> 1. "All the brothers of a father are equally fathers to his children (this where there is now no polyandry). 2. All the children of several brothers are brothers and sisters to each other; all the grandsons of a man's brothers are his grandsons." These features of the system bear the stamp of a polyandrous origin; they are features of the system of relationship which might be expected to accompany the higher polyandry. The schedules returned to Mr. Morgan show that among the Tamul and Telugu, peoples of Southern India, numbering about twenty-four millions, "all the brothers of a father are usually called fathers, but in strictness, those who are older than the father are called *great fathers,* and those who are younger, *little fathers.*" And both Tamul and Telugu are still, as we have seen, to some extent polyandrous. The same system of relationship is found among the Puharies, a people on the skirts of the Tibetan region, and that manifestly practised polyandry till a late date. With the Puharies, all the brothers of a father are equally fathers to his children.

Thus Morgan's *Systems,* in the embryonic form of the circular letter of 1859, had already entered the nascent ethnological community and become a voice in its debates. And it had become an influential voice, one with a life and destiny all its own. McLennan fastened upon just those elements of Morgan's early formulation—matrilineal descent and polyandry—that Morgan himself was rejecting as explanations of the classificatory system in the 1865 version he was writing as McLennan's book was coming off the press. One wonders, without being able to decide the issue one way or the other, whether Morgan's circular letter may not have been *the* formative influence on these

---

[37] The same, p. 84 and n. 43.
[38] The same, p. 85.

two aspects of McLennan's doctrine. Perhaps it also contributed to his curious idea of exogamous "tribes," through a misunderstanding of Morgan's use of the word *tribe,* really referring to exogamous clans interior to the Indian nations. McLennan generally applies the word *tribe* (as do we) to what Morgan called *nations.* It is possible, therefore, that he mistook Morgan's meaning when he says, "no man is allowed to marry a woman of his own tribe, all the members of which are consanguinei."[39]

However that may be, Morgan purchased McLennan's book in February 1867 and thought himself forestalled in some particulars. One may guess what these were: McLennan's stage of "general promiscuity" (in evidence of which he refers to some of the very peoples of antiquity McIlvaine had written Morgan about in 1864![40]), the general notion of a prehistory of marriage forms, and the exogamy idea. Although the two corresponded and were on friendly terms during Morgan's European tour, their relations did not remain amiable. The very similarity of their ideas made them rivals.

As to Maine's *Ancient law,* McLennan speaks of it several times and at some length, criticizing Maine's patriarchal theory of the primitive family repeatedly. The essence of his critique is that Maine confines his attention to "races which were far advanced at the earliest dates to which their history goes back"[41] but that "many stages of progress had to be traversed" before that condition had been attained.[42] Maine, "trammelled by notions derived from Roman jurisprudence," would not have written as he had "had he examined the primitive races now extant."[43] Here a Rubicon is being crossed. The literature of ancient Greece and Rome, together with the Bible, had been the only reliable guides'to the primitive state of humankind under the short chronology. Now that a long chronology has overthrown the traditional one, those guides become trammels. Ethnological attention is turned away from the writings of the ancients and toward the "primitive races now extant." McLennan abandons the philological design of ethnological research because its historical reach is suddenly shown to be much too shallow.

---

[39] Morgan cited in the same, p. 51, n. 19.
[40] Massagetae, Agathyrsi, ancient Spartans.
[41] McLennan, *Primitive marriage,* p. 48, n. 16.
[42] The same, p. 91.
[43] The same, p. 48, n. 16.

An earlier publication, a long unsigned article on "Law" written for the eighth edition of the *Encyclopaedia britannica* (1857), is a valuable index of the development of McLennan's thought, for it is evident that his conversion to a longer chronology and to an ethnographic approach to law took place after this, his first major publication, and before the appearance of *Primitive marriage* eight years later.[44]

In the *Encyclopaedia britannica* article, McLennan's conception of law as "an expression of will, in the form of a command, sanctioned by applicable penalties, proceeding from a competent authority, prescribing to free agents a rule of action for a particular end, and resulting, generally, in a uniform line of conduct on the part of those to whom it is given"[45] is well within the terms of the Benthamite or utilitarian tradition. He discusses natural law and the state of nature; he invokes the Benthamite "greatest good" standard, and among the authorities he cites many are of this tradition or congenial to it: Bentham himself, James Mill, J. S. Mill, Comte, Austin, Grote. He draws especially heavily on J. S. Mill and Comte for his conceptions of social science. Sociology or "the social science" is for him the necessary basis for a science of law; and it has the function of supplying the legislator with "general rules and principles for solving practical problems."[46] The piece is shot through with an optimistic belief in progress, a belief that "all things work together for good," [47] and a vision of law as "an active force, restricting and directing the various social activities, so as, though in small part, beneficially to determine the character of social progress." Accordingly there is a long section on the growth of law framed according to a vision of "the fulness of the idea of law" which "has not been reached by the whole of any system of law now administered" but which everywhere directs the progress of civilization.[48] Thus it is a sign of the uneven development of law that "women everywhere, to this day, are without equal rights." Moreover, "in Europe, where the states are interested in maintaining the balance of power, an approach to equity is made in the regulation of relations of states great and small; but

---

[44] Rivière identifies this and other unsigned articles in his edition of *Primitive marriage,* p. xlix.

[45] McLennan, "Law," p. 253.

[46] The same, p. 264.

[47] The same, p. 261.

[48] The same, p. 255.

outside Europe—in India, China, Japan, Africa—the European states practise the morality of superiors, and gratify every desire, however iniquitous, in satisfying which they are not led into conflict with one another."[49]

In these allegiances McLennan put himself at odds with positions Maine was to take in *Ancient law* and in his professional life. Both, to be sure, are wedded to the view that law progresses in a predetermined direction—that is, to an evolutionism of a fundamentally optimistic kind. Within that common ground, however, Maine develops a highly effective critique of the prevailing Benthamite tradition with which McLennan had identified himself, and Maine's attack is the expression of a Tory politics with which McLennan, a lifelong Liberal, could not have found himself sympathetic.

I cannot agree, therefore, with Burrow—whose excellent book, *Evolution and society,* has otherwise done so much to advance our understanding of the British pioneers of anthropology—when he suggests that Maine's *Ancient law* may have been of profound importance in McLennan's intellectual development, bringing about the great changes we see between the 1857 article and *Primitive marriage* in 1865.[50] To the contrary, in a passage from the *Encyclopaedia britannica* article to which Rivière draws our attention,[51] McLennan embraces the very patriarchal theory he later so emphatically opposed. Rejecting the "fiction" of the social compact theory of the origin of civil society, and its supposition that "society was formed by the aggregation of solitary beings," he goes on to say,[52]

> Society obviously commences in the family: the society of parents into which every human being is born, and in which are to be found the germs of that subordination to, and recognition of authority which are essential to the civil state; the state where the government is patriarchal is indeed the direct prolongation of the family. As the banyan tends to surround itself with a forest of its own offshoots, so the family tends to multiply families around it, till it becomes the centre of a tribe. The feelings of kindred which connect families into tribes tend, though with a feebler force, to bind tribes together in nations; and the sentiment of humanity, which is the feeling of kindred refined and diffused, tends, though more feebly still, to unite nations in the great society of mankind. While such

---

[49] The same, p. 258.
[50] J. W. Burrow, *Evolution and society,* pp. 231–232.
[51] Rivière, introduction to *Primitive marriage,* p. xxx.
[52] McLennan, "Law," pp. 255–256.

is the gradual development, the specialities of the composition of families and of tribes vary, of course, with race, geographical position, climate, and the prevailing religious beliefs.

Rivière cites the following passage from *Primitive marriage* in which McLennan rejects the theory he had once espoused in nearly identical language, including the image of the banyan tree:[53]

> The old theory of the composition of States, was based upon the tendency of families to multiply round a central family, whose head represented the original progenitor of them all. The family, under the government of a father, was assumed to be the primary group—the elementary social unit; in it were found at once the germs of the State, and of sovereign authority. Many circumstances recommended this theory, and none more than its apparent simplicity. It was easy to find abundant analogies for the prolongation of the family into the State. A family tends to multiply families around it, till it becomes the centre of a tribe, just as the banyan tends to surround itself with a forest of its own offshoots. And it is obvious, to follow up this figure, by remarking that the feelings of kindred which hold families together in tribes, tend to bind together, in nations, tribes which, like the Greek races, trace back their descent to kinsmen.

Thus although it is certain that McLennan read *Ancient law* between the 1857 article and the writing of *Primitive marriage* and that Maine's work made a considerable impression on him, the development of McLennan's ideas is, if anything, in a direction that puts him into *greater* disagreement with Maine. If Maine was a major influence on McLennan, it was in a decidedly negative way that his influence worked. Indeed, the obsessional character of McLennan's later attacks upon Maine incline one to Rivière's suggestion that Maine was "an ideal representation of everything to which McLennan was either antagonistic or to which he had aspired and had failed to achieve." Thus

> Maine was a successful lawyer and academic, part of the establishment, the recipient of a knighthood and many other honors, certainly a conservative and occasionally a Tory, and a man whose ideas received popular acclaim. McLennan came from a humbler background, was a comparative failure as a lawyer, a Liberal, never obtained an academic post, and

---

[53] McLennan, *Primitive marriage,* pp. 106–107; Rivière, introduction, p. xxxi.

was accorded only minor academic honors, while his ideas were not popularly received.[54]

Rather than follow this rather tawdry and necessarily speculative path further, let us return to the main issue, which has now become: Why did McLennan reverse himself on the patriarchal theory between the 1857 article and the 1865 book? The answer must surely be, judging from the terms of his critique of the patriarchal theory, his conversion to a longer chronology. McLennan makes his opposition to the biblical chronology and his adherence to a longer chronology abundantly clear in a later article that speaks directly to the issue, "The early history of man," published in the *North British review* in 1869. Although he is not as forthright on the question in *Primitive marriage,* however, his critique of Maine therein makes it sufficiently clear that he had reached this position by 1865. Indeed, we can even name the probable source for his conversion, for the word *post-pliocene* by which he characterizes the limited temporal reach of philology was a neologism of a most influential book, Lyell's *Antiquity of man,* published in 1863.[55]

While Morgan looked helplessly on, his big book stuck in the quagmire of Smithsonian finances, McLennan had seized upon the time revolution to sweep away the old ethnology in tutelage to philology and ancient history and to clear a space for the new. This revolution in ethnological time now requires our close inspection.

---

[54] The same, p. xxxv.
[55] Charles Lyell, *The geological evidences of the antiquity of man,* p. 1.

9

Of Time and Ethnology

✦✦

In McLennan, as we have seen, ethnology begins its disengagement from philology; and it owes this coming of age to the sudden enlargement of the span of ethnological time. Let us now step back to get a deeper perspective upon this movement. We shall have to look to the Bible or, rather, to certain readings of the Bible (especially the book of Genesis) upon which the original unity of the short chronology, philology, and ethnology was based. Our first task is to survey the history of the short chronology, briefly but from the beginning to the beginning of the end in the 1860s. Then we must look at the biblical basis of the philological project and its inherent ethnological dimension. Finally, we shall consider the onset of the time revolution and some of its consequences for conceptions of mankind.

In Morgan's family Bible, as in many Bibles of his day, the chronology of Archbishop Ussher that had become traditional among English-speaking Protestants was printed in a central column of notes wedged between columns of the sacred text. It had become part of the Bible; if not the divine Word itself, it nevertheless was the mere explication of the Word. Typography conveyed the sense that it was a simple fact, beyond dispute. This was far from the case, however. The Ussherite chronology was but one of several competing chronologies of the Bible; and the historiographic culture these several chronologies expressed did not spring directly from the Bible without human aid and untroubled by alternatives. It was deliberately created, in the face of competing nonbiblical cultures of macrohistory. Sacred history had to defend itself against gentile histories from early on and to struggle toward internal consistency and textual groundedness as it developed. The short chronology of world history and of ethnographic time was an artifact of reflective thought and of intercultural polemics. In the course of this struggle a biblically based universal history was created.

Far from being natural, the shortness of the family of chronologies based on the Bible stands in sharp contrast to those of the other peoples in whose midst the ancient Hebrews lived. In the Egyptian chronology to be found in Manetho, for example, the reign of the gods, demigods, and spirits of the dead takes up 24,900 years, after which there commences the period of human history, whose span must accommodate the thirty dynasties of Egyptian kings. The chronological tradition of the Chaldeans is even more generous. The ten biblical patriarchs from Adam to Noah lived to a great age, no doubt, but the related Chaldean tradition of ten kings from the beginning of civilization to the universal deluge takes 120 *saroi* of 3,600 years each, or 432,000 years altogether according to Berossus; whereas the subsequent 86 kings, up to the taking of Babylon by the Medes, total 33,091 years, many times in excess of any reckoning based on the Bible. The Sumerian king lists have a chronology on the same order of magnitude, in the hundreds of thousands of years.[1]

Manetho and Berossus wrote in the late third century B.C. in Greek to explain their national cultures to their Hellenistic rulers, the Ptolemies and Seleucids, respectively. Josephus, in the late first century A.D., also wrote in Greek to defend the antiquity of Jewish culture—which he put at a round 5,000 years—not, indeed, against that of the Egyptians or Chaldeans but that of the Greeks. To do so he anchors Jewish history in Manetho's well-established Egyptian chronology, identifying the Jews with the Hyksos shepherd kings whose conquest of Egypt was finally overthrown by the kings of the eighteenth dynasty. Josephus makes no attempt to date the Creation, however, or to call into question the greater length of Egyptian or other gentile histories.[2]

The Christian chronographers were not content to leave the issue of the relation of sacred history to the various national histories outside the Bible text where Josephus had taken it. The idea that the duration of the world would correspond to the six days of Creation acquired its dominion over Christian chronology very early.

---

[1] Manetho, *Aegyptiaca*, Fr. 1. On Berossus see *The Babyloniaca*, pp. 19, 21. On Sumerians see Samuel Noah Kramer, *The Sumerians*, Appendix E., "Sumerian king list," p. 328 ff.

[2] Josephus, *Against Apion*, 1.1 (5000 years of Jewish history), 1.69–105 (its relation to Egyptian history).

Considering that a thousand years are as a day in the eyes of the Lord, the world would therefore last 6,000 years, after which would come the sabbath of eternity. Clement of Alexandria and Hyppolytus in the third century were the first of whom we have record to express the notion that the advent of Christ falls in the middle of the last of the six millenia. Ideally this would give an era in which the Incarnation occurred in Aera Mundi 5500 or 5501. But complicating factors were, first, the need to find a year some thirty years after the Incarnation in which the paschal moon fell on a Friday as a date for the Passion and, second, the desire to link the multiyear paschal cycles of the moon with the Creation in some simple ratio. The Byzantines finally settled on an era based on the creation of the world in 5507–5508 B.C.[3]

The project of finding a date for the Creation brought the Christian chronographers into direct conflict with the gentile chronologies. St. Augustine defends the six thousand years of macrohistory against the falseness of writings that speak of many thousands of years and specifically attacks a claim of greater antiquity for Egypt.[4] Christian chronographers made the first of Egypt's thirty dynasties commence after the Flood and the Dispersal of Peoples. As to the preceding period of Gods, demigods, and spirits of the dead, Syncellus' account records two different approaches. The first of these (which Syncellus favors) is to throw doubt on the "Egyptian writings against God and against our divinely inspired scriptures"[5] and to deny that Egypt was inhabited before the Flood; the second was to reinterpret Manetho, taking the years to be "lunar years"—that is, months—such that the 11,985 years of the gods are reduced to so many months, or 969 solar years; and also taking the 858 years of the remaining predynastic period as *horoi* (three-month periods), which thus become 214½ years, or a total of 1183½ years altogether, fitting nicely within the interval between the Creation and the Flood (2242 years, in the Septuagint). This alternative, which Syncellus attributes to Panodorus but in which Eusebius also participated, amounts to a reconciliation of Egyptian chronology with sacred chronology by reinterpretation. Berossus' chronology of Chaldean history was de-

---

[3] V. Grumel, *La chronologie* (*Traité d'études byzantines*) vol. 1, chap. 1, pp. 5–25.

[4] St. Augustine, *City of God*, 12.101, 18.39, 40, cited in Paolo Rossi, *The dark abyss of time*, p. 168.

[5] Manetho, Fr. 2 (Syncellus).

fanged in a similar manner. The *saros* of 3,600 years was reinterpreted as 3,600 *days*; whence the 120 *saroi* of the ten kings before the Flood become 1183 years, 6⅚ months, also well within the bounds of the era of Creation.

The greatest of the Christian chronographers was Eusebius of Caesarea, whose *Chronicle* became the basis of biblically oriented universal history until the Renaissance. Indeed, it can be said that all chronologies of the ancient history are so many footnotes to Eusebius. Paradoxically, the text on which at some point all such chronologies depend is lost, a victim of its own great popularity, if popularity can be attributed to a work so technical that it will appeal only to scholars. St. Jerome translated and added to its chronological tables, and his Latin version became the foundation of chronology in Latin Christendom. There is also an Armenian translation. Eusebius survives in Greek, however, only in the excerpts cited in the Byzantine chronographers, principally George Syncellus.

The restoration of Eusebius' text has occupied philologists since the seventh century, with no end in sight, making any characterization of it hazardous for the nonspecialist.[6] We can at least say without serious danger of error that the *Chronicle* was a world chronology covering over two millennia, commencing with the birth of Abraham and finishing with the Vicennalia of Constantine (A.D. 325). It consisted of two parts, the first of which was a series of excerpts of various authorities on the national histories of the Chaldeans, Assyrians, Hebrews, Egyptians, Greeks, and Romans, with king lists. The second part, the *Chronological canon,* was where Eusebius' real contribution lay. This consisted of a running chronological table. The table was built around columns of numbers representing the years since the birth of Abraham, to which were keyed parallel columns of the year numbers of the Greek system of Olympiads (after Aera Abrahami 1241) and those of the king lists of other nations. In the margins to either side of these columns of figures important historical events were noted at the horizontal level of the year of their occurrence.

In the *Chronological canon* Eusebius had created a simple and very effective instrument for the integration of world history. The

---

[6] I have found Alden A. Mosshammer, *The* Chronicle *of Eusebius and Greek chronographic tradition,* chap. 1, "The text of the *Chronicle,*" pp. 29–83 a most useful guide through this philological bog. My characterization of the text is based on the Armenian version in the German translation of Josef Karst.

several national chronologies are brought into relation to one another through the horizontal ordering of synchronisms at every point in the table; and the causal interconnection of the national histories became available to investigation through the record of events. Eusebius created a temporal grid into which the national histories of more distant nations could readily be added by taking advantage of known synchronic points with many of the nations already included. It was the historian's equivalent of the geographer's spatial grid of longitude and latitude by which increments of new knowledge of exotic places could readily be linked to existing knowledge. This frame for universal history was built up of synchronisms; not from abstract notions of homogeneous, empty time but the filled, significant time of national histories. In many ways we are still completing Eusebius' project, thickening and extending his *Chronological canon*.

Eusebius was aware of the discrepancies between different versions of the sacred text that render calculation of the date of Creation uncertain. Thus he notes that the Septuagint gives 2,242 years from Adam to the Flood, whereas the Hebrew text of the Jews gives 1,656 years and that of the Samaritans, 1,307.[7] His project is bounded by the shallow reach of biblical time, making of the Flood and consequent Dispersal of Peoples the starting point of universal history.

The spatiotemporal boundaries of the biblical culture of universal history thus created may be rapidly paced off. As we have seen, it arises in the Near East in opposition to environing traditions— Babylonian, Sumerian, Egyptian—that envision a longer (even a very much longer) chronology. These cleavages become apparent on the confrontation of cultures that Hellenistic rule brought about; in a sense the biblical tradition becomes conscious of itself in opposition to the others, of which it is forced to take notice in its search for a biblical synthesis of world history. The biblical tradition of history was, of course, Jewish as much as it was Christian. The Jewish Era of Creation which begins in a year corresponding to 3761 B.C. was determined by Mar Samuel (d. c. 250) according to a tradition that appears to be reliable—that is, in the period in which the Christian conception was taking form; but it came into common use only gradually, replacing the use of the Seleucid era.[8]

The biblical culture of history embraced Islam as well. Thus the

---

[7] In the Armenian version (Karst), pp. 38–41. In the Latin version of St. Jerome we have the birth of Christ 5199 years after the Creation; see Grumel, p. 24.

[8] *The Jewish encyclopedia,* s.v. "Era."

the universal history of Abu'l-Fidā (1273–1331) contains a well-worked-out chronology in which the expulsion of Adam from Paradise precedes the birth of Christ by 5,584 years.[9] To fix the outermost boundary of this culture of history, however, we may consult the greatest of the Muslim chronographers, al-Bīrūnī, whose two great works, the *Chronology of ancient nations* and the *Indica*, are fine expressions of the impulse to refine, correct, and extend Eusebius' temporal grid for universal history. In the *Chronology of ancient nations* al-Bīrūnī's stated purpose is to derive a single system of chronology from the comparison of all known systems. His discussion of the Era of Creation begins with the Persians and Magians, who think that the duration of the world is 12,000 years, of which 3,000 have passed from the Creation to the time of Zoroaster, and a further 258 years to the beginning of the Aera Alexandri. As to the Jews and Christians, al-Bīrūnī continues, they disagree over the interval from Adam to Alexander, the Jews giving 3,448 years and the Christians, 5,180. He has a long discussion of the weaknesses in their respective chronologies and judges that each makes assertions that cannot be supported except by false subtleties and doubtful interpretations. He further notes, in discussion of the Era of the Deluge, that the Persians deny the Flood, and in this the Indians, Chinese, and other eastern nations agree. Although al-Bīrūnī's purpose obliges him to concentrate on the discrepancies between the various systems of chronology, however, it will be apparent to us that they all—even, by chance, the Zoroastrian—belong to the same order of magnitude and constitute a family of related chronologies.[10]

By contrast, in the *Indica* al-Bīrūnī was aware that here he was dealing with a culture of history that was radically different. For not only were Indian conceptions of duration unimaginably long, they did not even believe in creation in a recognizable form, since the same clay persisted, according to them, from one world age to another; so that what they mean by creation is the working of a piece of clay into various forms and combinations.[11] India, with its concep-

---

[9] Abu'l-Fidā, *Abulfedae historia anteislamica*, pp. 5–10. "The *Mukhtaṣar ta'rīkh al-bashar,* a universal history covering the pre-Islamic period and Islamic history down to 729/1329, is in its earlier part based mainly on Ibn al-Athīr," *Encyclopaedia of Islam,* 2d ed., s.v. "Abu'l-Fidā;" see also art. "Ta'rīkh." I am indebted to my colleague Juan Cole for bringing this author to my attention.

[10] al-Bīrūnī, *The chronology of ancient nations,* translated by Sachau, chap. 3, pp. 16 ff.

[11] *Alberuni's India* (Ta'rikh al-Hind) (Sachau), pp. 321–322.

tion of immense cycles of time through which the world takes form, endures, declines into destruction and latency, and is formed again (which, I cannot help saying, seems so much more congenial a matrix for modern scientific conceptions than biblical time), clearly formed the outer frontier of this culture in al-Bīrūnī's time.

Among the Peoples of the Book, then—Jews, Christians, and Muslims—there grew up a family of related chronological systems that together constituted the substance of a single culture of universal history. Both textual differences (of the kind Eusebius notes) and theological differences were major sources of disagreement, and uniformity was never attained. Toward the latter end of the history of this historiographical culture the proliferation of competing schemes had reached proportions that were scandalous and that in themselves were an argument for its adversaries. "First get the more than seventy systems of your chronology to agree," wrote Voltaire, "and then you can laugh at the Chaldeans."[12] Voltaire's 70 systems were far short of the count. Des Vignolles (*Chronologie de l'histoire sainte*, 1738) had collected upward of 200 different systems, varying between extremes of 3,483 and 6,984 years from the Creation to Christ.[13]

In the Christian west a vigorous debate over world chronology had commenced with the work of Joseph Scaliger, whose *De emendatione temporum* (1583) revived the learning of the Greek Christian chronographers. Paolo Rossi's excellent study allows us to track the debate in great detail for the century leading up to Vico, 1650–1750.[14] It was precisely by invoking the extraordinary antiquity of the Chaldeans—and also that of the Mexicans, Peruvians, and Chinese—and by comparing the chronologies of those peoples to that of the Jews that Isaac Lapeyrère sustained, in 1655, the existence of the "preadamites," men who had populated the earth before Adam, the first man to come from the hands of the Lord. In this alarming view, the Bible lost its standing as universal world history and was reduced to being a summary of the particular history of the Hebrew people. The Deluge was no longer a universal catastrophe but became a particular episode in the history of one particular nation.

It is undeniable that after the publication of Lapeyrère's book chronology, which before 1655 had been a field open to free speculation and

[12] Cited in Rossi, *The dark abyss of time*, p. 145.
[13] *Encyclopaedia britannica*, 11th ed., s.v. "Chronology."
[14] Rossi, *The dark abyss of time*, pp. 133, 138–139.

controversy, became a sort of mined terrain over which movement was possible only with extreme caution. Reference to the early wisdom of the Egyptians and the Chaldeans took on different overtones after the hypothesis of the preadamites had been advanced.

Just as the biblical culture of macrohistory had had to define itself in opposition to the Egyptian and Chaldean cultures in the period of its formation, now Manetho and Berossus reappear in the guise of the inimical other, and those who call upon them in criticism of the short chronology are liable to be branded as "libertines and *esprits forts.*" In addition to these ancient antagonists, however, there is the problem of the historiographic traditions of exotic peoples being brought now for the first time to the notice of the Europeans, also very much longer than the biblical chronologies. One has the impression from Rossi that the Chinese national history in the reports of Jesuits made the greatest splash; but a host of newly discovered national chronologies flood in upon the scene at the same time: Mexican, Peruvian, Indian, Siamese, Persian—the list goes on and on. "Within eleven years of the publication of the first edition of the *Praeadamitae,* no fewer than seventeen works had been published with the specific aim of refuting its impious hypothesis,"[15] and a tension was thereby established between the requirements of religious belief and the expanding knowledge of other cultures.

Thus by the nineteenth century it was the Orientalists and the Americanists who brought refractory data to the debate over chronology, and it was to the new Orientalist archaeology of Egypt that critics of the short chronology especially appealed before midcentury. However, the role of Orientalism in the opening out of ethnological time was soon overtaken by the archaeology of fossil man. The Egyptological work of Champollion and Lepsius might extend human history back by a few thousand years; but the archaeologists of fossil man brought about a quantum leap in the scale of ethnological time that was sudden and the further limits of which were unknown.

It is well to keep in mind that the revolution in ethnological time was one of a series of expansions of the historical scale taking place in the nineteenth century and that these expansions, though related, took place in fairly discrete stages. We may put these developments (overschematically, no doubt) somewhat as follows. In the early part

---

[15] The same, p. 138.

of the century it had become possible and respectable to believe in a very long geological time while it continued to be a test of orthodoxy to believe in the recent creation of man, together with the other living inhabitants of the globe. This was the point Morgan had reached in his 1841 paper, "On geology." As for biological time, the prevailing doctrine, established by Cuvier and developed by William Buckland, admitted many epochs of creation and extinction prior to the creation of man and the present flora and fauna described in Genesis. Thus the fossil record achieved a time scale not limited by the Genesis narrative, which depicted, in this view, only the most recent of the epochs of creation. Under this doctrine the living biological species including the human continued to be recent creations. Then, in 1859, Darwin's *Origin of species* propounded a theory whereby the living species were brought into relation with the extinct species of the fossil record, and indeed the various strata of life forms in the whole of biological time were unified. In the same year the discoveries of fossil man at Brixham Cave by Hugh Falconer, William Pengelly, and Joseph Prestwich were publicly endorsed as testaments to a greater antiquity of man by Sir Charles Lyell in his presidential address before the Geological Section of the British Association for the Advancement of Science; in 1863 he would publish a book on the issue that gave it a very wide airing.[16] Mankind was suddenly assimilated to the fossil record and to its enlarged framework of time.

Western linguistic and ethnological projects down to the nineteenth century had been built upon certain readings of the Bible, specifically the macrohistorical narrative of Genesis. The seminal event for linguistic and ethnological theorists was the Tower of Babel story, shortly after the universal flood that had depopulated the world. The Confusion of Tongues by God in that story, and the subsequent repopulation of the world by the descent of Noah, permitted certain readings that proved very productive for linguistic and ethnological science. First, there was the genealogical conception of the interrelations of the different nations. Noah's sons, Shem, Ham, and Japhet, each gave rise to several lineages, which founded the

---

[16] On these several time revolutions (not always adequately distinguished) there is a largish literature. See especially Francis C. Haber, *The age of the world, Moses to Darwin*; Charles C. Gillispie, *Genesis and geology*; Donald K. Grayson, *The establishment of human antiquity*; Glyn Daniel, *The idea of prehistory*; and Jacob W. Gruber, "Brixham Cave and the antiquity of man."

several nations of mankind. Second, there was a genealogically guided taxonomic structure or levels of classification implicit in the narrative, such that, for example, Shemites or Semites, Hamites and Japhetites at the highest level of classification were more proximately related to nations of the same stock than to nations of the other stocks. Third, there was the underlying ultimate unity of the human family in Noah or, indeed, in Adam and Eve. Fourth, the relations among different languages were also genealogical in character, tracking the descent of Noah. Language history, then, was a movement from original unity in Adam's language to diversity, a process of ramification that was at the same time a process of corruption from the original perfection of the language in which Adam gave their true names to the beasts.

These conceptions inform the project of recovering the lost perfect language of Adam and of tracing the history of the nations through the systematic comparison of vocabularies or of standardized texts such as the Lord's Prayer in many languages. Hans Aarsleff, whose admirable researches have greatly illuminated the state of language theories prior to the nineteenth century, attributes the beginnings of this process to strong infusions of Jewish mysticism in cabalistic doctrines that became known to the West after 1492 with the expulsion of the Jews from Spain.[17] Mystical recovery of Adam's language was claimed by Jacob Boehme, and Rosicrusians believed that fragments of the Adamic language survived the Confusion of Tongues and could be recovered from the languages of the present through comparative study. In Leibnitz at the end of the seventeenth century we already find clear expression of the project of systematic comparison of vocabularies to decide questions of ethnic and language history, among them the question of American Indian origins long before Jefferson's formulation.[18] The "discovery" of Sanskrit itself in the closing decades of the eighteenth century occurred within this framework of ideas—indeed, was made possible and meaningful within this framework. Thus the French Jesuit Coeurdoux found the astonishing similarities of Sanskrit with Latin and Greek evidence that the Indians, like the Europeans, were descendants of Japhet. Sir William Jones' anniversary discourses to the Asiatic Society in which he specifies the relation of Sanskrit to European languages, are, taken

---

[17] Hans Aarsleff, *From Locke to Saussure,* p. 281.
[18] The same, pp. 93, 99, n. 39.

together, a universal history on the lines of the conceptions here outlined.

As we enter the nineteenth century therefore, when language study acquires scientific pretensions, the final objective of the philological program is already well formulated and its execution is in train. That objective is the comprehensive classification of the languages of the world upon historical principles, which would necessarily be a comprehensive delineation of the historical interrelations of languages, living and dead, and their derivation from the first language. (In many ways this prefigures the shape of the modern, Darwinian conception of the classification of species, also upon historical principles.[19]) The biblical basis of this program recedes into the background in the nineteenth century, except in such vestiges as the names Hamitic and Semitic; but because it is not acknowledged does not mean it is not there. The idea of the genealogical connections of languages (and nations), and the familiar figure of the family tree (Stammbaum) by which those connections are expressed, persist to the present. The short frame of traditional ethnological time is an integral part of the program. Its ideal end point, the recovery of the ancestry of all languages back to a primitive language or languages, presupposes a

---

[19] It is striking that Darwin, in his chapter on classification of species, introduces his "branching diagram" and then immediately turns to the classification of languages to illustrate his conception. "It may be worth while to illustrate this view of classification, by taking the case of languages. If we possessed a perfect pedigree of mankind, a genealogical arrangement of the races of man would afford the best classification of the various languages now spoken throughout the world; and if all extinct languages, and all intermediate and slowly changing dialects, had to be included, such an arrangement would, I think, be the only possible one. Yet it might be that some very ancient language had altered little, and had given rise to few new languages, whilst others (owing to the spreading and subsequent isolation and states of civilisation of the several races, descended from a common race) had altered much, and had given rise to many new languages and dialects. The various degrees of difference in the languages from the same stock, would have to be expressed by groups subordinate to groups; but the proper or even only possible arrangement would still be genealogical; and this would be strictly natural, as it would connect together all languages, extinct and modern, by the closest affinities, and would give the filiation and origin of each tongue" (*Origin of species,* pp. 422–423). The original "genealogical arrangement of the races of man" was that of Genesis. The affinity of Darwinian and philological classification made a strong impression upon August Schleicher, who wrote a pamphlet on the subject (*Die darwinsche Theorie und die Sprachwissenschaft*) that was widely read, English and French translations appearing soon after its publication in 1863.

past of only a few thousand years even to be conceived. And the parallel courses and unitary objectives of philology and ethnology, much remarked on in the nineteenth century, have their roots in these conceptions as well.

It is important to stress the continuity of nineteenth-century philology with what went before because the folk-history of linguistics that has prevailed until recently, written from a Neogrammarian viewpoint in the progressive, genealogy-of-ideas mode, exaggerates the discontinuity between the "philosophical" language study of the eighteenth century and the "scientific" linguistics of the nineteenth century.[20] Nevertheless, the perceived success of Indo-European comparative philology set in motion by Bopp and Rask in the second decade of the nineteenth century made it the leader and standard for other branches of the field and the defining type of language study in the public eye.

Such was the success of Indo-Europeanist philology that by midcentury it had achieved a reputation for having attained the rigor of an exact science, a reputation that extended well beyond the ranks of its specialist practitioners to embrace the reading public generally. It was a reputation it shared with political economy, for like political economy it purported to reduce aspects of human behavior to lawlike generalizations. Grimm's law, to be sure, was different in important ways from, say, Ricardo's theory of rent. Grimm's generalizations about sound shifts were particularizing ones, which applied only to certain languages of a single family, whereas Ricardo's formulations were to have been true of all times and places, springing from universal human nature in its interaction with external nature. Thus two essentially different models were offered to other aspiring human sciences, one directed toward the examination of cultures in all their particularity, the other the expression of a theory of human nature for which national and cultural differences are so much friction to the operation of its laws.

Let us follow, briefly, the fortunes of philology as a model for other disciplines. By midcentury Schleicher was asserting that the object of language study was natural rather than cultural, and that the new philology, *Glottik* as he named it, therefore had the exact character of the natural sciences and not just the probabilistic charac-

---

[20] This interpretation of the history of linguistics is epitomized by Holgar Pedersen's *The discovery of language, linguistic science in the nineteenth century*, which has been the standard work in English since its translation in 1931.

ter of the moral sciences.[21] He was joined in this view by Max Müller; and although there were demurers (most notably Whitney), the fact is that Müller was philology's greatest publicist in his day.[22] His lectures on the "science of language" were immensely popular and sold widely when published (they were, as we have seen, of great significance to Morgan), and Müller went on to speak of the "science of religion" and the "science of mythology," organizing comparative study of religion and myth along philological lines.

Thus it was that the prestige that encompassed philology extended far beyond its proper boundaries and brought other kinds of scholarship into its sphere of influence. We have already seen how Americanist ethnology—that of Schoolcraft, for example—was dominated by the philological classifications of its subject, the American tribes. Beyond such direct bearing of philology on other kinds of study, there was its influence as a model. Morgan is an excellent example of this; his kinship work is not philological, but it models itself upon the philological method and sets out from philologically determined classifications. Morgan is by no means unique in this. Other examples appear in quite different fields. Thus Maine's "comparative jurisprudence," Fustel's study of early Indo-European ancestor worship, and Robertson Smith's *Religion of the Semites* begin from a philological conception of the field of study and its subdivisions—that is, the radiating, treelike structure of related cultures (legal systems, religions)—and proceed by comparative study. They are not exactly clones of comparative philology, for they establish their own method by analogy, not by extension or imitation of philology. They are witness to the great influence and creative power of comparative philology under Indo-Europeanist leadership.

Before turning to the period of its greatest power in the second half of the nineteenth century, it is important to repeat of its origins in the eighteenth, that Indo-Europeanist philology was born of a scholarly culture of the study of languages and nations that had biblical moorings of which the short chronology was one. In the

---

[21] August Schleicher, *Die deutsche Sprache*, pp. 119–129; *Compendium der vergleichenden Grammatik der indogermanischen Sprachen*, p. 1.

[22] Max Müller, *The science of language*, lecture 1, "The science of language one of the physical sciences." Whitney, "Schleicher and the physical theory of language," *Oriental and linguistic studies*, art. 11; in "Physei or thesei—natural or conventional?" (Silverstein, ed., *Whitney on language*, art. 8) he comes down decisively in favor of the conventional character of language—which indeed had been his position from the first of the Smithsonian lectures of 1863.

famous anniversary discourses delivered before the Asiatic Society of Bengal, which he had founded in 1784—discourses that together formed a universal history—Sir William Jones adumbrated the genetic connection of Sanskrit to Greek, Latin, Gothic, Celtic, and Persian. But he also fitted Indian chronology to the Eusebian grid by observing that the first three avatars of Viṣṇu relate to the Universal Deluge, placing Kṛṣṇa 3,000 years ago, following a period of "the settlement of nations, the foundation of states or empires and the cultivation of civil society" subsequent to "the dispersion from Babel."[23] Slightly earlier Father Coeurdoux had speculated that the striking similarities of Sanskrit with Greek and Latin showed that the Indians (as the Europeans) were descendants of Japhet. In both cases what is being said is that Sanskrit is more closely related to the languages of Europe than it is to Hebrew, and that the date at which their differentiation commences is established by the Confusion of Tongues, the baseline for language history.

The lingering influence of the biblical conceptions in language study can perhaps best be illustrated by a diagram of Müller's that appeared in 1854.[24] Let us isolate the conceptual elements of this diagram (see figure 11). First there are the social-evolutionary stages: family, nomadic, political. Second, there are corresponding stages of the evolution of language. Third, there is the branching, treelike structure of genetic relations among particular languages, developing inexorably from few to many; the coexistence of the two great images, the genealogical tree and the staircase of the scale of mind, is as typical of the age as it is striking. Fourth, there is reference to the ethnological time horizon of the Bible in the starting point of the historical process, the antediluvian level, at which language is in its primitive form of simple roots. The Semitic and Aryan languages are on a level, and their original unity is assumed, at some point about halfway through history; the unity, that is, of the biblical and progressive nations vis-à-vis the others. Ultimately all languages derive from a single language or language type. In this conception, the

---

[23] William Jones, *Discourses delivered before the Asiatic Society*, p. 32.

[24] Max Müller, "The last results of the researches respecting the non-Iranian and non-Semitic languages of Asia or Europe, or the Turanian family of language" in Bunsen, *Outlines of the philosophy of universal history* (1854), pp. 263–487; diagram p. 487. Adam Kuper, "The development of Lewis Henry Morgan's evolutionism," draws attention to this diagram. There is no evidence that Morgan had read this work, however.

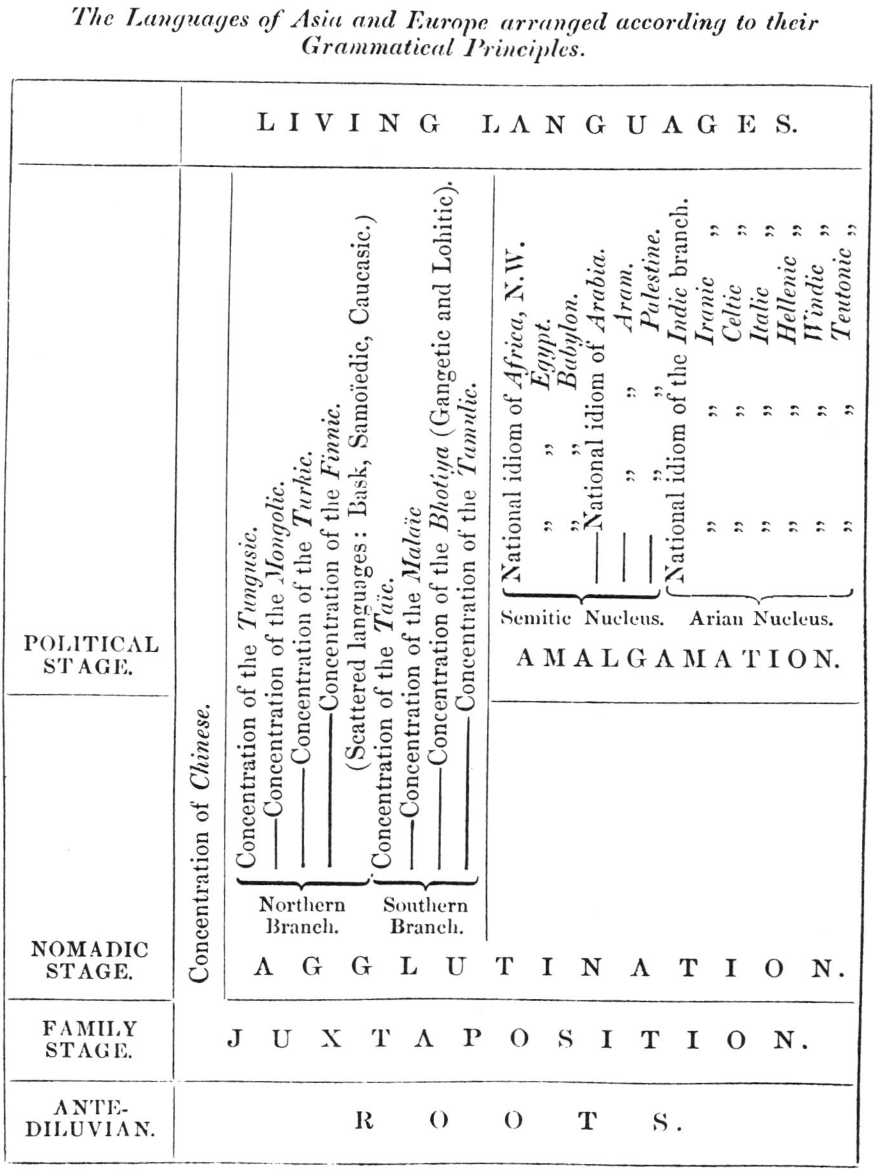

The Languages of Asia and Europe arranged according to their Grammatical Principles.

LIVING LANGUAGES.

Concentration of *Chinese*.

Concentration of the *Tungusic*.
— Concentration of the *Mongolic*.
— Concentration of the *Turkic*.
— Concentration of the *Finnic*.
(Scattered languages: Bask, Samoïedic, Caucasic.)
Concentration of the *Taic*.
— Concentration of the *Malaïc*.
— Concentration of the *Bhotiya* (Gangetic and Lohitic).
— Concentration of the *Tamulic*.

National idiom of *Africa*, N.W.
„ „ *Egypt.*
„ „ *Babylon.*
— National idiom of *Arabia.*
„ „ *Aram.*
„ „ *Palestine.*
— National idiom of the *Indic* branch.
„ „ *Iranic* „
„ „ *Celtic* „
„ „ *Italic* „
„ „ *Hellenic* „
„ „ *Windic* „
„ „ *Teutonic* „

Semitic Nucleus.   Arian Nucleus.

POLITICAL STAGE.

AMALGAMATION.

Northern Branch.   Southern Branch.

NOMADIC STAGE.

AGGLUTINATION.

FAMILY STAGE.

JUXTAPOSITION.

ANTE-DILUVIAN.

ROOTS.

Fig. 11. Max Müller's classification of languages.

capacity of philology to recover linguistic roots in analysis is tantamount to a capacity to recover the beginnings of language itself.

Let us now consider the revolution in ethnographic time and its effects upon philology, ethnology, and the relation between the two.

In any analysis of historical change, everything depends upon the specifics of rate and directionality. As to rate, the revolution in ethnological time was very sudden, and it divided the scholarly lives of Morgan and his generation in two. The generational character of the change is dramatic. To many scholars born around 1820, whose publications commenced in the 1840s or 1850s and who continued to publish into the 1860s and 1870s, the time revolution was the central intellectual event, an earthquake that rearranged the parts of the intellectual landscape decisively and beyond recall. Those born later and beginning their scholarly careers after the earthquake took the new lay of the land for granted; they could not recapture the intensity of the change as lived experience, and their readings of the work of their predecessors was quite different, being shaped by an assumed long chronology. Sudden as the revolution was, it was as quickly normalized.

We are safe in saying that the revolution in ethnological time presented a very sharp profile, but there is yet a great deal to be learned about the exact character of its onset, which was by no means uniform. The onset cannot simply be fixed by the date of the Brixham Cave and other excavations. It is a matter not of objective events but of interpretations of those events, of the presentation of those interpretations to the public, and of their reception by various segments of the public, in each stage of which process there may be considerable range of variation. For example, if we consider the intellectual environment in which Morgan became converted to the long chronology, we find that as early as the 1850s the "scientific racism" of Gliddon and Nott appealed both to Egyptology and to the excavation of American Indian sites in their attack upon the biblical chronology; but the blatant parson-baiting clangor of their work and its offensive support of slavery did not commend it to Morgan and his circle. It was generally perceived to be unorthodox. Conversely, the annual reports of the Smithsonian Institution, which Morgan regularly read and to which, under Joseph Henry's leadership, he was strongly inclined to give most favorable readings, took notice of archaeological findings that challenged the short chronology distinctly later and handled them more gingerly. In the 1860s the annual reports begin publishing one or more articles in each number on what we would call prehistoric archaeology. In spite of the great interest in the emerging challenge to the short chronology these articles attest, however, the reader of today finds it striking how reluctant the articles are to come out and state conclusions that cross the historical threshold of the Flood. The presentation, then, of the new interpretations of the span of human history that inform archaeological activity is variously bold (Nott and Gliddon) or cautious (Smithsonian *Annual reports*)—and, of course, the receptivity of readers was also various. For many in the English-speaking world, I suspect, the appearance of Lyell's *Antiquity of man* (1863) was decisive, presenting the new chronology in a way that was seen to be impeccably scientific but also not antireligious.

The directionality of the change is unambiguous. Nothing within the body of the built-up Eusebian time frame was directly affected by this revolution; it was only the beginning of history, hitherto held to a very recent date by the Flood narrative, that was changed beyond recognition. Time opened out indefinitely backward; we may truly say that the bottom dropped out of history, for not only was the new chronology very much longer than the old, its beginning was unknown and henceforth the frame of universal history and of ethnological time was unsettled and subject to continuous revision. The beginning of the story of mankind was further blurred by the Darwinian revolution in the species conception and the related idea of the long series of insensible steps by which the human species emerged from its prehuman ancestor.

The effects upon the conception of man were immense. The proximate range of historical time was unaltered in its contents, and yet everything acquired a new significance. As a linguistic relic of the short chronology we still divide "history" into ancient, medieval, and modern periods; but "history" is now preceded by "prehistory," a word that enters English, French, and other languages in the 1860s. The Middle Ages are no longer the middle of human history; nor is the ancient period the beginning. The Bible and Homer are no longer our sources of knowledge of man's original condition; indeed, there is no written testimony we may now consult for that, and prehistory perforce adopts the methods of geology, into whose time frame the story of mankind has now been absorbed. The 1860s marked the end of a long period in which universal histories commenced with the ancient Greeks, Romans, and Hebrews; the written word now lost its authority as a guide to origins. Constructions prior to the revolution, whose time horizon was provided by the ancient Greeks—constructions as diverse as Auguste Comte's three stages of knowledge (theological, metaphysical, positivist) beginning with the Greeks and ending with the French, and the fourfold dialectic of history in the *Communist manifesto* (the slave society of antiquity, feudal society, capitalism, socialism)—no longer encompass the whole human story as their authors had intended, and there is a shift in the readings that it is possible to give them. The radical revision of social science was inevitable.

We may state the matter of directionality and its consequences as follows. The story of civilization remained much as it had been prior to the revolution in time; but there now opened up a prior history that can only have been a period of savagery. Two consequences follow: the leading alternative to the law-of-progress theory is ruled out, the theory, namely, that God provided mankind with all the elements of civilized life at the beginning of history, and that modern savages were nations that had lost those arts. The sudden onset of the long chronology, then (as Morgan attests), had the effect of a decisive confirmation of the idea of progress. It also, however, altered the tempo of history in such a way as to change the relation of the savage to the civilized yet further. The chain of discoveries and inventions that constitute the recent part of the story of progress— that is, the part about civilization—remained unchanged; but the earlier period of savagery was slowed to a glacial pace such that the first discoveries and inventions came about much more gradually than recent ones and with long intervals between. The staircase of progress, the scale of mind or of civilization, was lengthened out in its lower steps. Morgan, following Lyell, figures the "ratio of progress" as a geometric progression.[25] The staircase, then, has a slope that describes a parabola, rising slowly at first and then more and more steeply. This was the new image upon which an increasingly self-confident Western civilization gazed and recognized itself.

The differential effects of the newly lengthened chronology upon the anthropologies of disciplines outside what we have come to call prehistoric archaeology may be illustrated by two of Morgan's contemporaries, Joshua Hall McIlvaine for theology and William Dwight Whitney for linguistics.

Joshua McIlvaine provides a case of Protestant Christian an-

---

[25] Morgan, *Ancient society*, p. 38.

thropology that lies near at hand. McIlvaine wrote two books of commentary on the Adam and Eve narrative in Genesis, from the creation of man to the banishment from Eden. So similar are these two books in their scope and chapter headings that we may regard the second book as a revision of the first. *The tree of the knowledge of good and evil* (1847) was written before the time revolution; *The wisdom of Holy Scripture, with reference to sceptical objections* (1883) was written after. Comparison allows us to isolate its effects.

In the 1847 book McIlvaine takes it for granted that the Adam and Eve narrative is historical. Its events are not only historical, however; they are "pregnant with meaning," "full of divine significance."[26] Thus the Genesis story is constituted of events that are also symbols, intended to instruct man in religious truth as well as to inform him of historical truth. The business of the book is to decode these symbols or sensible representations, and the interpretation is accordingly in some sort of the nature of allegory.

McIlvaine does not directly speak of chronology, but his disquisition on the rainbow reveals his assumptions in that regard. How is it that the rain is first mentioned at the time of the Flood and the rainbow, that "outward symbol for a new order of inward and spiritual things," came into existence only after the Flood, when it was wanted as a sign of God's promise to man? It has to do with the fact that the earth before the Flood was imperfectly drained; "the process of draining, by which God gathers the waters together into one place, and causes the dry land to appear" is still going on, as of old. The Great Lakes region of North America was underwater at a comparatively late date. Moreover, they are slowly running dry: "One day those lakes must be drained off, and their bottoms, except where they are on a level with the ocean, or shut in by impassible barriers, will be, like the surrounding country, covered with cornfields." At the beginning of this process rain could not form, because water was not drained off into large bodies on which the sun's heat could act to produce evaporation and hence clouds (and rainbows). The fossil record gives proof:[27]

> What confirms this view is, that the elephant, the hippopotamus, the tapir, the alligator, and animals of the same sort, the living but degenerate representatives of that huge, informe animal world whose fossil remains

---

[26] McIlvaine, *The tree of the knowledge of good and evil,* p. 18.
[27] The same, fn. pp. 193–195.

are found in the bones of the mammoth, the great saurians, and the like, are all lovers of the marshy and imperfectly drained portions of the earth. From this it would appear, that when the earth was inhabited by this sort of creatures, in numbers and species so much greater than now, it must have been less perfectly drained than now. During this period, also, the animal part of man, after he had been driven forth from Paradise, the high and drained situation of which is demonstrated by the mention of four great rivers which had their source in the garden, might naturally partake to some degree of this informe and gigantic character. Therefore the Scriptures, with all the earliest traditions of the human race, speak of giants.

What is more, the short chronology underlying McIlvaine's early book on the Genesis story is joined to the conception of a golden age of first innocence: "Here in Paradise, in the garden of delight, the race of man passed its innocent and happy, but alas! its brief and fleeting infancy. To this period it still looks back with fond and tender regret. The literature of the first ages, among all nations, retains the tradition of a *golden age,* when sin and sorrow were as yet unknown."[28] The overall conception of historical process is necessarily degenerationist.

Turning now to the 1883 book and the articles that are its early drafts, we find that McIlvaine is concerned to reconcile his Christian anthropology based on the Adam and Eve narrative with the anthropology of contemporary social science when possible, and to defend it against infidel scholars and materialists where necessary. In so doing the short chronology is openly disavowed:[29]

The Holy Scriptures leave science perfectly free within her own sphere— as in all other things so in this—to determine by her own methods the age of the world and the length of time during which it has been inhabited by man. They teach nothing opposed to any conclusions upon these and similar questions which may be established upon strictly scientific evidence. If it should be proved that the earth is millions of years old, and that it has been inhabited by man for a much longer time than has been supposed, Christians may accept these results with entire satisfaction, and without the least detriment to their faith in the Scriptures.

---

[28] The same, pp. 98–99.

[29] McIlvaine, "The miracle of creation" (1878), p. 832. This and "Organization the fundamental principle of social science" (1876) went into the 1883 book, *The wisdom of Holy Scripture, with reference to sceptical objections.*

Moreover, we hear no more of a golden age; McIlvaine's view is now decidedly a progressive one, in which "God is in all history working out his wise and holy and benign purpose, no less truly than in the world of nature";[30] "progress is a fundamental law of human society."[31]

The mental revolution that has taken place between the first and second commentary on Genesis affects McIlvaine's conception of the character of the story itself. Once constituted of events that were also symbols, the narrative now becomes wholly symbolic. As the biblical text had been historicized in prior centuries, now the substance of this part of the text at least has ceased simply to be historical; rather, it has become an object of historical understanding. Thus, for example,[32]

> the expression, "In the beginning," carries the mind back through all the dim ages of the past, in order to portray to the imagination the origin of all created things. Its indefiniteness is eminently suitable to the subject. For it does not chronologically determine any particular time when the creation took place, nor, indeed, is there in the subsequent Scriptures any information from which it is possible to form a satisfactory estimate of the age of the world. There has been no science of chronology revealed from heaven, any more than of other things which are the legitimate subjects of scientific investigation. There is no reason to think that the apostles or writers of the New Testament regarded the Scriptures as containing an inspired chronology. For they quoted from the Septuagint translation as freely as from the original, notwithstanding, if a full chronology could be made out from the sacred records, this version of the Old Testament would give nearly fifteen hundred years more for the age of the world than can be gathered from the Hebrew. They did not even notice this, nor similar discrepancies, which seems to warrant the inference that they did not regard them as of sufficient importance.
>
> It is true, indeed, that learned and able men have taken the greatest pains to work up a sacred chronology from the data supplied in the Hebrew Scriptures. But no two of them agree in their results, so that these are of no authority. Nor can this be a matter of surprise to any one who will take the trouble to examine for himself the materials out of which these elaborate systems are constructed, which are nothing else than the genealogies interspersed here and there in the historical records,

---

[30] McIlvaine, "Miracle," p. 846.
[31] McIlvaine, *Wisdom of Holy Scripture,* p. 447.
[32] McIlvaine, "Miracle," pp. 830–831.

and which a child may see were never intended, and are totally un-
trustworthy for any such purpose.

McIlvaine argues that if scriptural allusions to physical phenomena
had been scientifically accurate, they would have been unintelligible
to generations born before the birth of science. This relativizes the
Bible text, or at least aspects of it, to history, specifically to a progressive view of history. We hear no more of the physics of the
rainbow or of the Great Lakes running dry.

The first dozen books of Genesis have divided Protestant theologians in America ever since the revolution in ethnological time, and
their interpretation has become the diagnostic of liberal and fundamentalist differences. McIlvaine's was the historicist solution of the
hermeneutic problems it posed; the fundamentalist solution was,
rather, to reject the time revolution in the interests of preserving the
facticity of the Creation narrative. The Scopes Trial of the 1920s and
the "Creation Science" of today are so many landmarks in the struggle between competing chronologies and anthropologies.[33]

Quite different were the effects of the time revolution on the
country's most eminent linguist. Whereas it had obliged the theologian McIlvaine to alter his course sharply, it encouraged William
Dwight Whitney along a course he had already taken.

Whitney gave a series of six lectures on "the principles of linguistic
science" at the Smithsonian Institution in March 1864, a brief
abstract of which was published in the Smithsonian's annual report.
The following winter (December–January 1864–65) they were expanded into twelve lectures delivered before the Lowell Institute in
Boston. They were then further expanded and published in the latter
half of 1867 as *Language and the study of language*. Here again we
have two versions of the same text, from the period in which the
time revolution was beginning to unfold.

In the Smithsonian lectures Whitney expresses himself skeptical of

---

[33] Moreover, long after most Christian scholars had "made peace with the idea
of the Earth's antiquity," twentieth-century evangelicals have resurrected Flood
geology and a short chronology for the earth according to Davis A. Young's interesting review of the question (*Christianity and the age of the earth*, chap. 5). One can
still purchase Bibles in which, as in Morgan's, the Ussherite chronology is printed
in the central column—for instance, *The Scofield reference Bible* published by
Oxford University Press (New York).

philology's grander pretensions and draws attention to its limits as well as its strengths. Of the Indo-European language family he tells us that precisely where and when it originated is beyond the power of linguistics to determine. Continuing on this theme, he alludes to the beginnings of the time revolution, briefly but distinctly:

> That the time of Indo-European unity must have been thousands of years before Christ is very certain. Recent discoveries are proving that man's antiquity is much greater than has hitherto been usually supposed. Respecting the origin of particular races our knowledge is likely ever to continue exceedingly indefinite.[34]

As to the project Jefferson had launched, the question of an "affinity of American with Asiatic language," Whitney declared, "no linguistic evidence of any real value has as yet been adduced . . . nor has the time yet come for a fruitful discussion of the question."[35] Direct comparison of American and Asiatic languages is premature; the comparative philology of the separate families must first be worked out before we can decide the question of Asiatic derivation.

As to the other grand project, that of showing the unity of the human race, Whitney is wholly negative: "Linguistic science can never hope to give any authoritative decision upon the subject."[36] Linguistic science cannot, on the one hand, prove the ultimate variety of the human races because it has no internal chronology: "It cannot say how long a time may have been occupied in the formation of roots, or how long the monosyllabic stage may have lasted; and it must confess it altogether possible that an original human race should have separated into tribes before the formation of any language so distinctly developed, and of such fixed forms, as should leave traceable fragments in the later dialects of the sundered portions." On the other hand, unity is not excluded: "Among all the varieties of human speech there are no differences which are not fully explainable upon the hypothesis of unity of descent."[37] As to proving an original unity, it might be hoped that traces of such unity would be discoverable in all parts of human language. It is not theory but examination that impedes the way. "But investigation, however incomplete, has

---

[34] Whitney, "The principles of linguistic science," Smithsonian Institution, *Annual report* 1863, p. 104.

[35] The same, p. 112.

[36] The same, p. 113.

[37] The same, pp. 113–114.

already gone far enough to leave no reasonable expectation of making the discovery."[38]

These points are reaffirmed in the 1867 book.[39] In the discussion of linguistic and physical evidence of race in their bearing on the question of unity, however, Whitney invokes the new long chronology directly and at some length. Of the two branches of ethnological study, the linguistic and the physical, he says,[40]

> Both are legitimate and necessary methods of approaching the solution of the same intricate and difficult question, the origin and history of man on the earth—a question of which we are only now beginning to understand the intricacy and difficulty, and which we are likely always to fall short of answering to our satisfaction. There was a time, not many years since, when the structure and history of the earth-crust were universally regarded as a simple matter, the direct result of a few *fiats,* succeeding one another within the space of six days and nights: now, even the school-boy knows that in the brief story of the Genesis are epitomized the changes and developments of countless ages, and that geology may spend centuries in tracing them out and describing them in detail, without arriving at the end of her task. In like manner has it been supposed that the first introduction of man into the midst of the prepared creation was distant but six or seven thousand years from our day, and we have hoped to be able to read the record of so brief a career, even back to its beginning; but science is accumulating at present so rapidly, and from so many quarters, proofs that the time must be greatly lengthened out, and even perhaps many times multiplied, that this new modification of a prevailing view seems likely soon to win as general an acceptance as the other has already done. And the different historical sciences are seeing more and more their weakness in the presence of so obscure a problem, and confessing their inability to give categorical answers to many of the questions it involves.

Thus Whitney picks up on the emergent time revolution early on, and appeals to it briefly in the Smithsonian lectures and boldly in the book, to reinforce his more modest estimate of the power of the science of language to settle ethnological questions. On the issue of human unity, for example, the structure of the argument changes but the conclusion remains the same. In the lectures it is the lack of a

---

[38] The same, p. 114.

[39] Whitney, *Language and the study of language,* pp. 351 (Indians), 382 (unity of mankind).

[40] The same, pp. 382–383.

chronometer internal to linguistic methods—the lack of something in the nature of glottochronology, perhaps—that is the reason linguistic science is unable to get to the bottom of the matter. In the book Whitney is able also to point to a chronology external to linguistic methods, whose great length underscores his sense of limits. After the time revolution there will be no going back to the earlier, heroic age, when comparative philology expected to unveil the origin of language and with it, the origin of mankind.

Can we generalize the effects of the time revolution upon philology and upon its relation to ethnology? The advent of the long chronology within the philological world is clearly visible in the work of August Schleicher as early as 1860 (*Die deutsche Sprache*),[41] a figure often regarded as transitional to the Neogrammarians of Leipzig who redirected philology in the 1870s. How does the time revolution figure in that redirection? I believe it figures in several ways. The Neogrammarians, as the German name *Junggrammatiker* more clearly expresses, were a younger generation who, because their scholarly careers commenced after the long chronology had been established, took it for granted and readily abandoned those features of the philological tradition that had been fostered by the short chronology. The grand program of recovering the primitive speech of the Indo-Europeans, or of tracing all languages back to one or a few originals, and of the global classification of languages now lost its hope of final fulfillment and, with it, its glamor. Language history of this kind gradually lost its hegemony within the discipline; it became a part, but no longer the leader, of the science. The Neogrammarian program focused upon greater rigor in formulating the laws of sound change, laws that were now to be "without exception." And the programmatic change entailed was to give greater value to the recent, better-documented past and less to the distant, poorly documented past of Indo-European origins whose allure had diminished as the time revolution removed it from the period of the beginnings of language itself. The great prestige of antiquity was broken, reversed. Philology under the Neogrammarians undertook to make itself more rigorous by becoming more modest, orienting itself to more recent data and shedding its grander, philosophic dimension.

---

[41] August Schleicher, *Die deutsche Sprache,* p. 42: the development of Indo-European languages required not four thousand but twice five thousand years.

As comparative philology matured into historical linguistics, it abandoned the larger pretensions of the past, and the program of global classification of languages settled into a "normal science" mode. At the same time its glamor faded for other disciplines without. For ethnology it is perhaps correct to say that it has always had an alliance with linguistics but that the substance of the connection has changed with the changes in linguistics itself. In any case, it can certainly be said that the effect of the time revolution was to break up the package of biblically grounded conceptions that informed the original intermixture and collaboration of philology, ethnology, and universal history since the Renaissance in the recovery of the original state of mankind and the story of the Dispersal of Nations. In so doing it enabled the freeing of ethnology from philology's tutelage. It tended to redirect ethnology toward the study of contemporary savages and prompted it to look to excavation, rather than to ancient texts, for the study of the past.

10

Contributions to Knowledge

✛✛

Having examined the emergence of a public discourse on kinship in the 1860s, it remains to see Morgan's manuscript through press and into that discourse and to evaluate its "contributions to knowledge" as promised by the title of the Smithsonian series in which it was published, after much delay. We return to the private history of the *Systems of consanguinity and affinity of the human family* as Morgan is completing the final, or what I have called the 1867, version.

Morgan had sent the revised version of Part I to Joseph Henry on 29 October 1866 with a letter asking to hear whether it was satisfactory and what Henry's plans would be with reference to its publication. There was no reply.[1] On 21 February 1867 he wrote to say that Parts II and III of the final version were now complete. The letter shows considerable anxiety. Henry's continued delaying tactics had made Morgan doubtful of his intentions. He therefore asked to know those intentions before he sent the manuscript and the time within which it would be printed, if accepted. Another source of anxiety was his old fear of being forestalled, which had been aroused by the recent purchase of McLennan's *Primitive marriage.*[2]

---

[1] Morgan to Joseph Henry, 10/29/66, Smithsonian Institution Archives.

[2] Morgan to Henry, 2/21/67, Smithsonian Institution Archives. Morgan's inventory of books (Morgan Papers) shows that he purchased McLennan's book in February 1867. Adam Kuper's theory ("The development of Lewis Henry Morgan's evolutionism") that Morgan developed the conjectural history of the family after studying McLennan is untenable. The evidence shows that although McLennan's book had been published in 1865, Morgan purchased it only in February 1867, the same month in which he reports the completion of the 1867 version to Henry. Kuper's argument overlooks Morgan's explicit testimony as to the stimulus for the new theory (McIlvaine's suggestion based on the Hawaiian custom). Moreover, in the letter under discussion Morgan states that he has been *forestalled* by McLennan, which is quite different from being inspired by his ideas to devise a new theory.

I must now make it my constant effort to see this work published until it is accomplished. It is absolutely necessary that I should be relieved from it, and turn my attention to other matters. For nearly nine years I have given to this subject almost my entire time, and it will demand more or less of my time until it is printed. It is also necessary for another reason, lest I should be forestalled in some of its conclusions. This has already occurred, as to one or two points, by McLennan's work on Primitive Marriages.

If the preliminary questions are settled unfavorably, and I am obliged to seek another publisher, I ought to be free to do so at the earliest moment.

On 19 April Morgan still had not heard from Henry, and wrote asking for an explanation. Finally, on 2 May, Henry replied.

The acceptance for publication of so large and expensive a work involves much responsibility and I cannot venture to commence the printing of it until I am fully assured by those who are authorities in Ethnology that it contains important additions to knowledge, is unexceptionable as to style, and not unnecessarily increased by old matter. The first impression of one who has been engaged in physical research is that, in proportion to the conclusions arrived at, the quantity of material is very large, and on this account I was very anxious that it should be cut down as much as possible, the error in such cases being generally to produce a treatise on a given subject, instead of an original contribution to knowledge.

He had therefore submitted the revised Part I to "a gentleman who has given much attention to the subject of Roman Law," and subsequently to "a society of gentlemen who will probably make a final report as to its publication." This last was the American Oriental Society; Henry had in fact sent the manuscript of the revised Part I to the Society through William Dwight Whitney, its secretary, ten days after Morgan had written, asking "that it be examined by a committee with the view of ascertaining whether it is an article of sufficient originality and importance to merit a place in the Smithsonian Contributions to Knowledge." He added that he had not previously pressed the examination because funds did not permit him

---

Finally, of the two features of McLennan's theory that Kuper regards as stimuli for Morgan—promiscuity and polyandry—the latter, as we have already seen, had been proposed by McIlvaine and addressed in the 1865 version, which could not have been influenced by McLennan. If anything, the evidence shows that McLennan's theorizing was inspired—though in a degree it is impossible to measure—by Morgan.

to proceed with publication, but that he was now prepared to do so the "moment that we can be assured that it is of proper quality and in a proper condition to be adopted by the Institution."[3]

There is reason to think that the news of a second review committee came as a shock to Morgan. It certainly did to McIlvaine, who, writing to Morgan later that fall, expressed his pleasure "that the long agony of the Smithsonian over your M.S. is over." He continued, "I am done with Prof. Henry for not accepting our report upon it as final. He ought to have done so. I fear he deceived us."[4] If we may reconstruct Morgan's understanding of the status of his manuscript from this, it seems to have been that the issue of scholarly merit had been decided favorably and that Henry himself would decide whether Morgan's revisions met the requirements imposed by the McIlvaine-Green commission and by himself. In any case, Morgan responded to Henry's unwelcome news of a further review tersely, with the request that a final decision be reached by 1 July, adding that "as there seems to be a growing probability that the Institution will not accept it for publication I am becoming more restive each day with the loss of time, and wish to be free at the earliest moment, if such is to be the result, to take its publication into my own hands."[5]

Of course, the American Oriental Society committee had only Part I in hand, and on 10 July Whitney wrote to Henry that the committee could hardly draw an intelligent estimate of the whole from the preliminary and least valuable part of the manuscript that had been sent. Nevertheless, from Part I and the 1859 paper contained in the circular letter published by the Smithsonian, the committee said, "we are clearly and unanimously of opinion that the paper, as a whole, will contain materials of decided anthropological value, and will be worthy of inclusion among the publications of the Institution."[6]

This did not satisfy Henry. The 1867 version, he found, "still contains a redundancy of matter, and is not as well arranged as it might be."

As the cost will be great, I am desirous of having authority from the Oriental Society for its publication, and to be able to state this fact on

---

[3] Morgan to Henry, 4/19/67; Henry to Morgan 5/2/67; Henry to Whitney, 4/29/67, Smithsonian Institution Archives.

[4] McIlvaine to Morgan, 11/27/67, Morgan Papers.

[5] Morgan to Henry, 6/5/67, Smithsonian Institution Archives.

[6] W. D. Whitney to Henry, 7/10/67, Smithsonian Institution Archives.

the reverse of the title page. I would, therefore, prefer a formal letter of approval of adoption, signed by each of the Committee, together with such suggestions as may tend to improve the character of the work.

This would require that Morgan send the rest of the manuscript. Henry asked him to do so, but Morgan required a guarantee that, "as none of the preliminary questions have as yet been settled, . . . in case we should disagree with reference to any of them in which I have a direct interest, such as a reduction of the Tables, or the Dedication, you would return the manuscript to me immediately upon my asking permission to withdraw it." On 25 July having won satisfaction on that point, he sent Parts II and III and the long letter from which I have quoted in Chapter 7 characterizing the changes from the 1865 version.[7]

The American Oriental Society committee, consisting of Whitney, James Hadley, and James Hammond Trumbull, reported to Henry in September that "they find an extensive series of highly interesting facts, collected with unusual energy and thoroughness, presented with clear method, and discussed with marked ability. They believe that students of philosophy and ethnology, though they may not accept all the conclusions of the author, will welcome his memoir as a valuable contribution to science." Henry forwarded a copy of the letter to Morgan with the remark, "I send you a copy of a letter in which I think you will take great interest—There is a pleasure in laboring for an object of laudable ambition which is greatly enhanced by the assurance that the result of our labors is such as to gain the approbation of those who are best qualified to judge of their importance." He was prepared to commence publication at the beginning of the year, adding that all revisions should be made before it went to the printer to avoid expensive alteration in proof. Although the published *Systems* states on the title page that it was accepted for publication in January 1868, Henry had in effect committed himself in his letter of the previous October.[8]

In his reply Morgan vented his frustration over the delay:[9]

---

[7] Henry to Whitney, 7/13/67/; Morgan to Henry, 7/19/67; Henry to Morgan, 7/22/67; Morgan to Henry, 7/25/67, Smithsonian Institution Archives.

[8] Whitney, James Hadley, and James Hammond Trumbull to Henry, 7/?/67; Henry to Morgan, 10/5/67, Smithsonian Institution Archives.

[9] Morgan to Henry, 10/15/67, Smithsonian Institution Archives.

I can see that it makes but little difference with an Institution like the Smithsonian whether a particular memoir is examined, revised and published in two or six years; but it is very different with the author. It hinders his progress in other work, and consumes his time. I hope therefore that some of the lost time will be recovered by the rapidity of the publication.

There were to be further delays, however. In December Morgan wrote to Henry asking that the *Systems* be given a separate volume of the Contributions to knowledge series and that it be completed in the coming year. Henry replied that Part I would be put to press at the beginning of the year but in justice to other contributions now on hand and for budgetary reasons it could not be put through the press at once in the form of a single volume; at the end of the publication the parts would be made up into one volume for distribution. Morgan replied that at that rate the printing would consume three to five years; to which Henry said that provided there were no fresh misfortune from fire or the like, he thought they could finish in three years or less.[10]

Three years was nearly right. The Smithsonian preserves a voluminous correspondence recording the traffic among Morgan, the Smithsonian, and the printer for those years, but for the most part the *Systems* was completed in 1867, and we need not track it further. Suffice it to say that typesetting commenced on 1 May 1868 and finished in June 1870. Fijian and Tongan schedules collected by Lorimer Fison reached Morgan on 16 May 1870 and were added in an appendix; and other changes were being made up to the end of composition and Morgan's departure for a fourteen-month trip to Europe, which were more or less simultaneous.[11] The *Systems* bears a legend on the last page giving June 1870 as the publication date, but from a letter of Spencer Baird (Henry's assistant) to Morgan it appears that, although composition was completed then, the book had not been printed. Henry had also departed for Europe, leaving no instructions to Baird, who was in charge; and in view of the heavy demands on the publishing budget, Baird presumed Henry would wait until his return before ordering copies to be struck off. Morgan

---

[10] Morgan to Henry, 12/5/67; Henry to Morgan, 12/6/67; Morgan to Henry, 12/10/67; Henry to Morgan, 1/2/68, Smithsonian Institution Archives.

[11] Spencer Fullerton Baird to Morgan, 6/13/70; Morgan to Baird, 6/15/70, gives his departure date as 25 June. Smithsonian Institution Archives.

wrote from London on 12 August that Sir John Lubbock had wanted the *Systems* while writing his book (*The origin of civilisation*) just published: "There are now two books ahead of me which have been issued since my manuscript was finished [McLennan's *Primitive marriage* being the other], and Darwin has in press another on the 'Descent of Man,' which runs in the same direction."[12] Nothing further seems to have been done until December, when Henry, having returned from Europe, placed an order for a printing of the *Systems,* 1,000 copies bound and 250 copies in boards. Henry pressed the matter, but it was not so easily done. Correspondence with the printer shows that the plates of the diagrams were in the hands of another firm and had to be sent; when they arrived they were found to be "mere shells" and electroplate casts had to be made of them. Further, the printer needed preliminary matter from Henry; this Henry sent, predating the Advertisement 1870. Proofs of both had to be corrected and returned. It was not until April 1871 that the book was finally ready for press, and the first shipment, of 180 copies in paper, was sent before the month was out.[13]

The *Systems of consanguinity and affinity* had entered the public domain even before its publication and some considerable time before its anxious author clapped eyes on it. In October 1870, Joseph Henry sent an advance copy, bound in paper and almost certainly lacking plates and front matter, to Sir John Lubbock as a special consideration to the president of the Anthropological Institute, who had taken so direct an interest in the work. Henry solicited his opinion of it, and Lubbock replied that it is a work "of great merit and importance. Indeed it seems to me one of the most suggestive & original works on the philosophy of human progress, which has appeared for many years."[14] On 14 February 1871—still prior to the publication of the *Systems*—Lubbock gave a long paper on it before the Anthropological Institute under the title, "On the development of relationships." Morgan, who was touring the Continent at the time, knew nothing of these developments. Upon his return to Lon-

---

[12] Baird to Morgan, 6/18/70; Morgan to Baird, 8/12/70, Smithsonian Institution Archives.

[13] See especially J. W. Huff (attorney for T. K. Collins, printer) to Henry, 2/13/71 (plates); 2/6/71 (preliminary matter); 4/27/71 (180 copies in paper shipped yesterday) and subsequent notices of shipment. Smithsonian Institution Archives.

[14] Henry to Sir John Lubbock, 10/19/70; Lubbock to Henry, 11/8/71, Smithsonian Institution Archives.

don in June he heard of them from McLennan. He first saw his own work in the London Library, in which Lubbock had deposited the advance copy Henry had sent. Shortly thereafter he acquired a copy from the London agent of the Smithsonian Institution.[15]

How shall we evaluate the *Systems*?

When he submitted the 1865 version to the Smithsonian, Morgan believed that the criterion by which it should be judged was its success or failure as a "new instrument for ethnology" and proof of the Asiatic origin of the Indians. He wrote Henry,[16]

> You will remember that I told you this singular research would either lead to very important results, or prove a total failure:—that it would furnish a new instrument for the prosecution of ethnological investigations, more efficient than the grammatical structure of language, or come to nothing. For a long time I did not know where my facts would lead me, but I am now satisfied I have found solid ground to stand upon. I think I am safe in saying that the Asiatic origin of the Indian family as well as the unity of origin of all the Indian nations represented in the Tables, are demonstrated by moral proofs sufficient to satisfy the most exacting. If this is true (of which you can inform yourself through a competent scientific commission) it will be no disadvantage to the Institution to present the evidence in one of its series of publications. It is also a reason for doing it at the earliest practical time. Of course I may be mistaken in this conclusion, concerning which I may have deceived myself.

In its character as a new instrument for ethnology, the discovery process by which the Iroquois system was transformed into the classificatory system had two critical junctures, as Morgan saw it: discovery of the identity of the Iroquois system with that of the Ojibwa, and the identity of Iroquois and Tamil (Dravidian). For at each of these junctures the "new instrumentality" found unities that philology could not. The Iroquois-Ojibwa identity established, in principle, that there was a single American Indian kinship system, shared by distinct linguistic stocks; the Iroquois-Dravidian identity enlarged this American Indian system, in principle, to Asian-American dimensions. But do these identities hold? Is there such a

---

[15] *Extracts from the European travel journal of Lewis Henry Morgan,* pp. 368–371, entries for 7, 20, 21 July 1871.

[16] Morgan to Henry, 3/13/65, Smithsonian Institution Archives.

thing as the classificatory system of relationship? The answer to both questions must be no.

What does it mean to say that Ojibwa or Tamil is the same as Iroquois? For Morgan, to begin with, it does not mean identity of what he calls the *terms of relationship* or the *vocables*. These are properly objects of study for philology, and his interest is to find genetic (historical, genealogical) relations where philology cannot. It means, rather, a sameness in the pattern in which relationships that are given in nature are merged with one another or are left distinct. This is known through examination of the terms of relationship recorded in the schedules; not directly (through the vocables) but by means of their "translations," which is to say, the meanings in English of the native names for the relationships. These translations or meanings generally turn out to be the most proximate to ego of the several natural relationships denoted by the vocables in question; for example, the Seneca vocable *hä⊥nih* (F, FB, and so forth) means *father*. (The underlying conception is rationalized in Morgan's theory of the growth of nomenclatures of relationship: in the classificatory system, primary terms of relationship—for example, *father*—are generalized to secondary relationships, such as that of father's brother, in the evolution of the nomenclature.) Thus it becomes possible to say that the father's brother *is* a father, both in Iroquois and in Ojibwa, or both in Iroquois and in Tamil, and thus that Iroquois, Ojibwa, and Tamil are the same.

Even with the aid of the translations, however, it is not so simple, and the different schedules are not rendered exactly the same. On Ojibwa, for example, Morgan finds himself obliged to say, as one of its indicative features, "my father's brother is my step-father" rather than "my father." He observes that the chief difference of the Ojibwa from the Seneca and the Yankton "consists in the substitution of the step-relationship for a portion of the primary"; and he is obliged to show how this difference does not upset the identity he is trying to establish: "[It] will be found to be simply a refinement upon an original system in all respect identical with the Seneca and Yankton. This is conclusively shown by the present condition of the system amongst their nearest congeners, the Mississippi nations, among whom the step-relationships are unknown in this connection."[17] Thus the identity of Seneca-Iroquois, Yankton Dakota, and Ojibwa is not direct but mediated by another term, an *original system* of

---

[17] *Systems*, p. 205.

which they are descendants. Similarly, in Tamil my father's brother is my father, but distinguished as *great* or *little* father by prefixes accordingly as he is older or younger than my father. Morgan brushes aside these differences from Iroquois, judging them to be minor.

The idea that the Iroquois-Ojibwa identity is mediated by an original system is quite reasonable and follows the philological model. It has the drawback, however, that discriminations of same and different are no longer straightforward and become subject to the interpreter's judgment, especially when there is no good outside evidence to corroborate the identity. The same may be said of the cavalier treatment of the *great/little* distinction in Tamil. I illustrate the problem of identity through a remarkable series of predictions Morgan made in the circular letter statement of 1 October 1859.

At that point Morgan had in hand the data from thirty-six widely scattered Indian nations, sufficient to establish to his satisfaction the existence of a unitary American Indian system of relationship. "The schedules, when compared, exhibit variations from uniformity, and occasional discrepancies, but the radical features of the system are constant in all."[18] For Tamil and Telugu he had only partially filled schedules recently obtained from the Rev. Henry M. Scudder. Morgan gives seven principal features, in which they are nearly identical to the unitary American Indian system the existence of which he believes he has established. He makes several predictions as to other features that will be discovered when complete schedules are obtained. I give these predictions in full, indicating which proved true and which false:[19]

> Whether all the sons and daughters of a man's brothers are called his sons and daughters [they are]; and whether all the sons and daughters of a woman's sisters are her sons and daughters [they are], these schedules do not show. It is to be inferred that they are, from the use by these persons of the correlative terms.
>
> If, in addition to these particulars, the grand-fathers and grand-mother's brothers and sisters are all alike grand-fathers and grand-mothers [they are]; if the grand-sons of a man's brothers and sisters are his grand-sons [they are]; and if the son of a man's female cousin is his nephew [he is not; rather, a son], and the son of this nephew is a

---

[18] "Circular in reference to the degrees of relationship among different nations," p. 4.

[19] The same, pp. 10–11.

grand-son [he is], then all the radical features of the American Indian are present in the Telugu and Tamilian system of relationship.

The fulfillment of all these predictions but one must have been very gratifying, and Morgan regarded the identity as established. The failed prediction respects the classification of the children of one's cross cousins in Dravidian, and he notes the discrepancy in the *Systems*:[20]

> It is a little singular that the children of my male cousin, *Ego* a male, should be my nephews and nieces, instead of my sons and daughters, and that the children of my female cousins should be my sons and daughters instead of my nephews and nieces, as required by the analogies of the system. It is the only particular in which it differs materially from the Seneca-Iroquois form; and in this the Seneca is more in logical accordance with the principles of the system than the Tamilian. It is difficult to find any explanation of the variance.

It is scarcely surprising that Morgan regarded this difference as of little moment. In fact, anthropologists for nearly a century after Morgan wrote the circular letter continued to believe in the essential identity of Iroquois and Dravidian kinship terminologies, though only in a morphological or typological sense, as members of the bifurcate-merging or Iroquois class, not in a genetic sense as descendants of a unitary ancestral system—that is, Morgan's classificatory system of relationship. In 1964 Lounsbury published a paper reanalyzing Morgan's Seneca terms, however, and showed that Iroquois and Dravidian terminologies are radically different. The demonstration concerned the logic by which kin are sorted into "cross" and "parallel" classes along a dimension of "bifurcation." Lounsbury corrected "a classic but erroneous anthropological view concerning the nature of the 'Iroquois type' of kinship system." This view was that Iroquois classifications were explainable on the basis of exogamous, unilineal moieties or clans (a view Morgan originated in the *League of the Iroquois*). Lounsbury shows that the predictions of this clan or moiety theory for Iroquois are wrong in half the cases. He goes on to say,[21]

> There do exist systems which classify kin-types in the way that the Iroquois type was imagined to. These are the "Dravidian" type of sys-

---

[20] *Systems*, p. 391.
[21] Floyd G. Lounsbury, "The structural analysis of kinship semantics," p. 134.

tems. Interestingly, they are *not* generally founded on clan or moiety reckoning, but on a mode of reckoning of bifurcation that, unlike the Iroquois, takes account of the sexes of all intervening links.

In sum, Iroquois cross/parallel classifications are radically different from Dravidian ones, so that what anthropologists call by the same name in the two cases is not the same thing at all. Details of the differences between Iroquois and Dravidian are sufficiently complex that, rather than burden this text with them, I shall refer interested readers elsewhere.[22] Suffice it to state that Lounsbury's proof that Iroquois and Dravidian are not identical centers on exactly those differences Morgan refers to in the *Systems,* and to the failed prediction of the circular letter. Proof of the failure of Morgan's "new instrument" in this matter came a century later, long after anthropologists had ceased to believe in the historical connection of Iroquois and Dravidian terminologies, and it centered on the one point in which Morgan's 1859 predictions were not borne out.

The reason the two systems differ, as we now know, is that the Dravidian is based on the rule of cross cousin marriage, whereas the Iroquois do not have and are not known to have had such a rule. With the benefit of a hindsight informed by all the kinship research that Morgan's work stimulated we can now see that the argument of the *Systems* would have taken a different and sounder direction had Morgan responded differently to McIlvaine's suggestion. For the latter's solution of the Turanian (or Tamil) system had two parts, the "Hawaiian custom" and cross cousin marriage, or rather the promiscuous intercourse of cross cousins, which he considered to be a "slight extension" of the Hawaiian custom. Morgan embraced the Hawaiian custom and to all intents and purposes rejected cross cousin marriage. He would have done better to do the reverse. For the supposed Hawaiian custom is at best a report of a practice no longer in existence, and if we follow the critique of Handy and Pukui we will come to the conviction that it is pure invention, the artifact of missionary exaggeration of the sexual license of Hawaiians prior to the advent of Christianity.[23] Even granting the Hawaiian custom, the difficulties of explaining Tamil by Hawaiian, as previously explained (chapter 7), carried problems of logical integration unan-

---

[22] Trautmann, *Dravidian kinship,* pp. 86–87, 176–185.

[23] E. S. Craighill Handy and Mary Kawena Pukui, *The Polynesian family system in Ka-ʿu, Hawaiʿi,* pp. 60–65.

ticipated by McIlvaine, which led Morgan to develop a complex series of marriage forms, his conjectural history of the family.

The notion that Tamil terms of relationship encoded a form of marriage that might be identified through a process of decoding the terminology was not wrong; but Morgan chose exactly the wrong one of McIlvaine's two suggestions. He should have seized on the partial recognition of cross cousin marriage and elaborated it into a fully-blown illumination of the Dravidian system. Cross cousin marriage was the road not taken. Why was it not?

What makes the matter more perplexing is the fact that McIlvaine was not the only one to bring to Morgan's attention the connection of cross cousin marriage with the Tamil terminology. The two-page vocabulary of Tamil terms of relationship that the Rev. Henry M. Scudder first supplied Morgan has many entries that make the mergers of kin indicative of cross cousin marriage perfectly transparent to anyone who is prepared to see.[24] For example, the entry for the term *māman* reads, "Brother of the mother. Also means *the father of one's wife*, or *the father of one's husband*, & a *father's sister's husband*, as well as a *mother's brother*" (see figure 5). If the mother's brother is also the spouse's father, it would not be rash to infer that one may marry his child. Or again, for *maittuni*: "may designate any one of *the wife's sisters*, but is most commonly used for *the wife's younger sister*. Also means a man's *younger brother's wife*; also a cousin, who is the *mother's brother's* daughter, or the *father's sister's daughter*." If the wife's (younger) sister is also the mother's brother's daughter, it would be reasonable to infer that a wife is also a mother's brother's daughter.

Although Scudder provided information from which one may readily infer cross cousin marriage, his brother, the Rev. Ezekiel C. Scudder, also a missionary at Vellore, refers to it directly as current custom in a letter of 8 April 1864. Speaking of the problem of fixing upon the correct "translation" for Tamil terms in Morgan's schedule, he says,[25]

> You will find one or two variations in the English translation of the terms, but they are not of much importance. E.g. Husband's Father in the Tamil [schedule of terms of relationship which the writer had sent earlier] was translated Uncle. Father in law is perhaps quite as appro-

---

[24] "*Tamil*. Rev. Henry W. Scudder," pp. 1234–1235, Morgan Papers. See fig. 5.

[25] Ezekiel C. Scudder to Morgan, 4/8/63, Morgan Papers.

priate. One is expected to marry an uncle's daughter or son, and thus the two relationships are combined in one.

The same applies to Wife's Father.

Nevertheless, in the 1865 version of the *Systems* there is no mention of cross cousin marriage. The astonishing thing is not that McIlvaine read that manuscript and spontaneously invented cross cousin marriage; rather, it is that Morgan did not do so himself. We may well ask why.

Given that the cohabitation of cross cousins could explain those features of Dravidian in which it differed from Iroquois, we might conclude that because he had built his book around the Iroquois-Dravidian identity, as proof of the Asiatic origin of native American peoples, Morgan was not kindly disposed toward an explanation of the Dravidian that tended to drive a wedge between it and the Iroquois and accordingly minimized it. Nevertheless, it is possible to imagine an alternative conjectural history in which cross cousin marriage lay at the bottom of the Iroquois-Dravidian identity and in which *Iroquois* departures from a *Dravidian* norm were explained as local innovations. Moreover, Morgan generally gives full treatment to possible explanations that he rejects; here there appears to be a pattern of reluctance to see and of minimizing what is thrust before him. There is, I believe, a personal factor at work.

When we examine the intellectual life of an individual, we cannot help becoming aware of the force of exiguous factors of a purely personal nature, factors that have no relation to prevailing intellectual tendencies and that disappear when our attention shifts from the individual to the intellectual community of which he is a part. Such I think is the case here, for Morgan's successors showed no such obtuseness in connection with the Dravidian marriage rule.

The personal factor I have in mind is the fact that *Morgan had himself married his mother's brother's daughter*; a cousin, that is, of the kind of relationship that anthropologists later come to call the relationship of cross cousin. Resek's biography of Morgan tells us that his wife, Mary Steele Morgan, was a cousin, and seems to say that she was his mother's brother's daughter, but the passage in question is not free of ambiguity.[26] I have verified the relevant genealogical connections through Morgan's entries in the family Bible and in published genealogies of the Morgan and the Steele

---

[26] Resek, *Morgan, American scholar*, p. 48.

families.[27] The facts are simply stated. Jedediah Morgan of New York married Harriet Steele of Hartford, Connecticut, in 1812. It was the second marriage for both of them, each having been widowed some time before. Their son Lewis Henry Morgan was born in 1818; in 1851 he married Mary Elizabeth Steele, the daughter of Lemuel Steele of Albany, who was the brother of Morgan's mother Harriet Steele. Marriage is a matter for state law under the American constitution, and the marriage of first cousins is prohibited in several states; but an examination of the New York statutes of the time shows that first cousin marriage was beyond the degrees prohibited by law—as, of course, Morgan, a lawyer, would have made it his business to know.[28]

Morgan can scarcely have contemplated McIlvaine's hypothesis of "a promiscuous intercourse of cousins" without thinking of his own marriage in terms of the structuring of the Tamil terminology; and the underlying valuations that attach to his global constructs were such as to make it distasteful to associate the marriage he had entered into with the classificatory system that opposed that of the civilized nations. McIlvaine's speech before the Pundits puts those valuations more strongly than Morgan ever does and goes on to account for what he calls the "permanent type of degradation and inferiority" of the Turanian and American Indian peoples by the deleterious consequences of the practice of intercourse among cousins, as a species of inbreeding: "For these the blood, instead of dispersing itself more & more widely, is constantly returning upon itself."[29] This part, too, of McIlvaine's argument cannot but have been personally repugnant to Morgan, and he did not adopt a theory of degeneration through inbreeding. Nor did he believe in the permanent inferiority of the cultural other, as we have seen.

Morgan's own view about the criterion by which the *Systems* should be evaluated seems to have shifted as he was writing. The

---

[27] Nathaniel H. Morgan, *A history of James Morgan of New London, Connecticut, and his descendants*, pp. 177–179; Daniel Steele Durrie, *The Steele family, a genealogical history of John and George Steele (settlers of Hartford, Conn.) 1635–6, and their descendants*, pp. 23, 44–45; Family Bible, Morgan Papers. I am grateful to Ms. Joan R. Frye of the New York Genealogical and Biographical Society and Mr. Karl Kabelac of the Rush Rhees Library of the University of Rochester for help in verifying this point.

[28] *The revised statutes of the state of New-York, as altered by subsequent legislation*, vol. 2, p. 321.

[29] McIlvaine, "The organisation of society" (MS., Morgan Papers), p. 26/31.

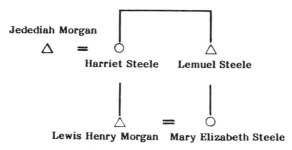

Fig. 12. Morgan's marriage.

time revolution overtook his project between the two major versions of the *Systems*, and the conjectural history of the family in his attempt to come to grips with the vast changes it had wrought. Thereafter the proof of Indian unity and Asian origin that had motivated the very existence of the kinship project fades into the background. The project had moved beyond its original *raison d'être*. Morgan now believed that the conjectural history of the family was its most important achievement. His contemporaries agreed. Morgan became the leading theorist of kinship in his day.

Morgan's relations with his peers are a complicated tale of the many disputes that broke out even before the *Systems* was bound and published and continued long after, of which perhaps the loudest was the one with McLennan, as we shall see later. Here I should like to illustrate the state of play by concentrating upon the central debate around which the emergent anthropological community took on definition—the debate, namely, over the patriarchal theory and alternative theories of the primitive state. The issue was far from antiquarian; it had political resonances and very direct bearing upon relations between the sexes. With such ramifications it gave the nascent discipline of anthropology an issue of the widest significance for which it could claim expert knowledge. The question of mankind's primitive state had been thrown wide open in the 1860s by the revolution of ethnological time, and many addressed the issue of the seventies, eighties, and nineties—so many, indeed, that to do it justice would require a study of its own. Here I can merely illustrate the extremes, taking Maine and Darwin on the one hand and Marx and Engels on the other. First, however, we must follow the further development of Morgan's kinship project after the *Systems*.

Briefly, then, when the *Systems* was finally published in 1871, it took its place in a body of recent work, together with that of Bachofen, McLennan, and Lubbock, the common effect of which was to displace the patriarchal theory in favor of an account of the primitive state that included promiscuity and descent through females. This conjuncture encouraged Morgan along the path he had somewhat tentatively embarked upon in the *Systems,* as we find in his 1877 book, *Ancient society.*

The core of *Ancient society* has two parts. The first of these is the "growth of the idea of government" in which Morgan returns to his original interest in the Iroquois constitution and brings it to bear upon the understanding of early Greece and Rome. The Iroquois system is built up of four levels beginning with the tribe (clan), or *gens,* as he now calls it. The Iroquois gens, phratry, tribe, and confederacy correspond to the archaic Grecian gens, phratry, tribe, and nation and the Roman gens, curia, tribe, and populus. Thus the Greeks and Romans are ethnologized and brought into a comparative framework with Iroquois as the type of advanced prestate societies. But the Iroquois are matrilineal and the Greeks and Romans are not. Morgan is now able to revive the theory of Amerindian matriliney and to universalize it as a stage of social evolution, followed by the "change of descent from the female to the male line." He can now return to a formulation we met in the Ojibwa notes in 1858 and say, "thus, among the Ojibwas descent is now in the male line, while among their congeners, the Delawares and Mohegans, it is still in the female line. Originally, without a doubt, descent was in the female line in the entire Algonkin stock."[30] The example of Bachofen certainly was an encouragement here.

The second major part of *Ancient society* is the "growth of the idea of the family," which is an elaboration of the findings of the *Systems.* The section closes with a scheme of five stages in sixteen steps of the "sequence of institutions connected with the family" into which the gentile organization is integrated (see figure 13). In this scheme, after the zero of promiscuous intercourse we find the consanguine family accounting for the Malayan system of relationship and the punaluan family accounting for the Turanian and Ganowánian systems, in agreement, more or less, with the doctrine of the *Systems* (chapter 7, this volume). Also, at the end of the scheme we find the monogamian family—that is, the marriage of single pairs—accounting for the Aryan, Semitic, and Uralian systems, again in agreement with the earlier book. It is the two intermediate stages that are novel and require comment. The syndyasmian or pairing family is based

---

[30] *Ancient society,* p. 344.

First Stage of Sequence.

I.   *Promiscuous Intercourse.*

II.   *Intermarriage of Brothers and Sisters, own and collateral, in a Group: Giving,—*

III.   *The Consanguine Family. (First Stage of the Family): Giving,—*

IV.   *The Malayan System of Consanguinity and Affinity.*

Second Stage of Sequence.

V.   *The Organization upon the basis of Sex, and the Punaluan Custom, tending to check the intermarriage of brothers and sisters: Giving,—*

VI.   *The Punaluan Family. (Second Stage of the Family): Giving,—*

VII. *The Organization into Gentes, which excluded brothers and sisters from the marriage relation: Giving,—*

VIII. *The Turanian and Ganowánian System of Consanguinity and Affinity.*

Third Stage of Sequence.

IX.   *Increasing Influence of Gentile Organization and improvement in the arts of life, advancing a portion of mankind into the Lower Status of barbarism: Giving,—*

X.   *Marriage between Single Pairs, but without an exclusive cohabitation: Giving,—*

XI.   *The Syndyasmian Family. (Third Stage of the Family.)*

Fourth Stage of Sequence.

XII. *Pastoral life on the plains in limited areas: Giving,—*

XIII. *The Patriarchal Family. (Fourth, but exceptional Stage of the Family.)*

Fifth Stage of Sequence.

XIV. *Rise of Property, and settlement of lineal succession to estates: Giving,—*

XV. *The Monogamian Family. (Fifth Stage of the Family): Giving,—*

XVI. *The Aryan, Semitic and Uralian system of Consanguinity and Affinity; and causing the overthrow of the Turanian.*

Fig. 13. Sequence of institutions connected with the family, from *Ancient Society.*

on marriage between single pairs "but without an exclusive cohabitation" and readily dissolved by either husband or wife. This is Morgan's understanding of the present condition of the Iroquois as distinct from the ancestral condition (the punaluan family) that accounts
for their system of relationship. As Tooker says,[31]

> Morgan apparently was led to this conclusion by Iroquois practice and
> that of some other Indians. Among the Iroquois, although divorce was
> frequent, marriage was quite thoroughly monogamous; an Iroquois had
> only one spouse at a time, although over the course of a lifetime he might
> have several. But since generally in the nineteenth century "patriarchy"
> (and polygamy) as indicated in the Bible was regarded as being a later
> development than the systems of more "primitive" societies, Morgan
> could not suggest that the monogamian family developed directly from
> some pre-patriarchal one. Hence, he could only emphasize the difference
> between the Iroquois system and the later ones—stability of marriage—
> and to view this feature as the reforming one.

The patriarchal stage that follows the syndyasmian family and precedes the modern, monogamian one, however, is distinctly labeled
exceptional. Morgan does not regard it as a universal stage or as
accounting for the indicative features of the descriptive (Aryan, Semitic, Uralian) system of relationship. Not only is the patriarchal
family relegated to a late stage in social evolution, it is pushed to
one side. The "striking features of the patriarchal families, so unlike
any form previously known, have given to it a commanding position;
but the Hebrew and Roman forms were exceptional in human experience." In the *patria potestas* of Rome "paternal authority passed
beyond the bounds of reason into an excess of domination."[32] Far
from being the primitive state, it was a late and pathological form.
So much for Sir Henry Maine, whose predicament we must now
consider.

Maine's patriarchal theory had been undermined by the time revolution, and it came under the increasingly pointed attack of the
newly adumbrated alternatives of Morgan, McLennan, and Lubbock.
In his books of the 1870s, *Village-communities in the east and west*
(1871) and *Lectures on the early history of institutions* (1875), he
takes note of the new theories at some length but in general adopts

---

[31] Elisabeth Tooker, foreword to *Ancient society,* p. xxii.
[32] *Ancient society,* pp. 466, 467.

a policy of Olympian nonengagement with them, always a good strategy under such circumstances. Accordingly these books have a more narrow, Indo-European horizon, and the universalist ambitions of the earlier book are put on the shelf. Of *patria potestas* he says,[33]

> I need not here repeat to you the proof which I have attempted to give elsewhere, that a great part of the legal ideas of civilised races may be traced to this conception, and that the history of the development is the history of its slow unwinding. You may, however, be aware that some enquirers have of late shown themselves not satisfied to accept the Patriarchal Family as a primary fact in the history of society. Such disinclination is, I think, very far from unnatural. The Patriarchal Family is not a simple, but a highly complex group, and there is nothing in the superficial passions, habits, or tendencies of human nature which at all sufficiently accounts for it. If it is really to be accepted as a primary social fact, the explanation assuredly lies among the secrets and mysteries of our nature, not in any characteristics which are on its surface.

Maine's artificialist interpretation of kinship is very much the continuation of a theme laid down in *Ancient law*. Perhaps under further encouragement from the book of Fustel with its forthright rejection of a naturalistic origin for the patriarchal Aryan family in favor of a religious one, Maine stresses even more the role of legal fictions in extending the scope of kinship in the archaic Indo-European legal systems he studies. Adoption, slavery, coresidence, common membership of a guild, god-parenthood, fosterage, and the relation of teacher and pupil: all, he shows us, have at one time or another been brought under the idea of kinship. Some of the finest passages of Maine are those that sound this theme.

Then, in the 1880s, he abruptly reversed course. He found unexpected support from Darwin and exchanged the artificialist explanation of the patriarchal family for a naturalistic one that would now guarantee its antiquity.

Darwin's intervention in the debate had come as early as 1871, in *The descent of man*. It appears in his discussion of sexual selection. So long as the pairing of man or of any other animal is left to mere chance, with no choice exerted by either sex, there can be no sexual selection. Thus it is that Darwin is bound to address the theory of communal marriages or promiscuous intercourse raised by Lubbock's *The origin of civilisation,* McLennan's *Primitive marriage,*

---

[33] Henry Sumner Maine, *Village-communities in the east and west,* pp. 15–16.

and Morgan's "A conjectural solution of the origin of the classificatory system of relationship," under the rubric of causes that prevent
or check the action of sexual selection with savages. The treatment
assimilates human marriage to the animal world and speaks of it as
do naturalists when they speak of monogamous or polygamous
species of animals, even though Darwin acknowledges that the writers under discussion "imply by the term marriage a recognized right
protected by the tribe."[34] His conclusion is that although it is probable that the habit of marriage in the strict sense developed gradually
and almost promiscuous or very loose intercourse was once extremely common,

> nevertheless, from the strength of the feeling of jealousy all through the
> animal kingdom, as well as from the analogy of the lower animals, more
> particularly of those which come nearest to man, I cannot believe that
> absolutely promiscuous intercourse prevailed in times past, shortly before
> man attained to his present rank in the zoological scale. . . . Therefore,
> looking far enough back in the stream of time, and judging from the
> social habits of man as he now exists, the most probable view is that he
> aboriginally lived in small communities, each with a single wife, or if
> powerful with several, whom he jealously guarded against all other men.[35]

Maine was slow to find comfort in this quarter. But when he did
so in *Dissertations on early law and custom* (1883), and again in an
anonymous review of McLennan's parting shot, a posthumous attack
upon him completed by his brother and titled *The patriarchal theory*
(1885), Maine fashioned a very effective reply to his tormentors, "the
two zealous inquirers, now lost to us, J. F. McLennan and L. H.
Morgan."[36] The argument is that the marriage regimes propounded
by McLennan and Morgan are exceptional, temporary, or pathological whereas the patriarchal family is typical, being based upon a
constant of human nature, the sexual jealousy of the male. Maine
relies heavily on the authority of Darwin, quoting the above mentioned passages, with reference to Letourneau and Gustav Le Bon

---

[34] Charles Darwin, *The descent of man and selection in relation to sex*, p. 893
(chap. 20).

[35] The same, pp. 895, 896.

[36] Maine, *Dissertations on early law and custom*, p. 195. Maine's unsigned
review of McLennan's *Patriarchal theory* appeared in the *Quarterly review*, January–April 1886, pp. 181–209.

for incidental support. The end result is a rejection of unilineal evolution in favor of a pattern that is pluralistic, but guided in a specific way by "a strong force lying deep in human nature."

Whereas McLennan and Morgan sought a theory agreeable to the long chronology in the customs of savages, abandoning the patriarchal theory of Homer and the Bible, Maine was able to go one further, with Darwin's aid, and establish an argument upon a feature of enduring human nature by appeal to biology. Thus was the patriarchal family naturalized and its claim to great antiquity shored up; but at the cost of a retreat from the considerable promise of his earlier, artificialist interpretation in favor of an argument from human nature for which he had once excoriated Rousseau and his ilk.

It is the peculiar property of the social evolutionism of Morgan and those in his camp that it both validates modern Euroamerican institutions, as the vanguard of the sequence of forms, and undermines their authority by showing that they have not always been and will not always be. The doctrine is susceptible of conservative readings, and Morgan was indeed so read in America by the Social Darwinism of the following generation. At the same time it is serviceable to those who wish to find in it arguments for social change. Thus it is that what Victorian gentlemen such as Morgan, McLennan, and especially Bachofen were saying about matriarchy has ever since been of use to feminism; and thus it is that, through Marx and Engels, Morgan has become a household god in the socialist world.

During the winter of 1880–1881, Karl Marx took up Morgan's *Ancient society* and filled ninety-eight pages of a notebook with extracts and comments. Examining these notes, which have been published by Lawrence Krader, one is struck by Marx' interest in the most technical of Morgan's detail, be it the evidence for the punaluan family, the rules governing Australian (Kamilaroi) marriage classes, or the intricacies of the Iroquois gentile organization. Marx also took notes, though much less extensive ones, on John Budd Phear's *The Aryan village*, Maine's *Early history of institutions*, and Lubbock's *Origin of civilisation*.[37]

This turning toward the new anthropology in the last years of his

---

[37] Marx, *The ethnological notebooks of Karl Marx* (*studies of Morgan, Phear, Maine, Lubbock*), edited by Lawrence Krader.

life is part of a broad interest in archaic forms of property, including serious study of traditional collective peasant tenures in Russia.[38] There is reason to think that this program of study was impelled by a desire to restore the rent fabric of a theory of universal history that the time revolution had parted. Marx did not live to publish on these matters, but a note by Engels to the 1888 English edition of the *Communist manifesto* makes it clear what place the new anthropology and Morgan in particular were to have played in the larger scheme of Marx' thought. The *Manifesto* is above all a universal history, from ancient Rome to the present and indeed into the future. It was written, however, before the time revolution had rendered its starting point much too recent in the lengthened ethnological time to sustain such universalist claims. When therefore it says in the opening sentence, "The history of all hitherto existing society is the history of class struggles," Engels' 1888 note adds,[39]

> That is, all *written* history. In 1847, the pre-history of society, the social organization existing previous to recorded history, was all but unknown. Since then, Haxthausen discovered common ownership of land in Russia, Maurer proved it to be the social foundation from which all Teutonic races started in history, and by and by village communities were found to be, or to have been, the primitive form of society everywhere from India to Ireland. The inner organization of this primitive Communistic society was laid bare, in its typical form, by Morgan's crowning discovery of the true nature of the *gens* and its relation to the *tribe*. With the dissolution of these primeval communities society begins to be differentiated into separate and finally antagonistic classes. I have attempted to retrace this process of dissolution in: *Der Ursprung der Familie, des Privateigenthums und des Staats,* 2nd edition, Stuttgart, 1886.

The supposed discovery in Morgan that communism was the primitive state might be appropriated to tie up the ends of a new, socialist universal history conforming to the newly lengthened chronology, a universal history in which the origin of the historical process was replicated in its goal. Morgan's interests in collective forms of property holding and transmission, in collective living arrangements such as the Iroquois longhouse, and in collective sexual relations as the

---

[38] See Teodor Shanin, "Late Marx: gods and craftsmen" in Shanin, ed., *Late Marx and the Russian road, Marx, and "the peripheries of capitalism,"* pp. 3 ff.
[39] Cited in Dirk J. Struik, *Birth of the Communist manifesto,* p. 89.

basis of early family forms all contributed to this program. Engels' version of his friend's intentions in this regard are largely confirmed by a sentence in a draft reply, dated 8 March 1881, to a letter from Vera Zasulich concerning agrarian problems and the village commune in Russia. Marx says, only slightly mangling the wording from Morgan's *Ancient society*,[40]

> In a word, [the rural commune] finds [the modern social system] in a crisis which will end only by its elimination, by a return of modern societies to an 'archaic' type of communal property, a form in which—as an American author who is not at all suspected of revolutionary tendencies, supported in his work by the government in Washington, says— "the new system" toward which modern society tends "will be a revival in a superior form of an archaic social type."

According to Engels, it had been Marx' intention "to present the results of Morgan's researches in the light of the conclusions of his own—within certain limits I may say our—materialistic explanation of history, and thus to make clear their full significance."[41] After Marx died Engels made use of his notes on Morgan in what he regarded as the execution of a bequest, the writing of the work referred to in his note to the *Manifesto, The origin of the family, private property and the state, in the light of the researches of Lewis H. Morgan* (1884). Although the book is far more than a recital of Morgan's work, it is sufficiently similar that we need not go into it for present purposes. Engels' further remarks on the nature of Morgan's contribution, however, are of considerable interest.

"Before the beginning of the sixties," Engels says in the preface to the fourth edition, in which he gives an impassioned and not always discreet review of the new anthropology,[42]

> Before the beginning of the sixties, one cannot speak of a history of the family. In this field, the science of history was still completely under the influence of the Five Books of Moses. The patriarchal form of the family, which was there described in greater detail than anywhere else, was not

---

[40] Cited in Marx, *The ethnological notebooks*, p. 87. The Morgan passage is from *Ancient society*, p. 552. Of "the next higher plane of society" he says, "it will be a revival, in a higher form, of the liberty, equality and fraternity of the ancient gentes."

[41] Friedrich Engels, *The origin of the family, private property and the state*, p. 71.

[42] The same, pp. 74–75.

only assumed without question to be the oldest form, but it was also identified—minus its polygamy—with the bourgeois family of today, as if the family had really experienced no historical development at all.

Morgan's discovery that the American Indian gens organized by mother right was the earlier form of the later Greek and Roman gens organized according to father right was decisive. "The Greek and Roman gens, the old riddle of all historians, now found its explanation in the Indian gens, and a new foundation was thus laid for the whole of primitive history."[43]

> This rediscovery of the primitive matriarchal gens as the earlier stage of the patriarchal gens of civilized peoples has the same importance for anthropology as Darwin's theory of evolution has for biology and Marx's theory of surplus value for political economy. It enabled Morgan to outline for the first time a history of the family in which for the present, so far as the material now available permits, at least the classic stages of development in their main outlines are now determined. That this opens a new epoch in the treatment of primitive history must be clear to everyone. The matriarchal gens has become the pivot on which the whole science turns; since its discovery we know where to look and what to look for in our research, and how to arrange the results. And, consequently, since Morgan's book, progress in this field has been made at a far more rapid speed.

Thus Morgan's discoveries, in this reading, swept away the patriarchal theory and provided Marx and Engels a vantage from which the critique of the bourgeois family might proceed. It also created an entire scientific prehistory. Morgan was, for Engels (although there is no evidence he saw himself so), a kind of scientific Rousseau. "Reconstructing thus the past history of the family, Morgan, in agreement with most of his colleagues, arrives at a primitive stage when unrestricted sexual freedom prevailed within the tribe, every woman belonging equally to every man and every man to every woman. Since the 18th century there had been talk of such a primitive state, but only in general phrases."[44] In the *Discourse on the origin of inequality,* Rousseau had propounded the theory of a primitive state before the family in which individuals lived isolated from one another and came together only temporarily for sex, a state without

---

[43] The same, p. 83.
[44] The same, p. 97.

the domination of one class by another or of women by men. In Holy Scripture, however, the first man, "having received enlightenment and precepts directly from God," was not himself in the state of nature; wherefore Rousseau found it necessary to launch his enquiry into human nature with the declaration, whose impudence is still shocking these two centuries hence, "Let us therefore begin by setting all the facts aside, for they do not affect the question."[45] Rousseau's was a pure conjectural history if ever there was one; by comparison, Morgan's conjectural history of the family was grounded in a mass of carefully elicited evidence. Morgan was Rousseau with data.

Morgan had since died, but there is every reason to think he would have been alarmed at this appropriation of his ideas for socialist ends. Indeed, Morgan's charm for Marx was exactly that he was a "yankee Republican" and a capitalist, in that his contributions were therefore beyond suspicion. McIlvaine, however, lived on and could have read the *Ursprung der Familie* in its original German edition. One cannot help wondering whether the Presbyterian minister and Princeton professor ever learned of his unwitting collaboration, through Morgan, with a pair of German radicals.

But that was long ago, and the most durable contributions of a work that opens up a new field of inquiry do not always prove to be those upon which the attention of its contemporaries fastens. Such is the case with Morgan's kinship work, if we accept the evaluations of the practitioners in the discipline that he did so much to create. The debate over the conjectural history of the family—which began not with Morgan but with Bachofen's *Mutterrecht* (1861) and McLennan's *Primitive marriage* (1865)—dominated ethnological discussion for the remainder of the nineteenth century and lingered beyond. Edvard Westermarck's *History of human marriage,* first brought out in 1891 and subsequently expanded to three large volumes, purporting to refute the hypothesis of primitive promiscuity on more or less Darwinian lines, is something of an end point for this debate. Although champions of primitive promiscuity and the matriarchal theory appear subsequently, the mainstream of the new discipline has passed them by. Nevertheless, it is worth saying in the face of the dismissive evaluations of this side of Morgan's work on the part of his professionalized heirs that it performed the service of dealing an effective blow to the traditional patriarchal theory and in

---

[45] Jean-Jacques Rousseau, *The first and second discourses,* pp. 102–103.

pioneering the vast new terrain of prehistory that had just opened up. If his work had *not* been superseded, we would have cause for concern over the state of anthropology.

The evaluations of Morgan from within the discipline have been many, impassioned, and heterogeneous, although there is a distinct difference between early critiques and those of the twentieth century that is worth investigating. Lubbock and McLennan are important early critics, and both provoked Morgan to issue rejoinders.

Lubbock's criticism was that there are two theses in the *Systems,* not one: that the classificatory system is "arbitrary, artificial, and intentional" on the one hand and, on the other, that it is natural, being "true to the nature of descents." The point is an acute one, which seized upon the fact (though Lubbock could not have known it) that the artificialist language of the 1865 version of the *Systems* had been carried over into the final version and in some places had not been suitably qualified to bring it into harmony with the new, naturalistic interpretation. In his reply to Lubbock, Morgan admits that such qualification should have been added to what has now become the *prima facie* view:[46]

> There are three or four places, and perhaps more, in that volume in which I speak of the system of a particular people as "artificial and compli-cated," and as "arbitrary and artificial," without the qualification in each case which should, perhaps, have been inserted. Thus, commenting on the same system (Con. p. 392), I remark that "the chain of consanguinity has been followed with great particularity, that the artificial and compli-cated character of the system might be exhibited, as well as the rigorous precision with which its minute details are adjusted." One who had read my work through could not have been misled by this statement, which was intended to characterise this system as it appeared on its face, and apart from all considerations respecting its origin.

McLennan, in his critique of Morgan, was especially effective in seeking out the weak spots in the conjectural history of the family, although neither his argument that the classificatory system is "a

---

[46] Morgan, "Systems of consanguinity," in *Nature,* 3 June 1875, p. 86; Lubbock's reply (June 17) is also titled "Systems of consanguinity," as is Morgan's surrejoinder (August 10). See also Lubbock's comments on Morgan in "On the development of relationships" and *The origin of civilisation and the primitive condition of man,* chaps. 3–5.

system of mutual salutations merely"[47] nor his alternative account of its origins can be said to improve upon what he seeks to demolish; and in his contests with him, Morgan had the unanswerable advantage of having firsthand knowledge of McLennan's preferred ethnological subjects, the savages of the present day.

What is noteworthy is that both these critics, and others, accept the existence of the classificatory system (as a problem to be explained) and its evolutionary priority; what they dismiss is Morgan's "theory" of these "facts" and provide their own explanations to take its place. Lubbock's conclusion to a review of Morgan's *Ancient society* is representative of early evaluations from England. "What Mr. Morgan has added to our stock of facts will endure, but his theories are doomed to rapid natural decay."[48] Much of those facts, however, were the product of theory.

Twentieth-century evaluations of Morgan are fashioned in a radically changed environment. Morgan's naturalism is replaced by an artificialist interpretation of kinship terminologies, closer to the "arbitrary, artificial, and intentional" treatment of the classificatory in the 1865 *Systems* that he so emphatically repudiated in his exchange with Lubbock. Structural-functionalism replaces evolutionism as the dominant mode of explanation. The "facts" that Morgan elicited acquire new meanings; the classificatory system, for example, becomes a structural type and ceases to be a genealogical or an evolutionary class.

Morgan's relation to the field he created is complex and difficult

---

[47] McLennan, *Studies in ancient history*, p. 273. The critique of Morgan takes up pp. 249–315. Morgan's reply is published in a long note in *Ancient society*, pp. 509–521.

[48] Lubbock, "Morgan's ancient society," p. 21. Engel's charge, that "the chauvinistically inclined English anthropologists are still striving their utmost to kill by silence the revolution which Morgan's discoveries have effected in our conception of primitive society, while they appropriate his results without the slightest compunction" (*Origin of the family*, p. 74) is hardly fair, but an element of national feeling does seem to have entered into the initial reception of Morgan's work in England. If that is so, Morgan himself is unlikely to be without blame, judging by the highly unflattering things he has to say about English (and Continental) society as compared with that of the United States in his European journal. Morgan's Americanism often overpowered his Anglo-Saxonism. In one of his earliest articles, "Thoughts on Niagara," the differences between the American and the Canadian falls become a metaphor for a patriotic meditation on the differences between the United States and Great Britain.

to specify. Was he, as McIlvaine and Engels thought, the Newton and Darwin of his science? The idea of a Kuhnian paradigm does not seem to fit well as a characterization of what Morgan accomplished or as an explanation of the intellectual principle that governs the activity of anthropology, unlike that of physics or biology. He did not create a paradigm for an established field; he invented a field, and he bequeathed it some descriptive and analytic devices, together with an ambitious and unfinished project: the global classification of kinship systems, the working-out of their historical interconnections, and the elucidation of the links between kinship institutions and the semantic patternings of the terminology of kinship. Twentieth-century ethnology consequently has a greater internal heterogeneity than physics or biology, which is reflected in widely varying estimates of Morgan's contribution. The extremes of these estimates are represented by Leslie A. White, for whose unfashionable evolutionism Morgan was a hero and a club with which to tax his Boasian enemies on the one hand to, on the other, Malinowski, who complained of "the bastard algebra of kinship" that Morgan had created, and David M. Schneider, who took the centenary of the publication of the *Systems* as occasion to announce that "'kinship,' like totemism, the matrilineal complex and matriarchy, is a non-subject since it does not exist in any culture known to man."[49] The one thing upon which all sides of this turbulent, not to say anarchistic, scholarly community appear to be agreed is, in Lowie's words, that "Morgan's unique distinction . . . [is] in literally creating the study of kinship systems as a branch of comparative sociology."[50]

We need not recount these various evaluations. The fact that anthropologists have felt called upon to return to Morgan's work to assess and reassess it so frequently and so vociferously demonstrates of itself and aside from the substance of their evaluations the continuing significance for the discipline of his accomplishment, and at the same time the absence of a "normal science" phase in that discipline. In ways for which it is not true of Newton and Darwin, Morgan's writings are of continuing interest for researchers. In spite of the variety within the discipline, however, there is an identifiable main-

[49] B. Malinowski, "Kinship," p. 19; David M. Schneider, "What is kinship all about?" p. 59 and *A critique of the study of kinship*, p. vii.
[50] Robert Lowie cited in Meyer Fortes, *Kinship and the social order, the legacy of Lewis Henry Morgan*, p. 11.

stream, and Meyer Fortes' reassessment of Morgan's work is a telling expression of the mainstream view.

The appealing generosity of Fortes' appraisal of Morgan is heightened when, in confessional mode, he informs us that he first heard of Morgan as a false prophet of the discipline in Malinowski's seminars at Cambridge and gradually worked his way around to the diametrically opposed view. Examining the genealogy of his own, structural-functionalist brand of anthropology, he sees an intellectual lineage extending back through Lowie, Radcliffe-Brown, and Rivers to Morgan and Maine, representing the sources of social-structural concepts and theories, and combining with a second lineage representing the cultural approach extending back through Kroeber, Malinowski, and Frazer to Tylor and, to some extent, Boas. "I claim that Morgan's substantive discoveries and intuitively elaborated methods of analysis constituted the foundations of what we now call structural theory in social anthropology. I maintain that the analytical procedure implicit in his work foreshadowed and stimulated, in a striking manner, the development of theory which we owe above all to the lead given by Radcliffe-Brown."[51] Morgan's works especially "can be seen to constitute the basic charter of modern structural theory in social anthropology."[52]

Morgan's basic failing, in this reading, is that he did not discriminate between synchronic and diachronic systems and relations. When we concentrate upon the synchronic element of Morgan's work, we find in it the beginnings of structuralist analysis: not only, then, a superb body of newly elicited kinship data but the conception (which guides collection, description, and analysis) that in each case the data constituted a *system,* the determination that it is identity of underlying *ideas* (rather than vocabularies) that constitutes the subject of comparison between kinship systems, the abstraction of "indicative features" as the beginnings of *analysis,* and above all the discovery, in Rivers' words, of "the close connection between the terminology of the classificatory system of relationship and forms of social organization."[53] Morgan, says Fortes in the Newtonian imagery that had been used in McIlvaine's funeral address, was "a discoverer, one not unworthy to be ranked with a discoverer of a new planet."[54]

---

[51] The same, p. 18.
[52] The same, p. 15.
[53] W. H. R. Rivers cited in the same, p. 26.
[54] The same, p. 8.

In addition to the generous recognition of his structuralism, Fortes is equally generous with his condemnation of Morgan's historicism. "Morgan's supreme vice of method was to leap indiscriminately from what was effectively synchronic observation to pseudo-historical deduction."[55] Having seen how slow he was to take up the conjectural history of the family, the words "to leap indiscriminately" will appear far from judicious, but the point remains. Fortes says in effect that Morgan is a much better anthropologist when we leave the history out, and he says so from the vantage of a tradition that has endeavored to do better anthropology by leaving the history out. This latter is the program of Radcliffe-Brown for whom "conjectural history" was a word of reproach with which he castigated Morgan's evolutionism—more aptly than he knew—in order to reorient anthropology along lines of structural-functionalism. Fortes avers, however, that Radcliffe-Brown got much of his structural-functionalism from Morgan, specifically from deeply reading the *Systems*. This interpretation of Morgan's anthropology is a consequence of the decision to assess it from the vantage of one of its descendant intellectual lineages, which approach Fortes deliberately adopts in preference to trying to understand Morgan in the context of his own times. It is at one and the same time an assessment of Morgan and a description of the shape of current anthropology—or, at any rate, one version of it. Morgan's structuralism with the history left out is what anthropology has become.

What is most fascinating about this assessment is not the nature of the praise and blame that is meted out—for these are more or less determined by the approach Fortes has chosen—but what it does not say. One would not have thought it possible to read the *Systems* and completely miss the philological design of the entire kinship project. Fortes' silence as to this philological design is stunning. Yet he cannot have seen it and represented Morgan's work as he did. The supposed synchronic observations were defined, framed, and motivated by a diachronic conceptualization modeled upon comparative philology; that is, by a form of historicism other than the evolutionism of which Fortes exclusively speaks.

The way in which that philological conceptualization in Morgan has been obscured and forgotten can be seen in the destiny of his global typology of systems of relationship. In the construction of new

---

[55] The same, p. 15.

typologies under the regime of structural-functionalism, anthropology owes more to Morgan than it knows, but also less.

The originating problem of the *Systems*—the Indian unity and Asian origin question—obliged Morgan to be a lumper rather than a splitter and to resolve all empirical instances into one of only two systems, the classificatory and the descriptive; subordinate classes were philological ones such as Aryan and Semitic, Malayan and Turanian. At these and lower levels of classification the groups are genetic or genealogical ones—that is, they are based on descent from a common ancestor.

Independently of each other, Lowie and Kirchhoff invented a taxonomy that in effect doubled Morgan's fundamental scheme by dividing both taxa in two.[56] The new scheme recognizes four patterns by which the father, father's brother, and mother's brother may be merged or distinguished (see figure 14). Distinctions in Morgan subordinate to the classificatory/descriptive difference reappear under a new, structural guise. Thus Lowie's "generational" and "bifurcate-merging" reproduce Morgan's Hawaiian and Iroquois (or Malayan and Ganowánian) subclasses of the classificatory system, but as structural, not genealogical or genetic, classes. (What Morgan identifies as secondary differences between Iroquois and Tamil, or Ganowánian and Turanian, gets overlooked in this scheme and has to be rediscovered by Lounsbury much later.) And the difference between "bifurcate-collateral" and "lineal" reproduces Morgan's distinction within the descriptive system of the "Celtic method," which holds the relatives distinct and the "unlimited generalization" of collateral relationships to be found in English words such as *uncle*. Murdock bases his sixfold taxonomy on a different criterion, the ways of classifying cross cousins, following Spier. His Hawaiian, Iroquois, Sudanese, and Eskimo types correspond to Lowie's types as indicated in figure 14, and in addition to these, he recognizes Crow and Omaha types.[57] Both of the latter have the attributes of Lowie's bifurcate-merging class but are distinguished from the Iroquois type by their merging of cross cousins with kintypes of generations junior or senior to them. The distinctions come ultimately from Morgan him-

---

[56] Lowie, "A note on relationship terminologies" (1928); P. Kirchhoff, "Verwandtschaftsbezeichnungen und Verwandtenheirat" (1932). See also Trautmann, *Dravidian kinship*, pp. 82–90 for a more extended discussion of this issue and other legacies of Morgan.

[57] George Peter Murdock, *Social structure*, pp. 223–224.

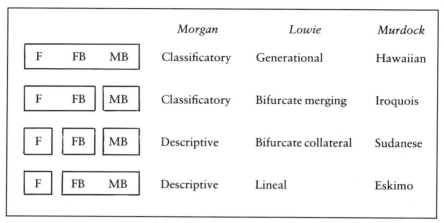

Fig. 14. Global taxonomies of kinship systems.

self. Of the way in which different Amerindian tribes classify cousins, he said,[58]

> There are four different methods of disposing of them found among the Ganowánian nations; by the first the children of a brother and sister are cousin and cousin; by the second uncle and nephew when males, and mother and daughter when females; by the third, son and father when males, and granddaughter and grandmother when females; and of the fourth, brother and sister.

These distinctions correspond to Murdock's Iroquois, Omaha, Crow, and Hawaiian types, respectively.

Thus in redesigning the global typology of kinship systems, Morgan's classes have been freely appropriated, but they have been turned into structural ones by stripping them of genealogical significance. The terms of discourse have been decisively changed. To debate whether Iroquois and Dravidian are the same does not have, for us, the momentous historical implications it had for Morgan. And to say that English and Japanese kinship terminologies come under the Eskimo type may amuse or cause one to question the value of structuralist typologies. For Morgan, however, it would have posed an intolerable problem threatening to overturn his entire treatment of kinship.[59]

---

[58] Morgan, *Systems*, p. 80.

[59] Discussed in Edward Norbeck, "Lewis Henry Morgan and Japanese terms of relationship: profit through error," pp. 208 ff.

We have to recognize that there is not merely one kind of historicism to be found in Morgan but two: evolutionism and what I shall call "genealogism." Although the two historicisms are logically independent of each other, neither Morgan nor his contemporaries seems to have thought so. Again and again in nineteenth-century Euroamerican thought we encounter the stepwise progression from lower to higher forms of the scale-of-nature or scale-of-mind idea combined with the treelike branching structure of what Darwin calls "the genealogical arrangement of the races of man," whose original is the narrative of the descent of Noah. This latter figure of a family tree carries no necessary implication of a "law of progress" and of a hierarchy of higher and lower forms, but it was invariably so understood by its many nineteenth-century users. Evolutionism and genealogism combine in the philology of Müller, the biology of Darwin, the comparative jurisprudence of Maine, and the comparative kinship of Morgan. But their combination is not organic. Dissolve the evolutionism in Morgan and something other than structuralism remains: the idea of the branching off from the parent stock of cultural forms over time, of an irreversible movement from unity to difference. It is upon this idea that the *Systems* was built.

With this idea in mind, and hoping to explain the exoticism of Iroquois kinship, Morgan took up the very inadequate research device provided by the philology of his day—the vocabulary list—and, moving from theoretical workshop to field trials and back again several times, forged it into something that reached well beyond its original purpose, the recording of a nomenclature. He devised the conception of kinship as a system of ideas, as a semantic pattern, and the research instrument to reveal it. And he devised as well a program of comparative study the objective of which was to elicit genealogical connections among kinship systems. In all of this his ideas were essentially sound and durable, although he overestimated the power of his method to uncover distant relationships, under the influence of the short time frame of the ethnological process as he first conceived it. And although his first formulation of the *Systems* recognized artifice in kinship (at least in the classificatory system), he abandoned that promising beginning when he saw a way to naturalize his subject.

Anthropology's forgetfulness of the genealogism in Morgan is not complete, and his contribution in this area is part of a submerged tradition within the discipline. Historical linguistics, whose heroic project of recovering lost unities that cross continents and oceans was hatched before the time revolution, has since settled into a "normal science" mode that seeks the more modest goal of elucidating genealogical relationships over, perhaps, the last two or three millennia. Historical linguistics, however, continues to practice word-by-word reconstruction of vocabulary, even when dealing with kinship terms, and has done rather little in semantics.[60] Morgan's project of discovering genetic connections through the comparison of terms of relationship conceived semantically, as systematic, internally patterned wholes, is susceptible of being transformed by fairly simple operations into a normal science mode that operates within well-defined linguistic regions and a time frame of a few thousand years. In the study of Native American kinship the collaboration between linguistics and anthropology is so well established that comparison of systems naturally follows linguistic groupings.[61] In the study of kinship in India the tradition of Morgan is also alive and well.[62] Indeed, there are some kinds of facts that can be discovered in no other way, neither by structuralism nor by linguistic comparison of lexica, between which Morgan's method occupies a middle ground. I have in mind the existence of systems whose kinship lexicon is of one language family but whose semantic pattern is of another. Morgan's method is especially valuable in clarifying the frontiers among different kinship systems.

Anthropologists will continue to reevaluate, and disagree about, Morgan's contribution to knowledge. Those who have struggled with the complexity of the *Systems* and been inspired by it—one thinks of Fison; of Rivers; of Radcliffe-Brown on Fortes' showing; of Lévi-Strauss, who dedicated *The elementary structures of kinship*

---

[60] Émile Benveniste, *Le vocabulaire des institutions indo-européenes*, 2 vols., is an outstanding example of what historical comparative semantics might accomplish. Unfortunately, in his treatment of kinship terms (vol. I, pp. 223 ff.) he stumbles badly; see *Dravidian kinship*, pp. 349–356.

[61] Examples are too abundant to list. On the lexical versus the semantic approach, compare Isidore Dyen and David F. Aberle, *Lexical reconstruction, the case of the Proto-Athapaskan kinship system* (1974) with John Ives, "Northern Athapaskan social and economic variability" (1985).

[62] Irawati Karve's *Kinship organization in India* (2d ed., 1965) is the foremost representative of Morgan's tradition for India, and my *Dravidian kinship* (1981) is in the same spirit. On the Tibeto-Burman periphery of the subcontinent, see N. J. Allen, "Byansi kinship terminology" (1975). For Munda, see R. J. Parkin, "Munda kinship terminologies" (1985).

to the memory of Morgan—form an impressive list. I have reason to believe that his contribution lies by no means wholly in the past. I agree with Elisabeth Tooker, who has said that in some respects anthropology has yet to catch up with Morgan.

Bibliography

++

Manuscript Collections

Lewis Henry Morgan Papers, Rush Rhees Library, University of Rochester.
Office of the secretary, correspondence, Smithsonian Institution Archives.
Official correspondence, American Oriental Society.
Ely S. Parker Papers, American Philosophical Society.
Leslie A. White Papers, Michigan Historical Collections, Bentley Historical Library, The University of Michigan.

Lewis Henry Morgan's Published Writings

"Aristomenes the Messenian." *The Knickerbocker* 21 (January 1843): 25–30. Signed "Aquarius" and dated Aurora, November 1842.

"Thoughts at Niagara." *The Knickerbocker* 22 (September 1843): 193–196. Signed "Aquarius."

"Mind or instinct, an inquiry concerning the manifestation of mind by the lower orders of animals." *The Knickerbocker* 22 (November, December 1843): 414–420, 507–515. Signed "Aquarius" and dated October 1843.

"Vision of Kar-is-ta-gi-a, a sachem of Cayuga." *The Knickerbocker* 24 (September 1844): 238–245. Signed "Aquarius."

"Iroquois laws of descent." In *Notes on the Iroquois*. Edited by Henry Rowe Schoolcraft, 495–497. Albany: Erastus H. Pease & Co., 1847. From a letter to Schoolcraft dated Rochester, 7 October 1845.

"Letters on the Iroquois, by Skenandoah: addressed to Albert Gallatin, LL.D., President New York Historical Society." *American Whig review* 5 (February 1847): 177–190; (March 1847): 242–257; (May 1847): 447–461; (November 1847): 477–490; (December 1847): 626–633.

"From Lewis H. Morgan, of Rochester"; "Additional donations received from Mr. Morgan, December 8, 1848." New York State Museum, *Reports on the Cabinet of Natural History* 2 (1849): 74–76.

"Communications from Lewis H. Morgan, Esq. of Rochester." New York State Museum, *Reports on the Cabinet of Natural History* 2 (1849):

81–91. Letters dated 31 October 1848 and Rochester, 13 November 1848.

"Reports to the regents of the University, upon the articles furnished the the [*sic*] Indian collection: by L. H. Morgan. December 31, 1849." New York State Museum, *Reports on the Cabinet of Natural History* 3 (1850): 67–97.

"Schedule of articles obtained from Indians residing in western New-York, being the product of their own handicraft and manufacture, for the New-York historical and antiquarian collection, under the direction of Lewis H. Morgan, of Rochester." New York State Museum, *Reports on the Cabinet of Natural History* 3 (1850): 57–60.

"The fabrics of the Iroquois." *Stryker's American register and magazine* 4 (July 1850): 319–343.

League of the Ho-dé-no-sau-nee, or Iroquois. Rochester: Sage and Brother, 1851.

League of the Iroquois. Introduction by William N. Fenton. New York: Corinth Books, 1962. Reprint of the 1851 edition.

Diffusion against centralization, a lecture delivered before the Rochester Athenaeum and Mechanics' Association, on its third anniversary, January 6, 1852. Rochester: D. M. Dewey, 1852.

"Report on the fabrics, inventions, implements and utensils of the Iroquois, made to the regents of the University, Jan. 22, 1851, by Lewis H. Morgan, illustrative of the collection annexed to the State Cabinet of Natural History, with illustrations by Richard H. Pease, Albany." New York State Museum, *Reports on the Cabinet of Natural History* 5 (1852): 67–117.

"Schedule of articles obtained from Indians residing in western New-York and on Grand River in Upper Canada, being the product of their own handicraft and manufacture for the historical and antiquarian collection in the State Cabinet of Natural History, by Lewis H. Morgan, Esq., of Rochester." New York State Museum, *Reports on the Cabinet of Natural History* 5 (1852): 51–54.

"Athenian democracy." *The New-York quarterly* 2 (October 1853): 341–367.

"Laws of descent of the Iroquois." *Proceedings of the American Association for the Advancement of Science* 11 (1857): 132–148.

"The Indian mode of bestowing and changing names." *Proceedings of the American Association for the Advancement of Science* 13 (1859): 340–343.

Circular letter dated "January   , 1859," including within a paper under the title, "Laws of consanguinity, and descent of the Iroquois." Rochester: Steam Press of A. Strong & Co., 1859.

"Memorandum of tools, &c., from Cuddapah, India, presented to agricultural museum, by L. H. Morgan of Rochester." *Transactions of the New*

York State Agricultural Society 19 (1859): 756–758.

"Suggestions relative to an ethnological map of North America, 36 by 44 inches." Smithsonian Institution, *Annual report* (1861): 397–398.

"Circular in reference to the degrees of relationship among different nations." *Smithsonian miscellaneous collections* 2 (1862): 5–33. Circular letter dated 1 October 1859 and schedule of "Degrees of relationship in the language of the   nation." Circular and schedule were sent out with cover letter by Joseph Henry, Secretary of the Smithsonian Institution, dated 20 January 1860 and cover letter by Lewis Cass, Secretary of State, dated 5 January 1860. Reprinted in *The Cambrian journal* (2d ser.) 3 (1860): 142–158 under the title, "The Welsh Indians," with cover letter by D. W. Nash, and Welsh terms of relationship entered into the schedule by the Rev. Mr. John Williams ab Ithel.

"Migrations of the Indians." *Transactions of the Albany Institute* 4 (1858–64): 299–300. Minutes of the meeting of 1 April 1862.

"The stone and bone implements of the Arickarees." New York State Museum, *Reports on the Cabinet of Natural History* (1868): 23–46. Dated Rochester, January 1868.

"A conjectural solution of the origin of the classificatory system of relationship." *Proceedings of the American Academy of Arts and Sciences* 7 (1868): 436–477. Delivered at the meeting of 11 February 1868.

"The 'seven cities of Cibola.'" *North American review* 108 (April 1869): 457–498.

"Indian migrations." *North American review* 109 (October 1869): 391–442; 110 (January 1870): 33–82.

The American beaver and his works, 1868. Facsimile reprint, New York: Burt Franklin, 1970.

Systems of consanguinity and affinity of the human family. Smithsonian contributions to knowledge, vol. 17. Washington, D.C.: Smithsonian Institution, 1871. "Accepted for publication, January, 1868."

"Oxford." *Appletons' journal* 4 (22 April 1871): 497–498.

"The Simplon Road over the Alps." *Appletons' journal* 6 (9 December 1871): 654–657.

"Australian kinship; with appendices, by Rev. Lorimer Fison." *Proceedings of the American Academy of Arts and Sciences* 8 (1872): 412–438. Paper read at the meeting of 12 March 1872.

"Chadbourne on instinct." *The nation* 14 (2 May 1872): 291–292. Review of *Instinct, its office in the animal kingdom, and its relation to the higher powers in man*, by P. A. Chadbourne.

"The city of the sea." *Harper's new monthly magazine* 45 (September 1872): 481–501.

"The human race." *The nation* 15 (28 November 1872): 354. Review of *The human races*, by Louis Figuier.

"Architecture of the American aborigines." In *Johnson's new universal cyclopaedia, a scientific and popular treasury of useful knowledge,* vol. 1, 217–229. New York: A. J. Johnson & Son, 1875.

"Arts of subsistence." *Proceedings of the American Association for the Advancement of Science* 24 (1875): 274–281.

"Ethnical periods." *Proceedings of the American Association for the Advancement of Science* 24 (1875): 266–274.

"Systems of consanguinity." *Nature* (3 June 1875): 86. Reply to Lubbock, dated Rochester, 19 April.

"Systems of consanguinity." *Nature* (19 August 1875): 311. Surrejoinder to Lubbock, dated Rochester, 20 July.

"Montezuma's dinner." *North American review* 122 (April 1876): 265–308. Review of *Native races of the Pacific states,* vol. 2, *Civilized nations,* by Hubert Howe Bancroft.

"Houses of the mound-builders." *North American review* 123 (July 1876): 60–85.

"The hue-and-cry against the Indians." *The nation* 23 (20 July 1876): 40–41. Dated Rochester, 10 July.

"Factory system for Indian reservations." *The nation* 23 (27 July 1876): 58–59. Dated Rochester, 20 July.

Ancient society, or researches in the lines of human progress from savagery through barbarism to civilization, 1877. Reprint with a foreword by Elisabeth Tooker. Tucson: University of Arizona Press, 1985.

"Migrations of the American aborigines." In *Johnson's new universal cyclopaedia, a scientific and popular treasury of useful knowledge,* vol. 3, 481–484. New York: Alvin J. Johnson & Son, 1878.

"Tribe." In *Johnson's new universal cyclopaedia, a scientific and popular treasury of useful knowledge,* vol. 4, 1704–1708. New York: Alvin J. Johnson & Son, 1878.

"The Indian question." *The nation* 27 (28 November 1878): 332–333. Dated Rochester, 22 November.

"A study of the houses of the American aborigines; with suggestions for the exploration of the ruins of New Mexico, Arizona, the valley of the San Juan, and in Yucatan and Central America, under the auspices of the Archaeological Institute." Archaeological Institute of America, *First annual report of the executive committee* (1879–80): 27–80. "Presented at the annual meeting of the Institute, Boston, May 15, 1880."

"On the ruins of a stone pueblo on the Animas River in New Mexico; with a ground plan." *Twelfth annual report of the trustees of the Peabody Museum of American Archaeology and Ethnology* 2 (1880): 536–556. "This paper was read to the American Association for the Advancement of Science, at the St. Louis Meeting, August, 1878."

Houses and house-life of the American aborigines. U.S. Geological survey, Contributions to North American ethnology 4. Washington, D.C.: Government Printing Office, 1881.

"Government and institutions of the Iroquois," ed. Arthur C. Parker. *Researches and transactions of The New York State Archaeological Association, Lewis H. Morgan Chapter* 7 (1928): 1–30. Title page of the original: "Address by Schenandoah on the government and institutions of the Iroquois delivered before the Turtle Tribe of the Nundawaronoh at the falls of the Genesee before the monthly council Nov. 7, 1845. Before the New York Historical Society April 6, 1846. A people without a city—a government without a record."

"Extracts from the European travel journal of Lewis H. Morgan," ed. Leslie A. White. Reprinted from *Rochester Historical Society publications* 16 (1937): 219–389.

Lewis Henry Morgan, the Indian journals 1859–62, ed. Leslie A. White. Ann Arbor: University of Michigan Press, 1959.

Other Publications

Aarsleff, Hans. *From Locke to Saussure, essays on the study of language and intellectual history.* Minneapolis: University of Minnesota Press, 1982.

Adu'l Fidā, Ismā'īl ibn 'Alī, 'Imād al-Dīn, al-Aiyūbi. *Abulfedae historia anteislamica (Mukhtaṣar taʾrīkh al-bashar).* Translated by Henricus Orthobius Fleischer. Leipzig: F. C. G. Vogel, 1831.

Agassiz, Louis. "The diversity of origin of the human races." *Christian examiner* 160 (July 1850): 110–145.

Allen, Don Cameron. *The legend of Noah, Renaissance rationalism in art, science, and letters.* Urbana: University of Illinois Press, 1949.

Allen, N. J. "Byansi kinship terminology: a study in symmetry." *Man* (n.s.) 10 (1975): 80–94.

Anderson, Rufus. *History of the missions of the American Board of Commissioners for Foreign Missions in India.* Boston: Congregational Publication Society, 1874.

Armstrong, William H. *Warrior in two camps: Ely S. Parker, Union general and Seneca chief.* Syracuse: Syracuse University Press, 1978.

Auburn Theological Seminary. *General biographical catalogue of Auburn Theological Seminary 1818–1918.* Auburn: Auburn Seminary Press, 1918.

Bachofen, Johann Jakob. *Das Mutterrecht,* 1861. Reprinted in *Johann Jakob Bachofens gesammelte Werke.* Edited by Karl Meuli, assisted by Harald Fuchs, Gustav Meyer and Karl Schefold, vols. 2–3. Basel: Benno Schwabe & Co., 1948.

———. *Myth, religion and mother right, selected writings of J. J. Bachofen (Johann Jakob Bachofen: Mutterrecht und Urreligion.* Edited by Rudolf Marx, enlarged ed., 1954), translated by Ralph Manheim with preface by George Boas and introduction by Joseph Campbell. Bollingen series 84. Princeton: Princeton University Press, 1967.

Barker, T. Childe. *Aryan civilization: its religious origin and its progress, with an account of the religion, laws, and institutions, of Greece and Rome, based on the work of De Coulanges.* London: Parker; Chipping Norton: G. B. Smith, 1871.

Benison, Saul. "Railroads land and iron: a phase in the career of Lewis Henry Morgan." Ph.D. dissertation, Columbia University, 1953.

Benveniste, Émile. *Le vocabulaire des institutions indo-européenes,* 2 vols. Paris: Les Editions de Minuit, 1969.

Berkhofer, Robert F., Jr. *The White Man's Indian; images of the American Indian from Columbus to the present.* New York: Vintage Books, 1979.

Berossus. *The* Babyloniaca *of Berrosus.* Edited and translated by Stanley Mayer Burstein. Sources from the ancient Near East vol. 1, fascicle 5. Malibu: Undena Publications, 1978.

Bieder, Robert E. *Science encounters the Indian, 1820–1880.* Norman and London: University of Oklahoma Press, 1986.

Bingham, Hiram. *A residence of twenty-one years in the Sandwich Islands; or, the civil, religious, and political history of those islands: comprising a particular view of the missionary operations connected with the intro- duction and progress of Christianity and civilization among the Hawaiian people.* Hartford, Conn.: H. Huntington; New York: S. Converse, 1847.

al-Bīrūnī, Abū Raihān Muhammad ibn Ahmad. *Alberuni's India,* 2 vols. in one (*Ta'rīkh al-Hind*). Translated by Edward C. Sachau, popular ed. London: K. Paul, Trench, Trübner, 1914.

———. *The chronology of ancient nations* (*Athār-ul-Bākiya*). Translated by Edward C. Sachau. London: William H. Allen and Co., 1879.

Blackstone, William. *Commentaries on the laws of England.* With notes by Thomas M. Cooley, 3d ed., 2 vols. Chicago: Callaghan and Co., 1884.

Bock, Kenneth E. "Comparison of histories: the contribution of Henry Maine." *Comparative studies in society and history* 16 (1974): 232–262.

Bozeman, Theodore Dwight. *Protestants in an age of science, the Baconian ideal and antebellum American religious thought.* Chapel Hill: University of North Carolina Press, 1977.

Bunsen, Christian Charles Josias. *Outlines of the philosophy of universal history, applied to language and religion.* 2 vols. London: Longman, Brown, Green, and Longmans, 1854.

Burrow, J. W. *Evolution and society, a study in Victorian social theory.* Cambridge: Cambridge University Press, 1966.

———. "The uses of philology in Victorian Britain." In *Ideas and institu- tions of Victorian Britain, essays in honour of George Kitson Clark.* Edited by Robert Robson, 180–204. London: G. Bell & Sons, 1967.

Caldwell, Robert. *A comparative grammar of the Dravidian or South- Indian family of languages.* London: Harrison, 1856.

Calhoun, John C. *A disquisition on government and a discourse on the constitution and government of the United States.* Edited by Richard K. Cralle. New York: D. Appleton & Co., 1854.

Champion, Edouard. *Les idées politiques et religieuses de Fustel de Coulanges (d'après des documents inédits).* Paris: Honoré Champion, 1903.

The Club. *The Club, si quid veri inveneris profer, 1854–1937.* Rochester: The Club, 1938.

Coke, Edward. *The first part of the institutes of the laws of England; or, a commentary upon Littleton.* 17th ed., 2 vols. London: W. Clarke and Sons, 1817.

Coulson, Thomas. *Joseph Henry, his life and work.* Princeton: Princeton University Press, 1950.

Cross, Whitney R. *The Burned-over District, the social and intellectual history of enthusiastic religion in western New York, 1800–1850.* New York: Harper & Row, 1965.

Daniel, Glyn. *The idea of prehistory.* London: C. A. Watts and Co., 1962.

Darwin, Charles. *On the origin of species.* A facsimile of the first edition. Cambridge, Mass., and London: Harvard University Press, 1964.

————. *The origin of species by means of natural selection* (1859) and *The descent of man and selection in relation to sex* (1871). Reprint. New York: Modern Library, n.d.

Dörmann, Johannes. "War Johann Jakob Bachofen evolutionist?" *Anthropos* 60 (1965): 1–48.

————. "Bachofens 'Antiquarische Briefe' und die zweite Bearbeitung des 'Mutterrechts,'" Nachwort to J. J. Bachofen, *Antiquarische Briefe,* edited by Johannes Dörmann and Walter Strasser, *Johann Jakob Bachofens gesammelte Werke.* Edited by Karl Meuli, vol. 8, 523–603. Basel, Stuttgart: Schwabe & Co., 1966.

————. "Bachofen-Morgan." *Anthropos* 63 (1968): 129–138.

Durrie, Daniel Steele. *The Steele family, a genealogical history of John and George Steele (settlers of Hartford, Conn.) 1635–6, and their descendants.* Albany: Munsell & Rowland, 1859.

Dyen, Isidore, and David F. Aberle. *Lexical reconstruction, the case of the Proto-Athapaskan kinship system.* Cambridge: Cambridge University Press, 1974.

Engels, Friedrich. *Der Ursprung der Familie, des Privateigenthums und des Staats, im Anschluss an L. H. Morgan's Forschungen.* Zurich: Hottingen, 1884.

————. *The origin of the family, private property and the state, in the light of the researches of Lewis H. Morgan.* Translated by Aleck West, introduction and notes by Eleanor Burke Leacock. New York: International Publishers, 1972.

Eusebius Pamphili, bishop of Caesarea. *Die Chronik.* Translated from the

Armenian version by Josef Karst. *Eusebius Werke,* vol. 5. Die griechischen christlichen Schriftsteller der ersten drei Jahrhunderte vol. 20. Leipzig: J. C. Hinrichs for the Kirchenvater-Comission der konigl. preussischen Akademie der Wissenschaften, 1911.

Feaver, George. *From status to contract, a biography of Sir Henry Maine 1822–1888.* London and Harlow: Longmans, Green and Co., 1969.

Filmer, Robert. *Patriarcha and other political works of Sir Robert Filmer.* Edited by Peter Laslett. Oxford: Basil Blackwell, 1949.

First Presbyterian Church, Rochester. *A catalogue of the members of the First Presbyterian Church, in Rochester: June, 1850.* Rochester: Smith & Clough, 1850.

Fortes, Meyer. *Kinship and the social order, the legacy of Lewis Henry Morgan.* Chicago: Aldine Publishing Co., 1969.

Freeman, John F. *A guide to manuscripts relating to the American Indian in the library of the American Philosophical Society.* Philadelphia: The American Philosophical Society, 1966.

Fustel de Coulanges, Numa Denis. *La cité antique, étude sur le culte, le droit, les institutions de la Grèce et de Rome.* Paris: Durand, 1864.

———. *The ancient city, a study on the religion, laws, and institutions of Greece and Rome.* Translated by Willard Small, foreword by Arnaldo Momigliano and S. C. Humphreys. Baltimore and London: The Johns Hopkins University Press, 1980.

———. "Une leçon d'ouverture et quelques fragments inédits de Fustel de Coulanges." Edited by Henri Berr. *Revue de synthèse historique* 2 (1901): 241–253.

Gallatin, Albert. "A synopsis of the Indian tribes within the United States east of the Rocky Mountains, and in the British and Russian possessions in North America." *Transactions and collections of the American Antiquarian Society* 2 (1836): 1–419.

———. "Hale's Indians of North-west America, and vocabularies of North America; with an introduction." *Transactions of the American Ethnological Society* 2 (1848): xxiii–clxxxviii (introduction), 1–234 (Hale's Indians of North-west America).

Gibson, Charles. "Lewis Henry Morgan and the Aztec 'Monarchy.'" *Southwestern journal of anthropology* 3 (1947): 78–84.

Gilchrist, Donald B. "Lewis Henry Morgan's gifts to the University of Rochester." *Rochester Historical Society publications* 2 (1923): 79–81.

———. "Bibliography of Lewis H. Morgan." *Rochester Historical Society publications* 2 (1923): 83–97.

Gillispie, Charles Coulston. *Genesis and geology, a study in the relations of scientific thought, natural theology, and social opinion in Great Britain, 1790–1850.* Cambridge, Mass.: Harvard University Press, 1951.

Giraud-Teulon, Alexis. *Études sur les sociétés anciennes, la mère chez certains peuples de l'antiquité.* Paris: E. Thorin, 1867.

Gossman, Lionel. "Orpheus philologus: Bachofen versus Mommsen on the study of antiquity." *Transactions of the American Philosophical Society* 5 (1983): 1–89.

Gould, Stephen Jay. *The mismeasure of man.* New York, London: W. W. Norton & Co., 1981.

Grave, S. A. *The Scottish philosophy of common sense.* Oxford: Clarendon Press, 1960.

Grayson, Donald K. *The establishment of human antiquity.* New York: Academic Press, 1983.

Gruber, Jacob W. "Brixham Cave and the antiquity of man." In *Context and meaning in cultural anthropology.* Edited by Melford E. Spiro, 373–402. New York: The Free Press; London: Collier-Macmillan, 1965.

Grumel, V. *La chronologie. Traité d'études byzantines,* vol. 1. Paris: Presses universitaires de France, 1958.

Guiraud, Paul. *Fustel de Coulanges.* Paris: Librairie Hachette et Cie., 1896.

Haas, Mary R. "Grammar or lexicon? The American Indian side of the question from Duponceau to Powell." *International journal of American linguistics* 35 (1969): 239–255.

———. *Language, culture, and history; essays by Mary R. Haas.* Edited by Anwar S. Dil. Stanford: Stanford University Press, 1978.

Haber, Francis C. *The age of the world, Moses to Darwin.* Baltimore: Johns Hopkins University Press, 1959.

Handy, E. S. Craighill, and Mary Kawena Pukui. *The Polynesian family system in Ka-ʻu, Hawaiʻi,* new ed. Rutland, Vt., and Tokyo: Charles E. Tuttle, 1972.

Haven, Samuel F. *Archaeology of the United States or, sketches, historical and bibliographical, of the progress of information and opinion respecting vestiges of antiquity in the United States.* Smithsonian contributions to knowledge. Washington, D.C.: Smithsonian Institution, 1856.

Healy, Frances Patricia. "A history of Evelyn College for Women, Princeton, New Jersey, 1887 to 1897." Ph.D. dissertation, Ohio State University, 1967.

Henry, Joseph. *The papers of Joseph Henry.* Edited by Nathan Reingold, sev. vols. Washington, D.C.: Smithsonian Institution Press, 1972– .

———. *A scientist in American life, essays and lectures of Joseph Henry.* Foreword by Lewis Thomas, edited by Arthur P. Molella, Nathan Reingold, Marc Rothenberg, Joan F. Steiner, and Kathleen Waldelfels. Washington, D.C.: Smithsonian Institution Press, 1980.

Herzfeld, Ernst. *Zoroaster and his world,* 2 vols. Princeton: Princeton University Press, 1947.

Hinsley, Curtis M., Jr. *Savages and scientists, the Smithsonian Institution and the development of American anthropology 1846–1910.* Washington, D.C.: Smithsonian Institution Press, 1981.

Hodge, Charles. "The unity of mankind." *Princeton review* 31 (1859):

103–149. Unsigned. Attribution in index vol. for 1825–68.

Humphreys, S. C. "Fustel de Coulanges and the Greek 'genos.'" *Sociologia del diritto* 3 (1982): 35–44.

Ives, John Watson. "Northern Athapaskan social and economic variability." Ph.D. dissertation, University of Michigan, 1985.

Jefferson, Thomas. *Notes on the state of Virginia; written in the year 1781, somewhat corrected and enlarged in the winter of 1782, for the use of a foreigner of distinction, in answer to certain queries proposed to him . . . The works of Thomas Jefferson.* Edited by Paul Leister Ford, vol. 3. New York: Knickerbocker Press; London: G. P. Putnam's Sons, 1904.

Jones, William. *Discourses delivered before the Asiatic Society, and miscellaneous papers, on the religion, poetry, literature, etc. of the nations of India.* Edited by James Elmes, 2 vols. London: Charles S. Arnold, 1824.

Josephus, Flavius. *Against Apion. Josephus.* Text and English translation by H. St. J. Thackeray, vol. 1. London: William Heinemann; New York: G. P. Putnam's Sons, 1926.

Karve, Irawati. *Kinship organization in India,* 2d ed. Bombay: Asia Publishing House, 1965.

Kirchhoff, Paul. "Verwandtschaftsbezeichnungen und Verwandtenheirat." *Zeitschrift fur Ethnologie* 64 (1932): 41–72.

Kramer, Samuel Noah. *The Sumerians, their history, culture, and character.* Chicago and London: The University of Chicago Press, 1963.

Kuper, Adam. "The development of Lewis Henry Morgan's evolutionism." *Journal of the history of the behavioral sciences* 21 (1985): 3–22.

Lévi-Strauss, Claude. *The elementary structures of kinship (Les structures élémentaires de la parenté,* 1949). Rev. ed. Translated by James Harle Bell and John Richard von Sturmer, edited by Rodney Needham. London: Eyre & Spottiswoode, 1969.

Lounsbury, Floyd G. "The structural analysis of kinship semantics." In *Proceedings of the Ninth International Congress of Linguists.* Edited by Horace G. Lunt, 1073–1093. The Hague: Mouton, 1964.

Lovejoy, Arthur O. *The great chain of being, a study of the history of an idea.* Cambridge, Mass.: Harvard University Press, 1936.

Lowie, Robert H. "A note on relationship terminologies." *American anthropologist* 30 (1928): 263–267.

Lubbock, John. *The origin of civilisation and the primitive condition of man, mental and social condition of savages* (1865), 4th ed. London: Longmans, Green, and Co., 1870.

———. "On the development of relationships." *Journal of the Anthropological Institute of Great Britain and Ireland* 1 (1871): 1–29. Read at the meeting of 14 February 1871.

———. "Systems of consanguinity." *Nature* (17 June 1875): 124–125. Reply to Morgan.

———. "Morgan's ancient society." *The Saturday review* (5 January 1878): 19–21.

Lyell, Charles. *Principles of geology, being an inquiry how far the former changes of the earth's surface are referable to causes now in operation* (1830–33), 2 vols., 1st American ed., from the 5th London ed. Philadelphia: James Kay, Jun. & Brother, 1837.

———. *The geological evidences of the antiquity of man, with remarks on theories of the origin of species by variation.* London: J. Murray, 1863.

Lynch, James P., and Elisabeth Tooker. "The public reception of *Systems of consanguinity and affinity,* 1873." Unpublished.

McKelvey, Blake. *Rochester, the water-power city 1812–1854.* Cambridge, Mass.: Harvard University Press, 1945.

———. *Rochester, the flower city 1855–1890.* Cambridge, Mass.: Harvard University Press, 1949.

McIlvaine, Joshua Hall. *The tree of the knowledge of good and evil.* New York: M. W. Dodd, 1847.

———. *A discourse upon the power of voluntary attention, delivered before the Rochester Atheneum & Mechanics' Association.* Rochester: D. M. Dewey, 1849. Delivered 28 June 1849.

———. *A discourse upon ancient and modern divination.* Rochester: Erastus Darrow & Brothers, Publishers, 1855. Preached "about two years ago."

———. *The peace of the tabernacle.* Rochester: C. P. Dewey, 1857. Preached 14 June 1857.

———. *A nation's right to worship God, an address before the American Whig and Cliosophic Societies of the College of New Jersey.* Trenton, N.J.: Murphey & Bechtel, 1859. Delivered 28 June 1859.

———. "A nation's right to worship God." *Princeton review* 32 (1859): 664–697. Unsigned. Attribution in index vol. for 1825–68.

———. "Covenant education." *Princeton review* 33 (1861): 238–261. Unsigned. Attribution in index vol. for 1825–68.

———. "The relation of the church to the poor." *Princeton review* 34 (1862): 601–634. Unsigned. Attribution in index vol. for 1825–68.

———. "Malthusianism." *Princeton review* 39 (1867): 103–128. Unsigned. Attribution in index vol. for 1825–68.

———. "Introduction to a new system of rhetoric." *Princeton review* 43 (1871): 483–581.

———. "Organization the fundamental principle of social science." *Princeton review* 5 (1876): 628–653.

———. "The miracle of creation." *Princeton review* (n.s.) 1 (1878): 830–850.

———. *The life and works of Lewis H. Morgan, LL.D., an address at his funeral* (1882). Reprinted in *Rochester Historical Society publications* 2 (1923): 48–60. Delivered 21 December 1881.

―――. *The wisdom of Holy Scripture, with reference to sceptical objections.* New York: Charles Scribner's Sons, 1883.

McIlvaine, Joshua Hall, and Chester Dewey. "Examination of some reasonings against the unity of mankind." *Princeton review* 34 (1862): 435–464. Unsigned. "Rewritten and prepared for the press" by McIlvaine after Dewey's death, according to McIlvaine, *The wisdom of Holy Scripture,* p. 60.

McLennan, John Ferguson. "Law," *Encyclopaedia britannica,* 8th ed. 1857, vol. 13, 253–279. Unsigned. Attribution in Rivière, intro. to McLennan, *Primitive marriage.*

―――. "Hill tribes in India." *The North British review* 34 (1863): 392–422. Unsigned. Attribution in Rivière, intro. to McLennan, *Primitive marriage.*

―――. *Primitive marriage, an inquiry into the origin of the form of capture in marriage ceremonies* (1865). Reprint, edited with an introduction by Peter Rivière, Classics in anthropology. Chicago and London: The University of Chicago Press, 1970.

―――. "The early history of man." *The North British review* 50 (1869): 272–290. Unsigned. Attribution in Rivière, intro. to McLennan, *Primitive marriage.*

―――. *Studies in ancient history, comprising a reprint of primitive marriage, an inquiry into the origin of the form of capture in marriage ceremonies.* London: B. Quaritch, 1876.

McLennan, John Ferguson, and Donald McLennan. *The patriarchal theory, based on the papers of the late John Ferguson McLennan.* Edited and completed by Donald McLennan. London: Macmillan and Co., 1885.

Maine, Henry Sumner. *Ancient law, its connection with the early history of society and its relation to modern ideas* (1861), 10th ed. With introduction and notes by Frederick Pollock. Reprint. Gloucester, Mass.: Peter Smith, 1970.

―――. *Village-communities in the east and west.* London: J. Murray, 1871. "Six lectures delivered at Oxford."

―――. *Lectures on the early history of institutions.* New York: Henry Holt and Co., 1875.

―――. *Dissertations on early law and custom.* London: John Murray, 1883. "Chiefly selected from lectures delivered at Oxford."

―――. Review of *The patriarchal theory,* by John Ferguson McLennan and Donald McLennan. *The quarterly review* 157 (January–April 1886): 181–209. Unsigned. Attribution in George Feaver, *From status to contract.*

Malinowski, B. "Kinship." *Man* 30 (1930): 19–29.

Manetho. *Manetho.* Text and translation by W. G. Waddell. Cambridge, Mass.: Harvard University Press; London: William Heineman, 1940.

Marsden, George M. *The evangelical mind and the New School Presbyterian experience.* New Haven and London: Yale University Press, 1970.

Marshall, P. J., and Glyndwr Williams. *The great map of mankind: perceptions of new worlds in the Age of Enlightenment.* Cambridge, Mass.: Harvard University Press, 1982.

Marx, Karl. *The ethnological notebooks of Karl Marx (studies of Morgan, Phear, Maine, Lubbock).* Transcribed and edited by Lawrence Krader. Assen: Van Gorcum & Co., 1972.

Marx, Karl, and Friedrich Engels. *Birth of the Communist manifesto (text, prefaces, early drafts and supplementary material).* Edited and annotated by Dirk J. Struik. New York: International Publishers, 1971.

Meek, Ronald L. *Social science and the ignoble savage.* Cambridge: Cambridge University Press, 1976.

Meuli, Karl. "Nachwort," in J. J. Bachofen, *Das Mutterrecht (Johann Jakob Bachofens gesammelte Werke,* edited by Karl Meuli, vol. 3), 1011–1128. Basel: Benno Schwabe & Co., 1948.

Morey, William Carey. "Reminiscences of 'The Pundit Club,'" *Rochester Historical Society publications* 2 (1923): 99–126.

Morgan, Nathaniel H. *A history of James Morgan of New London, Connecticut, and his descendants.* Hartford, Conn.: Lockwood and Brainard, 1869.

Morton, Samuel George. *Crania americana; or, a comparative view of the skulls of various aboriginal nations of North and South America.* Philadelphia: J. Dobson; London: Simpkin, Marshall & Co., 1839.

———. *Crania ægyptiaca; or, observations on Egyptian ethnography, derived from anatomy, history, and the monuments.* Philadelphia: J. Pennington; London: Madden & Co., 1844.

Mosshammer, Alden A. *The Chronicle of Eusebius and Greek chronographic tradition.* Lewisburg: Bucknell University Press; London: Associated University Presses, 1979.

Müller, Friedrich Max. "The last results of the researches respecting the non-Iranian and non-Semitic languages of Asia or Europe, or the Turanian family of language." In *Outlines of the philosophy of universal history, applied to language and religion.* Edited by Christian Charles Josias Bunsen, vol. 1, 263–487. London: Longman, Brown, Green, and Longmans, 1854.

———. *Lectures on the science of language, delivered at the Royal Institution of Great Britain in April, May, and June* (1861). Reprint. Delhi: Munshi Ram Manohar Lal, 1965.

Murdock, George Peter. *Social structure* (1949). Reprint. New York: The Free Press, 1965.

Nash, D. W. "The Welsh Indians." *The Cambrian journal* (2d ser.) 3 (1860): 142–159. Reprints Morgan's circular letter of 1 October 1859

and schedule of degrees of relationship with Welsh terms supplied by the
Rev. Mr. John Williams ab Ithel.

New York. *The revised statutes of the state of New-York, as altered by
subsequent legislation,* vol. 2. Albany: Gould, Banks; New York: Banks,
Gould, 1852.

Norbeck, Edward. "Lewis Henry Morgan and Japanese terms of relationship: profit through error." *Southwestern journal of anthropology* 19
(1963): 208–215.

Nott, Josiah C., and George R. Gliddon. *Types of mankind; or, ethnological
researches, based upon the ancient monuments, paintings, sculptures,
and crania of races, and upon their natural, geographical, philological,
and biblical history* . . . Philadelphia: Lippincott, Grambo & Co.; London: Trubner & Co., 1854.

———. *Indigenous races of the earth; or, new chapters of ethnological
inquiry, including monographs on special departments of philology,
iconography, cranioscopy, palaeontology, pathology, archaeology, comparative geography, and natural history.* Philadelphia: J. B. Lippincott
& Co.; London: Trubner & Co., 1857.

Parker, Arthur C. *The life of General Ely S. Parker, last grand sachem of
the Iroquois and General Grant's military secretary.* Buffalo: Buffalo
Historical Society, 1919.

Parkin, R. J. "Munda kinship terminologies." *Man* (n.s.) 20 (1985): 705–
721.

Pearce, Roy Harvey. *Savagism and civilization, a study of the Indian and
the American mind.* Baltimore: Johns Hopkins Press, 1967. Original
title: *The savages of America.*

Pedersen, Holger. *Linguistic science in the nineteenth century, methods and
results (Sprogvidenskaben i det nittende Aarhundrede, Metoder og Resul-
tater).* Translated by John Webster Spargo. Cambridge, Mass.: Harvard
University Press, 1931.

Powell, John Wesley. "Sketch of Lewis H. Morgan, President of the American Association for the Advancement of Science." *The popular science
monthly* 18 (1880): 114–121.

Princeton review. The Biblical repertory and Princeton review. Index volume from 1825 to 1868. Philadelphia: Peter Walker, 1871.

Pukui, Mary Kawena, and Samuel H. Elbert. *Hawaiian dictionary,
Hawaiian-English, English-Hawaiian.* Honolulu: University of Hawaii
Press, 1971.

Reid, Thomas. *The works of Thomas Reid. D.D.* Edited by William Hamilton, 4th ed. Edinburgh: MacLachlan and Stewart; London: Longman,
Brown, Green, and Longmans, 1854.

Resek, Carl. *Lewis Henry Morgan, American scholar.* Chicago: The University of Chicago Press, 1960.

Riggs, Stephen R. *Grammar and dictionary of the Dakota language.* Contributions to knowledge, vol. 4. Washington, D.C.: Smithsonian Institution, 1852.

Robinson, Charles Mulford. *First Church chronicles, 1815–1915, centennial history of the First Presbyterian Church, Rochester, New York.* Rochester: The Craftsman Press, 1915.

Rossi, Paolo. *The dark abyss of time, the history of the earth and the history of nations from Hooke to Vico* (*I segni del tempo*: *storia della terra e storia della nazioni da Hooke a Vico*). Translated by Lydia G. Cochrane. Chicago and London: The University of Chicago Press, 1984.

Rousseau, Jean-Jacques. *The first and second discourses.* Edited by Roger D. Masters, translated by Roger D. and Judith R. Masters. New York: St. Martin's Press, 1964.

Schele de Vere, Maximilian. *Outlines of comparative philology, with a sketch of the languages of Europe, arranged upon philologic principles; and a brief history of the art of writing.* New York: G. P. Putnam & Co., 1853.

Schleicher, August. *Die deutsche Sprache* (1859), 2d ed. Stuttgart: J. G. Gotta, 1869.

———. *Compendium der vergleichenden Grammatik der indogermanischen Sprachen,* vol. 1. Weimar: Hermann Bohlau, 1861.

———. *Die darwinsche Theorie und die Sprachwissenschaft.* Weimar: Hermann Bohlau, 1863.

Schneider, David M. "What is kinship all about?" In *Kinship studies in the Morgan centennial year,* edited by Priscilla Reining, 32–63. Washington, D.C.: The Anthropological Society of Washington, 1972.

———. *A critique of the study of kinship.* Ann Arbor: The University of Michigan Press, 1984.

Schoolcraft, Henry Rowe. *Notes on the Iroquois, or contributions to American history, antiquities, and general ethnology.* Albany: Erastus H. Pease & Co., 1847.

———. *Historical and statistical information respecting the history, condition and prospects of the Indian tribes of the United States,* 6 vols. Philadelphia: Lippincott, Grambo & Co., 1851–57.

Shanin, Teodor, ed. *Late Marx and the Russian road, Marx and "the peripheries of capitalism."* New York: Monthly Review Press, 1983.

Smith, Adam. *The theory of the moral sentiments, to which is added, A dissertation on the origin of languages.* New ed., with biographical and critical memoir of the author by Dugald Stewart. Bohn's standard library. London: George Bell and Sons, 1875.

Smith, Murphy D. "Peter Stephen Du Ponceau and his study of languages, a historical account." *Proceedings of the American Philosophical Society* 127 (1983): 143–179.

Smith, William Robertson. *Lectures on the religion of the Semites.* Edinburgh: A. and C. Black, 1889.

Spoehr, Alexander. "Lewis Henry Morgan and his Pacific collaborators." *Proceedings of the American Philosophical Society* 125 (1981): 449–459.

Squiers, Ephraim George. *Aboriginal monuments of the state of New-York.* Contributions to knowledge, vol. 2. Washington, D.C.: Smithsonian Institution, 1851.

Stanton, William. *The leopard's spots; scientific attitudes toward race in America 1815–59.* Chicago: The University of Chicago Press, 1960.

Stern, Bernhard J. "Selections from the letters of Lorimer Fison and A. W. Howitt to Lewis Henry Morgan." *American anthropologist* (n.s.) 32 (1930): 257–279, 419–453.

———. *Lewis Henry Morgan, social evolutionist.* Chicago: The University of Chicago Press, 1931.

———. "The letters of Asher Wright to Lewis Henry Morgan." *American anthropologist* (n.s.) 35 (1933): 138–145.

Stocking, George W., Jr. *Race, culture, and evolution, essays in the history of anthropology.* New York: The Free Press; London: Collier-Macmillan, 1968.

Stone, William L. *Life of Joseph Brant—Thayendanegea, including the border wars of the American Revolution, and sketches of the Indian campaigns of Generals Harmer, St. Clair, and Wayne; and other matters connected with the Indian relations of the United States and Great Britain, from the Peace of 1783 to the Indian Peace of 1795,* 2 vols. New York: Alexander V. Blake, 1838.

Thompson, Robert Ellis. *A history of the Presbyterian churches in the United States.* New York: The Christian Literature Co., 1895.

Tooker, Elisabeth. "History of research," "The league of the Iroquois: its history, politics and ritual," "Iroquois since 1820," and "Seneca" (with Thomas S. Abler). In *Handbook of North American Indians,* edited by William C. Sturtevant, vol. 15; *Northeast,* edited by Bruce G. Trigger. Washington, D.C.: Smithsonian Institution, 1978.

———. "Another view of Morgan on kinship." *Current anthropology* 20 (1979): 131–133.

———. "Isaac N. Hurd's ethnographic studies of the Iroquois: their significance and ethnographic value." *Ethnohistory* 27 (1980): 363–369.

———. Comment on "The mind of Lewis H. Morgan" by Elman R. Service. *Current anthropology* 22 (1981): 39–40.

———. "The structure of the Iroquois league: Lewis H. Morgan's research and observations." *Ethnohistory* 30 (1983): 141–154.

———. "Women in Iroquois Society." In *Extending the rafters, interdisciplinary approaches to Iroquoian studies,* edited by Michael K. Foster, Jack Campis, and Marianne Mithun, 109–123. Albany: State University of New York Press, 1984.

———. Foreword to *Lewis Henry Morgan, Ancient society.* Tucson: University of Arizona Press, 1985.

Tourneur-Aumont, J.-M. *Fustel de Coulanges 1830–1889*. Paris: Boivin & Cie., 1931.

Trautmann, Thomas R. *Dravidian kinship*. Cambridge studies in social anthropology 36. Cambridge: Cambridge University Press, 1981.

———. "Decoding Dravidian kinship: Morgan and McIlvaine." *Man* (n.s.) 19 (1984): 421–431.

Wayland, Francis. *A memoir of the life and labors of the Rev. Adoniram Judson, D.D.*, 2 vols. Boston: Phillips, Sampson and Co., 1853.

Westermarck, Edvard Alexander. *The history of human marriage*. London and New York: Macmillan and Co., 1891.

White, Leslie A. *Pioneers in American anthropology; the Bandelier-Morgan letters 1873–1883*, 2 vols. Albuquerque: The University of New Mexico Press, 1940.

———. "Lewis H. Morgan's journal of a trip to southwestern Colorado and New Mexico, June 21 to August 7, 1878." *American antiquity* 8 (1942): 1–32.

———. "Morgan's attitude toward religion and science." *American anthropologist* (n.s.) 46 (1944): 218–230.

———. "The Lewis Henry Morgan collection." *University of Rochester Library bulletin* 2 (1947): 48–52.

———. "Lewis H. Morgan's western field trips." *American anthropologist* 53 (1951): 11–18.

———. "How Morgan came to write *Systems of consanguinity and affinity*." *Papers of the Michigan Academy of Science, Arts, and Letters* 42 (1957): 257–268. Includes the entry for 19 October 1859, in Morgan's *Record of Indian letters*.

———. "The correspondence between Lewis Henry Morgan and Joseph Henry." *The University of Rochester Library bulletin* 12 (1957): 17–22.

Whitney, William Dwight. "Brief abstract of a series of six lectures on the principles of linguistic science, delivered at the Smithsonian Institution in March, 1864." Smithsonian Institution, *Annual report* (1863): 95–116.

———. "Schleicher and the physical theory of language." In *Oriental and linguistic studies*, 298–331. New York: Scribner, Armstrong & Co., 1873.

———. "Physei or thesei—natural or conventional?" *Transactions of the American Philological Association* (1874). Reprinted in *Whitney on language*, edited by Michael Silverstein. Cambridge, Mass., and London: MIT Press, 1971.

———. *Language and the study of language, twelve lectures on the principles of linguistic science*. New York: Charles Scribner & Co., 1867.

Williams, Gwyn A. *Madoc, the making of a myth*. London: Eyre Methuen, 1979.

Young, Davis A. *Christianity and the age of the earth*. Grand Rapids: Zondervan Publishing House, 1982.

Index

Designer:	U.C. Press Staff
Compositor:	Prestige Typography
Text:	11/13 Sabon Roman
Display:	Sabon
Printer:	Braun-Brumfield, Inc.
Binder:	Braun-Brumfield, Inc.